ASIAN SECURITY THE GREAT DEBATE

ASIAN SECURITY

THE GREAT DEBATE

ATTAR CHAND

Gian Publishing House

29/6 SHAKTI NAGAR • DELHI-110007 • INDIA

GIAN PUBLISHING HOUSE
29/6 Shakti Nagar, Delhi - 110007

I S B N 81-212-0087-3

PRINTED IN INDIA

Published by Mrs. Gayatri Garg for Gian Publishing House, Delhi and Printed at S.C. Sharma Printers, B-III, H-146, Vishnu Garden, New Delhi 110018.

PREFACE

During his four nations—Indonesia, Australia, New Zealand and Thailand—official visit, Prime Minister Rajiv Gandhi was able to explain India's positions on major international and regional issues—disarmament, Afghanistan, India-Pakistan relations, Kampuchea, non-alignment and Asia-Pacific security. He emphasized the inalienable rights of the "unfortunate" people of Kampuchea to decide their own destiny for which all foreign troops must withdraw from there on the basis of negotiations that ought to be initiated immediately.

On the recent the Gorbachev—Reagan Summit at Reykjavik, Iceland (October 11-12, 1986) the Prime Minister said the US Strategic Defence Initiative (SDI) had stalled that negotiations.

Earlier on August 11, 1986, Rajiv Gandhi declared in New Delhi that the "Delhi Six's"/ efforts for nuclear disarmament had Soviet support. The announcement at Vladivostok (July 28. 1986) and the suggestions made by Soviet leader Mikhail Gorbachev now and earlier, over a period of time were "positive".

Speaking at the Press Conference on October 12, 1986, at Reykjavik, Gorbachev went on record as saying that "this is the time for action, not just bombastic statements entailing no concrete steps. The World Is tried, the world is sick of empty talk, the world needs real progress : in disarmament, in eliminating nuclear weapons."

Appearing on Moscow Television (October 23, 1986) for the third time in 10 days since the Reykjavik summit, the Soviet leader observed : "All our proposals made in Reykjavik are objectively connected with the central weapons systems. Our concessions are also a part of the package. No package—no concession."

The Soviet peace programme, above all Asian security, is comprehensive. Apart from envisaging a radical reduction and ultimate elimination of nuclear-chemical and other weapons, it extends to all regions of the world, including Asia and the Pacific.

When on July 28, 1986 in Vladivostok, the Soviet leader Mikhail Gorbachev urged all Asian and Pacific nations to co-operation in the name of peace and security, his appeal was welcomed in many countries. Support for the Soviet initiative has been widely expressed in India, Afghanistan, Japan, Indonesia, Laos, Mongolia. Panama, the Philippines, Vietnam and other parts of our vast Asia-Pacific region.

The Soviet Union has put forward a concrete programme for eliminating all nuclear weapons by the end of this century and supported the declaration of the South Pacific as a nuclear-free zone, urging all other nuclear powers to guarantee its newly-adopted status. All this shows that the concern by the Soviet leaders about international security and peace coincides with the concerns and anxieties of the leaders of other states.

Increasingly more people are realising that the comples problems of today's world can no longer be resolved by using the nations which were characteristic of the previous centuries or even decades. The principal problem facing mankind today is the problem of survival. It is equally urgent for Europe, Africa, Asia and America, indeed for all countries. Hence the crying need for a new way of thinking and new understanding of international affairs.

Speaking at Vladivostok, Mikhail Gorbachev said that the USSR is going to withdraw part of its troops from Afghanistan by agreement with the Afghan Government. The new initiative shows that the USSR pursues a consistent foreign policy. It has repeatedly declared for the earliest possible return of the Soviet contingent from Afghanistan.

On October 15, 1986 some units of the limited Soviet contingent began leaving Afghanistan. By taking this serious step, the USSR seeks to speed up political settlement and give it another impetus.

Asia is still being kept astir by hotbeds of tension, by major and minor conflicts. What compounds the situation is that events are unfolding there outside the framework of any regional accords. The Asian and Pacific region has nothing so far to match the all-European process.

That is what accounts for the growing response to the Soviet Union's appeal for a co-operative effort to look for ways to strengthen peace, security and co-operation in Asia and the Pacific. The people of Asia and the Pacific have a common stake in a common and concerted approach to regional problems. The Soviet Union calls for bilateral and multilateral consultations to arrive at a settlement of the issues in dispute, build mutual confidence and gradually create the pre-conditions for an all-Asian forum as a joint effort in search of constructive solutions.

With its longest borders in Asia, the Soviet Union is sincerely anxious to prevent the Asian and Pacific region from every being a generator of tension and an area of military confrontation, and to see it actively involved in the general process of creating an all-embracing system of international security. The Soviet Union proposes resolving the issues of regional settlement of the issues of regional settlement, raising a barrier in the way of the spread and build-up of nuclear arms in Asia and in the Pacific, limiting naval activity in the Pacific, radically slashing the armed forces and conventional armaments in Asia, getting down to the actual discussion of confidence-building measures and of a pledge to renounce the use of force in the region.

Among the factors conducive to an all-Asian process are the growing authority and positive role of the non-aligned movement, the rising anti-war and anti-nuclear feeling, growing pressure for a new international economic order, and an appreciable improvement of Sino-Soviet relations.

It is the Soviet Union's conviction that promotion of regional cooperation responds to the basic interests of the nations of Asia and the Pacific. It will contribute not only towards their greater economic independence but also to their increased political role in international affairs and to a new period of renewal of world history.

Gorbachev's speech at Vladivostok is still in the focus of attention of the world community. Close interest is being displayed in the speech because it analyses in detail the reasons for the continued tensions in Asia and the Pacific. The Soviet leader suggested practical steps to normalise the situation and ensure good-neighbourly relations and co-operation.

The factors impeding peace and security in Asia are well known. But the Asia nations' desire for peace is much stronger than the contradictions created by history or artificially implanted by external forces. Convincingly, this is evidenced by reactions to Mikhail Gorbachev's speech which in most Asian countries was qualified as important and constructive.

Historical experience and current developments provide grounds for certain optimism in regard to the future of the region. In 1947, Asian nations held a representative conference in New Delhi to examine problems of peace and security on the continent. In Bandung, they elaborated the ten principles of peaceful co-existence and earlier in 1954, advanced the well-known five *Panchashila* principles. The other positive examples include the armistice in Korea, the 1954 Geneva Conference on Indochina, and the Indo-Pakistani agreement in Tashkent. Mikhail Gorbachev stressed in his Vladivostok speech that today a number of countries are also trying to tackle common economic problems and settle conflicts. India, Afghanistan, North Korea, Mongolia, and Indochinese countries have advanced peace initiatives. ASEAN nations have gained positive experience in regional co-operation. The South Asian Regional Co-operation (SAARC) has been set up.

Attaining durable peace and security in Asia is, without doubt, a complicated problem. Certain quarters inside and outside Asia do not wish to resolve conflicts and contradictions. They want not civil cargoes but bandits, murderers, saboteurs, and separatists to cross the borders of Asian countries.

The opponents of peace in Asia and the Pacific try to convince the public that the Soviet initiatives are only aimed at establishing domination in the region. The interest displayed by the USSR in the region, pointed out Gorbachev at Vladivostok, "is not a claim to privileges and special position, not egoistic attempts to strengthen our security at someone else's expense, not a search for benefit to the detriment of others. Our interest is in pooling efforts and in cooperation, with full respect for each people's right to live as it chooses and resolve its problems on its own in conditions of peace,"

The Soviet Union does not seek to impose its concepts on the Asian nations and does not try to involve them in closed military and political groupings and alliances such as the so-called Pacific Community. It is not going to have military bases in the Pacific or Indian Oceans and does not have military facilities in other countries. The Soviet Union sincerely wishes peace and security in Asia and the Pacific. It wants that key region of the world to be included in a common system of international security and to develop fruitful and mutually-advantageous trade, economic, scientific, and cultural ties with all its Asian neighbours. More so, since the Soviet Government is accelerating the economic development of Siberia and the Far East.

The interests of the Soviet Union and most Asian countries coincide. There are vast potentialities for extending business contacts with Japan and other industrialised capitalist countries of Asia. Positive shifts have taken place in political, economic, and trade relations between the Soviet Union and China. There exist possibilities for developing ties with ASEAN countries. Stable Indo-Soviet relations developing on a long-term basis have withstood the test of time.

Prime Minister Rajiv Gandhi, like other Prime Ministers of India starting with Jawaharlal Nehru and inclusive of Morarji Desai, could speak well of Indo-Soviet relations without any difficulty.

As recently as on July 26 this year, Rajiv Gandhi described the Soviet Union as "a staunch and proven friend" of India. He expressed the confidence that Indo-Soviet co-operation would continue to be "positive factor in the quest for global peace and well-being."

And on July 28, Gorbachev, speeking at Vladivostok, again hailed India and the non-aligned movement and declared :

"The great India, with its moral authority and traditional wisdom, with its specific political experience and huge economic potentialities, is the recognised leader of this movement ;

We highly assess its contribution to asserting standards of equitable co-existence and justice in the international community. Friendly relations between the USSR and India became a stabilising factor on a worldwide scale."

The good relations between India and the USSR are manufest through multifaceted co-operation—political, economic, cultural and so on. These provide the basic strength to this country enabling it to defy the imperialist pressures on the one hand and on the other to build a path towards economic independence.

Even small progress in the field of Asian security should be welcomed. But we have also to think of long-term prospects. Asia needs the spirit of Helsinki. In Vladivostok, Mikhail Gorbachev again declared for convening an Asian forum of the Helsinki Conference type. It would be just to hold such a forum in Hiroshima (Japan), the first victim of nuclear weapons. But, any other Asian city could well become its venue. The most important thing is to maintain dialogue or what I call the great debate in Asia as in Europe. This would stabilise the situation and lower the possibility of armed conflicts in the continent. It is such steps and not security based on military confrontation and the arms race that meet the interests of all Asian-Pacific nations, big and small.

Mr. Mikhail Goryanov has rightly stated : "The 8th Conference of the Heads of State and Government of Non-Aligned Countries. held in Harare, the capital of Zimbabwe, on September 1-7, 1986, once again corroborated the dedication of the movement's participants to the principles and aims of the policy of non-alignment. In a declaration dedicated to the 26, 25th anniversary of the founding of the founding of non-aligned movement, the leaders gathered in Harare states that the movement's efforts would continue to be directed at building a world without wars and promoting peaceful coexistence, an end to the arms race and universal disarmament; against all forms of interference and the use of threat of force; and towards achieving a peaceful settlement of international disputes, and eliminating racism and the remnants of colonialism. The Political Declaration of the conference stressed the close interconnection between the problems of disarmament and ensuring the right of self-determination and national independence. The nonaligned countries adopted a special declaration on South Africa denouncing the cooperation of the Western powers, especially the United States, with the apartheid regime and demanding the application of comprehensive and compulsory sanctions against that regime. The conference's economic declaration made particular mention of the necessity of the young states' attaining of economic independence and self-sufficiency." (See Nonalignment and Asian Peace and Security. New Delhi, 1986.

The conference also adopted the Harare Appeal to Mikhail Gorbachev, General Secretary of the CPSU Central Committee, and to Ronald Reagan, President of the United States, in which the nonaligned countries urged the USSR and the USA, as well as the other nuclear powers, to take immediate steps in the prevention of a nuclear war, and to continue the dialogue in order to stop the arms race and arrive at real agreements in the field of disarmament, including agreements to avert an arms race in outer space.

On the whole, the results of the conference in Harare have shown that the non-aligned movement remains a powerful force opposed to imperialism, neoclonialism and racism, and that it continues to contribute to the cause of peace and goodwill.

The Vladivostok speech of the Soviet leader Mikhail Gorbachev was a practical, realistic and positive exposition of Soviet policy, both internal and international. His reference to India and its efforts for peace, particularly as the recognised leader of the non-aligned movement have been highly appreciated both by the Government and by the people of India.

Mikhail Gorbachev's approach to the problem of peace, of good-neighbourly relations and his warning to imperialist powers not to interfere in the internal affairs of sovereign and newly-free countries have received laurels in India.

Security on the Asia-Pacific region is vital for world peace. The Soviet Union—two-thirds of its territory lies in Asia—is a bridge between the Atlantic and the Pacific Ocean. Similarly, India occupies a pivotal position in Asia. Peace and security in the Asia- Pacific region is vital to peace and security in Asia and throughout the world.

The Soviet Party Central Committee on October 18, 1986 issued an appeal to the people of the Asian and Pacific countries on the eve of the 69th anniversary of the Great October Socialist Revolution (November 7-8, 1986) urging them to "pool their efforts for ensuring international security and peaceful cooperation in the region."

The Party leadership urged the people of the world to step up the struggle for an improvement of the international situation, for constructive cooperation between states. The Party also called upon the peoples of the world to fight actively against the imperialist policy of violence, plunder, terrorist brigandage, and demand a political settlement of the conflict situations in Central America, in South Africa, in the Middle and Near East.

We in India are confident that the Asian Security idea will pick up particularly after Gorbachev has reiterated it and especially the form in which he has reiterated it. We must ward off that danger of the Pacific becoming a ring nf bases surrounding the countries in Asia and the Far East—the USSR, China and India. We must also extend this idea of security pact to the Indian Ocean, to the Arabian Sea, to the Arabian Gulf, to the hinterland and the littoral states around them.

I wish to express my sincerest thanks to the Librarians and staff of the libraries of Delhi University, Jawaharlal Nehru University, Nehru Museum Library, the Indian Council of World Affairs and to the Institute of Defence Studies and Analysis, New Delhi, for their generous help and cooperation in collecting the material for this study.

I am highly obliged to my Professor and Scholar friends for their valuable advice end guidance which enabled me to complete the manuscript.

ATTAR CHAND

Delhi
Deepawali
November 1, 1986

CONTENTS

CHAPTER ONE

THE REGION

THE POLITICAL MAP of Asia has undergone drastic changes over the last few decades. In the Asia-Pacific region, out of the rubble of colonial empires, dozen of new independent states have emerged whose role in global politics and in the world economy has been growing from year to year.[1]

From all points of view, Asia and the Pacific play a significant part in world affairs and their importance in all spheres of human activity continues to increase.

Nearly two-thirds of the world's population live in that vast region occupying 42 per cent of the Earth's surface. It has enormous labour, mineral and non-mineral resources, including fuel and strategic materials. The Gulf alone has nearly a half of the world's reserves of oil and the Indian Ocean countries account for almost 80 per cent of the world's production of gold, more than 50 per cent of tin and 30 per cent of manganese. Asia is also rich in natural rubber, bauxite, lead, nickel, iron ore and zinc.

The world's largest countries, such as the Soviet Union, China, the United States, India and Japan, which exercise increasing influence on world politics, are situated in close proximity to Asia and the Pacific.

The peoples of Asia and the Pacific are vitally interested in having most favourable conditions for their social, economic and cultural development and most of them consistently advocate the

1. Mikhail Isayev, *Peace Option her Asia.* Moscow, Novosti Press, 1986,

creation of an atmosphere of confidence, mutually beneficial co-operation, lasting peace and security in the region.

The Second World War did not leave Asia unscathed. It brought a lot of suffering and destruction to its countries and peoples. In Asia and the Pacific the war took a toll of nearly 11 million lives. It was in Asia that the first American atom bombs were dropped. They killed more than 300,000 people and burnt two Japanese cities, Hiroshima and Nagasaki, to ashes.

After the Second World War, Asia and the Pacific continued to suffer from the sinister consequences of the nuclear arms race. American imperialism is using its land and seas as a test site for new weapons of mass destruction. Asia has been a site of big and small conflicts and local wars, and tension persists in many of its regions. The aggressive policy pursued by imperialism and a number of other historical, social and economic factors have made that vast and important region of the world a tangle of many complicated international problems.

Being the largest Asian power with two-thirds of its territory situated in Asia and having close historical, political economic and cultural ties with its neighbouring Asian states, the Soviet Union does care about the course which the events in Asia and the Pacific will take. This is not the concern of a passive onlooker. The Soviet Union's interest is that of a country which for 70 years of its existence has been making tremendous efforts to lessen tension in Asia and make that continent a zone of peace, stability and good-neighbourly relations. Millions of Soviet people gave their lives to rid the peoples of Asia from the horrors of fascism and militarism.

The Bandung Conference of the Heads of State and Government of 29 countries of Asia and Africa, held in April 1955, convincingly demonstrated the desire of the countries for co-operation towards achieving peace, freedom and national independence. The Conference decisions reflected the idea – proposed by India and seconded by a number of Asian states—of setting up a zone of peace in Asia on the basis of the five principles of peaceful co-existence and of non-alignment to military blocs. The Ten Principles of God-Neighbourliness and Friendly Co-operation among the countries of Asia and Africa (the Principles of Bandung, adopted by the Conference) formed a solid basis in international law for the peoples' struggle for freedom, independence and peaceful future. The idea behind the Ten Principles of Bandung is to make Asia and Africa continents of peace and co-operation.

Security in Asia and in the Pacific and Indian Ocean is of great importance for the Soviet Union. The 27th Congress of the Soviet Communist Party, held from February 25 to March 3, 1986, precisely stated that Soviet foreign policy accorded growing importance to Asia and the Pacific. The Soviet Communist Party Congress also emphasized the importance of looking for ways of stabilizing the political situation in Asia and unravelling the knot of contradictions there.

These historic changes did not come as a gift to the peoples there. They had to endure many dramatic and sometimes tragic events in asserting their right to a peaceful and independent life. Even today in the international relations of the states on the multifaceted Asian continent we see the interaction, interlacing and clashing of diverse factors—historical, political, socio-economic, cultural and psychological. We have been acutely aware of the complex problems which the Asian peoples have inherited from both the distant and the recent past, above all from the colonial past : the gap in the levels of economic development of the various countries on the continent, the dependent status of many of them in the system of the world capitalist economy, territorial disputes, religious contradictions, ethnic differences, etc. The whole of this conglomerate of complicated problems becomes even more acute and to a greater extent undermines the foundations of peace on the Asian continent because of endless acts of subversion by forces hostile to the peace and freedom of Asian nations, and because of the aggressive circles of imperialism. As a result, instability still prevails in a number of regions in Asia, and in some places military clashes occur.[2]

"......We are for including the Asia-Pacific region into the general process of creating an all-embracing system of international security..." Soviet leader Mikhail Gorbachev said on July 28, 1986,

---

2. *Ibid.*

while speaking in Vladivostok (USSR). This idea is very topical. Although the Pacific region is not so militarised as the European one, dangerous militarist trends are gaining ground rapidly here.

In the second half of the 70s, the US took large-scale measures to build up its military might here. At present, according to military experts, it has in Asia the second largest naval and air force abroad, after the European continent. In particular, the Hong Kong magazine *Far Eastern Economic Review* believes that the US in Asia is now stronger than at any moment after the Vietnam war.

It is hard to disagree with this assessment. Suffice it to say that six carrier groups, now part of the US 7th Fleet, are considerably reinforced. They include the new aircraft carrier Carl Vinson, Los Angeles-Class submarines, Perry-Class patrol ships and Spruance-Class destroyers capable of carrying nuclear weapons. The forces based in the Pacific now have four Ohio-Classes submarines armed with intercontinental missiles. The number of American war planes in the Pacific has risen from 240 to 300 and will be additionally increased when two F-16 squadrons are added.

Where as in 1980 only 20 per cent of the US planes in the area were of the latest models, now their proportion has grown to 70 per cent. During the last year alone, the Pentagon increased the number of the newest Los Angeles-Class strike submarines from 8 to 13. Since June 1984, they are being equipped with nuclear-tipped Tomahawk cruise missiles. In the 80s, the Reagan administration plans to form a squadron of 10 Ohio-type nuclear submarines. Every one of these giant subs has the same displacement—18,700 tons—as a surface cruiser and 24 launchers for the latest Trident ballistic nuclear missiles. And all these military preparations are under way in the Pacific alone, regardless of what is being done directly on the Asian continent and in the Indian Ocean. Such a course of development is darkening the horizon not only in Asia but also in the world as a whole, adding to the risk of nuclear conflict.

What is to be done for the Pacific Ocean to be really Pacific. How can ensure that the skies over it, as well as over the Indian

Ocean and the ancient and young Asia, are not overcast with clouds of military threat ? These were the issues that were given priority treatment in the Vladivostok speech of Mikhail Gorbachev. It is important to stress that purely political measures to resolve the burning problems of the Asia and Pacific region were supplemented with proposals and offers relating to the military field.

The Soviet proposals advanced in Vladivostok are addressed not only to all states of the region, most of which are anyway worried by the situation developing near their coasts and frontiers, and by the unfolding of a new spiral in the nuclear missile arms race. They are also addressed to the United States and other developed Western states which have their interests in the Pacific and Indian Oceans. Common sense suggests that economic and political interests are easiest to protect in an atmoshere of good neighbourliness and co-operation, that regional problems are better tackled at the negotiating table than on the battlefield. Incidentally, the Soviet leader in his Vladivostok speech put forward new constructive proposals for the settlement of conflict situations in the Asia-Pacific region, and especially around Afghanistan, in South East Asia, and on the Korean Peninsula.

Counter-revolution and imperialism have turned Afghanistan into a bleeding wound. The Soviet Union supports that country's efforts to defend its sovereignty. Gorbachev has said that the Soviet Union should like, in the nearest future, to withdraw the Soviet troops stationed in Afghanistan at the request of its government. Moreover, the Soviets have agreed with the Afghan side on the schedule for their phased withdrawal as soon as a political settlement is reached that will ensure an actual cessation and dependably guarantee the non-resumption of foreign armed interference in the internal affairs of Afghanistan. It is in their vital, national interest that the USSR should always have good and peaceful relations with all its neighbours. This is a vitally important objective of the Soviet foreign policy.

The significance of the Asian and pacific direction is growing. In that vast region there are many tangled knots of contradictions and, besides, the political situation in some places is unstable. Here it is necessary, without postponement, to search for the relevant solutions and paths. Evidently, it is expedient to begin with the co-ordination and then the pooling of efforts in the interests of a political settlement of painful problems so as, in parallel, on that basis to at least take the edge off the military confrontation in various parts of Asia and stabilise the situation there.

This is made all the more urgent by the fact that in Asia and other continents the flashpoints of military danger are not being extinguished. The Soviet authorities are in favour of vitalising collective quests for ways of defusing conflict situations in the middle East, Central America, Southern Africa, in all of the planet's turbulent points. This is imperatively demanded by the interests of general security.

Crisis and conflicts are fertile soil also for international terrorism. Undeclared wars, the export of counter-revolution in all forms, political assassinations, the taking of hostages, the highjacking of aircraft, and bomb explosions in streets, airports, and railway stations—such is the hideous face of terrorism, which its investigators try to mask with all sorts of cynical inventions. The Soviet Union rejects terrorism in principle and is prepared to co-operate actively with other states in order to uproot it. The Soviet Union will resolutely safeguard its citizens against acts of violence and do everything to defend their lives, honour, and dignity.

Looking back over the years one will see that, by all the evidence, the pre-requisites for improving the international situation are beginning to form. But pre-requisites for a turn are not the turn itself. The arms race continues and the threat of nuclear war remains. However, international reactionary forces are by no means omnipotent. The development of the world revolutionary process and the growth of mass democratic and anti-war movement have significantly enlarged and strengthened the huge potential of peace, reason, and goodwill. This is a powerful counter-balance to imperialism's aggressive policy.

Meanwhile, the topical character of the problems of Asian security is to a great extent due to the importance of that continent in the world and the seriousness of the problems countered by the peoples and government of its countries. Asia is the largest continent and the biggest agglomeration of people in the world. Its countries not only have an old history but the processes taking place in them in the modern times considerably influenced world developments: a revolutionary wave which spread in Asia after Second World War resulted in the emergence of several socialist countries; Asia was the cradle of the contemporary national liberation movement; it was often at the head of the liberated countries' endeavour to strengthen their social progress, and became the cradle of the Movement of Non-Aligned Countries.

Asia is the scene of numerous conflicts, both latent and acute, concentrated often in dangerous hotbeds of international tension. The hotbeds of tension and conflicts in Asia are so dangerous to the further development of the continent and to world peace also because of all the developing continents, this part of the world was and still remains the target of the greatest aggressiveness of imperialism.

At the end to Second World War, there were only two socialist countries in Asia—the Soviet Union and Mongolia. More than 75 per cent of Soviet territory with 50 million inhabitants, important raw material resources and ever more significant energy and industrial complexes is situated in Asia. The Soviet Union has legitimate interests in the remaining part of Asia and is linked with its states by numerous ties and identical views on the solution of the continent's problems. It is interested in the development of all round relations with Asian countries, in the security of sea routes (mainly the only non-freezing link between the western and eastern part of the Soviet Union via the Indian and Pacific Oceans), in sea research and exploitation of sea resources.

The process of consolidating healthy principles in international relations, and of ensuring security on that continent is taking place in conditions of an aggravated confrontation between the two opposed lines in world politics—the course towards strengthening peace followed by the peace-loving forces there, and the militarist policy pursued by the imperialists and by the reactionary circles of that region which rally to them. There are powerful authoritative forces in Asia which firmly uphold the cause of peace. They are the socialist countries of Asia and a large group of non-aligned countries, as well as the growing movement of peace-loving, anti-war, and anti-nuclear forces, belonging to the progressive parties and public organizations of practically every country in the region. These forces are in the vanguard of the intensifying struggle for peace and stability on the Asian continent—a struggle which is acquiring an ever greater scale and purposefulness.

Present-day US neoglobalism aims at (a) encircling and overawing Soviet Union with military might and (b) wreck it up from inside.

And what has been the Soviet leader Mikhail Gorbachev's response? He has (a) invoked the spirit of renaissance for making friends in Asia Pacific and the rest of the world, and (b) adopted the policy of acceleration at home. At Vladivostock (July 1986), Gorbachev emphasised the need of having friendly relations with small and big countries of the region. The most difficult has been to deal with China. Believing that there is a real danger of a suicidal war, Gorbachev is extending the hand of friendship towards China, while further deep-ending the relations with India. It appears that he would placate the post-Mao leadership to a great extent.

China is pursuing its modernisations and opening itself up to Western capital and collaboration short of strategic understanding in public. Perhaps US-China relations on strategic matters are more below the ground, and if that is so this would be an example of classical secret diplomacy. The Soviet leadership cann't be unaware of this, and again it is making the Chinese commit to a no-nuclear first use in Asia. For an encircled people this is a significant break through. The navigation in the Amur river has begun and both USSR and China are happy. The Soviets must still be bothered about the Chinese conventional build-up on the Soviet Eastern front and the US would see to it that continues as part of their 'wedding' tactics in the Asian Pacific region. Almost every leader of the Socialist bloc is visiting Peking—Honecker of the German Democratic Republic and Jaruzelski of Poland. Will Gorbachev also visit Peking? Why not?

If Nixon-Kissinger can, why not Gorbachev? If Indian Foreign Minister can, why not Gorbachev?

But that is not all, Gorbachev has extended his hand of friendship in the Asia Pacific region. And quite long are the Soviet arms. They reach the Pacific region very well. For years US has been denying fishing rights to small and tiny islands of the region. Soviet Union has gone and joined up with them and recognised the fishing rights of some of these like the treaty with Kiribati. It has joined hands with the desire of the people of the Korean peninsula to have a 'zone of peace' there. Alongwith Vietnam, Laos and Kampuchea, the Central Committee of the CPSU declared for turning South-East Asia into a 'zone of peace', stability and good neighbourliness, for the establishment of good and mutually advantageous co-operation in the Asian-Pacific region. Will, this move towards some kind of multi-lateral or unilateral arrangements towards Asian security?[3]

As such China plays an important role in Asia from the geographical viewpoint. Its Asian policy, strongly influenced by nationalism and power ambitions, is subordinated to China's wider strategic objective—to become in the shortest possible time the leading economic, political and military power in the world. The expansion of relations between China and the United States (mainly in the military sphere) aroused considerable anxieties in Asia. However, what could be called actual alliance in the late 1970's has undergone great changes and nowadays China proclaims "a policy independent of the United States and the Soviet Union." A number of identical features in the socio-economic standard supports China's clean-cut orientation to developing countries, particularly in Asia, towards which it has ambitions to gain the leading position.

The China factor need not worry the Asian and Pacific region countries in evolving a system of comprehensive security there. The favourable developments in Sino-Soviet relations over the past few years, which have got accelerated of late, are not only not detrimental to any third country, but are likely to help improve the political climate in the entire region. Even A.P. Venkateswaran,

3. Rakesh Gupta. US Concern Over Asia-Pacific. *Patriot*, 9 October, 1986 ; p. 4

secretary to the Indian Foreign Affairs Ministry, admitted this in his talks with newsmen at the end of his visit to the Soviet Union on 5 October, 1986 when he said that "if there is any one who can really help us improve our ties with China it is none other than Mikhail Gorbachev."[4]

"The Soviet Union's striving to ensure durable peace and security in Asia has been shown convincingly again by the speech Mikhail Gorbachev delivered in Vladivostok." This has been stated by the Deputy Foreign Minister of Afghanistan Hodaidad Basarmal.

"Regrettably, the United States and its imperialist allies proclaim the whole world to be a zone of their vital interests. Some 30 US military bases are situated in the Indian Ocean basin alone. Due to the designs of the United States, the Asian-Pacific region has been turned into the second area in the world after Europe for the degree in which it is inundated with nuclear weapons", the Afghan Minister noted.

"People of the region oppose the United States diktat", he further said. "They can always count in this on the Soviet Union's support. We, Afghans, strongly support Mikhail Gorbachev's proposal for the convocation of a Pacific Conference patterned on the Helsinki Conference", he added.

"The Soviet Government's decision to return home several units of the limited contingent of the Soviet troops in the DRA reflects the Soviet Union's striving for an early peaceful settlement of the existing situation. This step is to exert a positive effect on the course of the Afghan-Pakistan talks in Geneva," Hodaidad Basarmal said.

Arithmetics is by no means irrelevant to politics. The material components of politics readily land themselves to numerical expression. At times, however, figures fail to convey the full magnitude of this or that political move. Western speculations over the Soviet leadership's decision to bring six Soviet regiments home from Afghanistan before the end of the year 1986 is a case in point.

---

4. See *Patriot*, 8 October, 1986.

The London Times wonders whether this figure is a large or small one and concludes that militarily the Soviet Union's initiative is not a big gesture. Washington's reaction to the Soviet decision was much the same. It has also hastened to dismiss the move as one of "little importance."

The figure—15 is the number of nuclear tests the United States has carried out since the declaration of the Soviet moratorium on its nuclear tests. Now, is this figure big or small? An absurd question, surely. For what matters, in the final analysis, is not the figure as such but the tendency behind it.

The six Soviet regiments returning home from Afghanistan are also evidence of a certain tendency. This is yet another concrete step along the path of building an all-embracing international security system mapped out by the 27th CPSU Congress. The purpose of the Soviet move is to help bring about a political settlement of the situation around Afghanistan, to give a new impetus to the Afghan-Pakistani negotiations now being held in Geneva through the good offices of the U.N. Secretary-General's representative. This first step of the Soviets may be followed by other similar steps. It was stated by Gorbachev in Vladivostok that in the event a final settlement was worked out, the Soviet side would be prepared to speed up the return of all its troops from Afghanistan with the Afghan leadership's consent.

The matter does not rest solely with the Soviets, however. The problem connected with Afghanistan have been created by those who hate the idea of other nations managing their own affairs. By its peace initiative the Soviet Union seeks to ease the tense situation around Afghanistan. It hopes that those who organize and carry out the armed intervention against Afghanistan will appreciate the Soviet Union's goodwill gesture and respond to it accordingly.

Prime Minister Rajiv Gandhi has said: "It is extremely important that Reagan and Gorbachev together build on the common perception they expressed at Geneva last year (1985) that a nuclear war cannot be won and must not be fought. The Soviet Union has, of course, unilaterally extended its moratorium on nuclear tests, and generally expressed its readiness to proceed with nuclear disarmament within the framework of the Six-Nation initiative, which has been endorsed by the Non-Aligned Movement. This is most gratifying. We hope for a similar response from the United States and other nuclear weapon powers."[5]

Prime Minister Rajiv Gandhi expressed happiness that the "six-nation" initiative had received support from the Soviet Union and its CPSU General Secretary Mikhail Gorbachev. "We are very happy with the steps offered by Mr. Gorbachev. The suggestions made at Vladivostok are positive," he said.[6]

Rajiv Gandhi was asked about Gorbachev's peace proposal especially the security idea for Asia and the Pacific region.

"We welcome the important and significant speech delivered by Mr. Mikhail Gorbachev at Vladivostok on July 28,1986. His continuous emphasis on nuclear disarmament and the unilateral moratorium on nuclear tests undertaken by the USSR have provided great encouragement and support to mankind to continue its efforts to rid the world of the threat of annihilation of whole civilisation". This has been said by Prof. S. Nurul Hasan, noted historian, former Indian Ambassador to the USSR. "We, in India, highly appraise Mr. Gorbachev's warm references to India, Indo-Soviet relations and the non-aligned movement. His forthright support to the unity and integrity of India, to the cause of peace in Asia and the Pacific regions and to the demilitarisation of the Indian Ocean are bound to be highly appreciated by the entire Indian people."

Japan, representing advanced capitalism in Asia, has become one of the world's imperialist centres in specific geographical and historical conditions, with U.S. support. It pursues an expansive economic policy in Asia. Although its military potential is not big, it keeps growing and must be taken into consideration in connection with alliance with the United States. This alliance, reflected also in identical attitudes to most of the Asian problems, has been substantially strengthened by the incumbent government of Prime Minister Y. Nakasone.

Mayor Takeshi Araki of Hiroshima said in Tokyo, on July 31, 1986 that he regards the proposal by Mikhail Gorbachev on

5. *Blitz* (Bombay) 11 October, 1986, p. 23.
6. *The Hindustan Times* (New Delhi) 12 August, 1986.

holding in Hiroshima of an international conference on security problems in the Asian and Pacific region as evidence of the fact that Hiroshima won recognition as a starting point on the road to peace.

Mikhail Gorbachev on August 11, 1986 met in Moscow with Chairman of the Presidium of the Central Committee of the Japanese Communist Party Tetsuzo Fuwa.

Gorbachev pointed out great importance of the very fact of the meeting of representatives of the CPSU and the Japanese Communist Party, which attests to the further development of their friendly relations, which become ever richer in content and more constructive. The two Parties, just as all fraternal Parties, are independent and equal, he stressed. But while being national forces and expressing the interests of their peoples, they are also forces of international character. The very course of world events, the vital need for the struggle for the prevention of new world war necessitate a greater interaction of communists of different countries. This must not be hampered in any measure either by the different conditions of their activity or the existing differences on some or other matter, he observed.

Summing up the main directions of the development of world politics, Gorbachev said that there still exist two lines, two approaches to the solution of vital problems. The line to which the Soviet Union adheres consistently, for which various forces that are sincerely interested in the consolidation of international security declare, is that of honest struggle for an end to the arms race, to confrontation, or transition to disarmament and broad international co-operation on the basis of the recognition of lawful interests and rights of all peoples, a realistic approach to the assessment of prospects of the development of civilisation from the viewpoint of nuclear menace. It is precisely this approach that prompts the peaceful initiatives of the USSR, of other socialist countries, since the 1985 Geneva meeting. The Soviet Union continues demostrating in practice the adherence to the ideas formulated in the Soviet-US-statement, Gorbachev said.

The other approach, that of the forces which declare for power methods of resolving world problems, without taking into consideration possible consequences of their use, is the unlimited build-up of the arms race, its spread into outer space, the continuation, of the confrontation, Gorbachev noted.

Pursuing clearly selfish purposes, these forces are obviously not going to lay down arms. This is reality and we should be aware of it, he added.

However, while realistically appraising the situation, we do not take a pessimistic stand, Gorbachev went on to say. These are great opportunities for the peace efforts and the potential of the peace keeps growing. There is very chance today not to surrender the destinies of peace into the hands of those who are irresponsibly guiding themselves by militarism and the arms race.

The Soviet Union, he stressed, will continue to work prese-veringly for the early accomplishment of the lofty strategic goal of the prohibition and elimination of nucler weapons and for the success of the ongoing talks, which presupposes the solution of partial, tactical problems that leads to that goal.

Mongolia is vitally interested in strengthening security in Asia. It fully supports the Soviet proposals and its own initiative of 1981 for concluding a Convention on mutual non-aggression and non-use of force among the states of Asia and the Pacific Ocean is of wider, all-Asian importance. The states of Indochina call for peaceful coexistence with the member countries of ASEAN. Similarly, the Democratic Korea, neighouring on the dictatorial regime in Seoul, which receives all round support of imperialism, focuses its attention mainly on this threat as on the problem of the country's reunification.

Mikhail Gorbachev on August 12, 1986 met Jambyn Batmunh, General Secretary of the Central Committee of the Mongolian People's Revolutionary Party (MPRP) and President of the Pre-sidium of the People's Great Hural of the Mongolian People's Republic in Moscow.

They spoke highly of broad and multifaceted Soviet-Mongo-lian co-operation but noted that the reserves available in this field are yet used far from fully. The task of further increasing the effectiveness of bilateral economic relations remains on the agenda.

Mikhail Gorbachev and Jambyn Batmunh expressed concern about international tensions persisting through the fault of bellicose US quarters. In these conditions, it is of prime significance to further strengthen the unity and cohesion of socialist countries and ensure their ever more vigorous interaction in working out and executing a concerted policy of fending off the threat of a nuclear war and consolidating universal peace.

Stress was laid on the role of processes taking place in the Asian-Pacific region, which determine in many ways the destiny of peace in general. Confidence was expressed that it is necessary to foster relations of peace, co-operation and good-neighbourliness there.

Jambyn Batmunh put a high value on the new Soviet initiatives meetings the interests of stronger security for the Asian and Pacific countries and of the limitation and reduction of arms, first of all nuclear arms. Consonant with these ideas is Mongolia's proposal, reiterated by the 49th Congress of the MPRP, for building a mechanism to rule out use of force in relations among states in that region as well as the known peace initiatives of the Democratic Korea, Vietnam, Laos and Kampuchea.

The Asian-Pacific people, politicians and public figures of different orientations are becoming increasingly convinced that resolute actions to save the world from the impending nuclear catastrophe are the urgent call of the day.

The committee working on a new constitution for the Philippines has suggested including in it an Article saying that the Philippines, in keeping with its national interests, has chosen and is pursuing a nuclear-free policy in its territory. "The Pentagon has no right to deploy nuclear weapons at Palau," the ruling of the Palau Special Appeal Court has said. Governmental spokesmen pointed in this connection that in its dealings with the Pacific countries, the USA ought to follow the example of the Soviet Union which has no military bases and nuclear weapons in the territories of other countries in the region.

During his recent talks with the French President Francois Mitterand, President Suharto of Indonesia voiced his resolute protest at continuing French nuclear tests in the southern Pacific, called for the elimination of nuclear arms, and stressed that the world is on the brink of a fatal disaster. He said that the funds spent on nuclear weapons should be better used for the abolition of hunger, disease and backwardness. He called on all countries to help end the arms race and work for disarmament.

The regional nations welcome the Soviet initiatives and concrete steps towards nuclear disarmament, notably, the Soviet decision to extend the unilateral moratorium on all nuclear tests until January 1987. "We are happy that the Soviet Union has extended its moratorium for the fourth time," Prime Minister Rajiv Gandhi of India said in an interview with the magazine *Asia and Africa Today.* It is utterly wrong that the other nuclear powers have so far failed to join the Soviet stand. But we hope that they will do that, he said.

"As we are working to clear our region from nuclear weapons" Efraim Kalsakol, General Secretary of the Trade Union Congress of Vanuatu, said in an interview with the Soviet newspaper *Trud,* "we welcome the Soviet Union's programme for establishing a stable peace and all-round constructive co-operation in Asia and the Pacific region."

In the years (1976-1986) since reunification, the Vietnamese working people have registered successes in all spheres of economic and cultural advance, in the development of the productive forces and the strenghtening and consolidation of the new, socialist relations of production. More than 300 major economic projects have been carried out, with the result that the country's production potential has substantially grown in many key branches of industry. The strengthening of the material and technical base and improvement of management in all branches of the economy made for a substantial increase in the growth rate of social production. For instance, the average annual growth rate of agricultural output during the last five-year-plan period (1981-85) increased to 5.1 per cent as against 2 per cent in 1976-80. In industry the corresponding percentages were 14 and 0.7. On the basis of the increase in production the scale of construction of housing and cultural facilities expanded. Strides were made in the development of culture, the arts, and medical care.

While resolving internal problems the Communist Party and the government of Vietnam devote much attention to foreign policy specifically the promotion of friendship and co-operation with all countries and peoples of the world. Particularly notable is the progress made in promoting multiform relations between Vietnam and our country. In January 1986 a protocol on completion of the co-ordination of state plans of the Soviet Union and Vietnam for 1986-90 was signed in Hanoi. The protocol provides for measures relating to the implementation of the most important provisions of the long-term programme of economic, scientific and technological co-operation signed by the two countries in 1983 and also of the decisions of the CMEA economic summit conference in 1984. The protocol provides for a 1.7 fold increase in Soviet-Vietnamese trade in the course of this five-year plan; the Soviet Union will increase aid to Vietnam in the construction of important economic projects.

The people of Vietnam are working indefatigably to strengthen their country. With substantial successes to their credit in the building of socialism and defence of their country, in the struggle to strengthen its international position the people of Vietnam are actively working with the fraternal peoples of Laos and Kampuchea for peace and security in Asia and the Pacific and throughout the world.

A meeting between Mikhail Gorbachev, and Truong Chinh, General Secretary of the Central Committee of the Communist Party of Vietnam and Chairman of Vietnam's State Council, was held on August 12, 1986, in Moscow.

The leaders of the two Parties exchanged views on various aspects of the present-day international situation and discussed the present state and prospects of the further development of Soviet-Vietnamese relations.

Mikhail Gorbachev and Truong Chinh stressed the identity of the Soviet and the Vietnamese assessments of the international situation. The major question, the question of war and peace, calls for the further mobilisation of all peace-loving and progressive forces for a resolute struggle for the prevention of nuclear war.

Both leaders voiced concern over the dangerous development of the situation in the Asian-Pacific region. It was observed that militarisation and the growth of the threat of war in that part of the world are starting to gather a dangerous speed. The Soviet Union and Vietnam are opposed to this course of events.

They see their interests in uniting the efforts of all countries and in promoting co-operation with full respect for the right of each nation to lead a life of its own choice and independently solve its problems in conditions of peace. Truong Chinh voiced unreserved backing for the new Soviet initiatives, advanced by Mikhail Gorbachev in his important speech in Vladivostok, for normalising the situation in the Asian-Pacific region and involving that region in the general process of building a comprehensive system of international security. He said that holding an Asian-Pacific conference with the participation of all the regions' interested sides would make a weighty contribution to fulfilling this task.

The Soviet Union and Vietnam together with fraternal Laos and Kampuchea stand actively for turning South-East Asia into a zone of peace, good-neighbourliness and co-operation. The Soviet Union and Vietnam reiterate their readiness to normalise relations with China, which would be very significant to improving the situation in the Asian-Pacific region and consolidating universal peace.

Asia's economic security is greatly jeopardised by Transnational corporations. In the past few years transnationals have spread their tentacles aggressively in Asia and the Pacific regions. US and Japanese corporations have displayed particular zeal in expanding their activities in many countries, penetrating new industries and bearing a strong impact on social affairs in the host countries.

Trampling underfoot the Asian national interests transnational corporations seek to gain control over emergent economies. By dominating local markets, transnationals seek to step exploitation of the Asian peoples, laying these under enormous tribute. According to some estimates, the overall profit milked by transnationals from different sources in the developing economies exceeds 100 billion dollars a year. A substantial amount of this money comes from Asian countries. Employees at factories run by foreign companies are mercilessly exploited. Wages paid to labour hired by American companies in Asia are ten times lower than those paid back at home to American workers with similar skills and working hours are 1.5 to 2 times longer. The same amount of money invested by transnationals in Asia brings three to four times more profit than when invested in a home country.

Transnationals have stepped up their pressure on Asian nations, playing on economic difficulties they face and their growing foreign debt, and putting ever more strains on their governments in an attempt to secure additional advantages. Inspired by transnationals, some international financial institutions, the International Monetary Fund above all, have sought to create a more suitable environment for foreign investment in Asia.

In many, an Asian country, the public sector has found itself under increasing pressure from transnationals. The latter have stepped up pressure on Asian governments in an attempt to force them to de-nationalise their state-run industries and by so doing consolidate their positions in Asian economies. Yielding to strong pressure, some Asian governments have substantially curtailed their public sector.

The Asian-Pacific peoples seem to increasingly realise that transnationals' aggressive expansion thwarts Asia's economic security and jeopardises Asian national interests. Progressives in many an Asian country have been more and more outspoken about the need to adopt economic policies rebuffing corporate pressure and promoting economic and political independence of emergent countries. It is for that reason that Asia reacted with so much interest to Soviet proposals concerning an overall security system in Asia presented by Mikhail Gorbachev in his Vladivostok speech in July 1986. The Soviet leader said such a system would promote peace in Asia, ensuring mutually advantageous and equitable co-operation between all its nations and paving the way for a resolution of the political and economic issues facing the continent,

A valuable contribution to this struggle is offered by the Soviet Union, one of the largest Asian and Pacific powers. At the 27th Congress of the Communist Party of the Soviet Union, held in Moscow in February-March 1986, an in-depth analysis was made of ways of ensuring security in Asia. The Political Report to the Congress, delivered by Mikhail Gorbachev, General Secretary of the CPSU Central Committee, noted : "The significance of the Asian and Pacific direction is growing. In that vast region there are many tangled knots of contradictions and, besides, the political situation in some places is unstable. Here it is necessary, without postponement, to search for the relevant solutions and paths. Evidently, it is expedient to begin with the co-ordination and then the pooling of efforts in the interests of a political settlement of painful problems so as, in parallel, on that basis to at least take the edge off the military confrontation in various parts of Asia and stabilize the situation there. This is made all the more urgent by the fact that in Asia and other continents the flashpoints of military danger are not being extinguished. We are in favour of vitalizing collective quests for defusing conflict situations in the Middle East,...in all of the planet's turbulent points. This is imperatively demanded by the interests of general security."

Asia is not formally divided as Europe has been into two hostile alliances reinforced by ideological divides. Why should it therefore be more difficult in Asia to create a forum where countries in Asia could exchange their views on problems of Asian security? Why a country like India, leader of the Non-aligned Movement, whose aim is peace, should shy away from discussing initially at any rate the question of Asian security? Even if such discussions are not possible at official level, we could certainly engage in such discussions in seminars and conferences of Asian intellectuals.[7]

The main objective of Islamabad and its mentors, however, is to drag Sri Lanka in the arms race on the pretext of fighting terrorism. Military expenditure of Sri Lanka had increased to six billion rupees, as against 3.6 billion allocated in the budget. The strength of Sri Lanka's armed force is also rapidly increasing—according toone estimate, from 13,000 to nearly 50,000. Over 200 Sri Lankan servicemen are already receivng training in Pakistan, according to a report. Ten-thousand strong "auxiliary detachment"

7. P.N. Haksar. Time Asia Worked for Security. *Patriot.*, 24 July, 1986, p. 4.

of Sri Lankans will be manned by Pakistani trained officers. Sri Lanka has begun to receive from the US and Pakistan military hardware, including aircraft, helicopters and patrol boats. Prisident Zia has announced that Islamabad would give 'moral and material support' to this island to "combat terrorism" while Gen V. Walters, US representative in the UN Security Council, has declared that security of this island demanded a continuous supply of arms. This is how the alleged "Soviet threat" is being used for militarisation of Pakistan and the so-called India's interference in the internal affairs of Sri Lanka being used to draw this country in the arms race.[8]

Thus, in the Pak-India-Sri Lanka triangle, the arms race is being stimulated by Washington, both overtly and covertly. This undoubtedly has created new security problems for India. That being the situation. New Delhi is vitally interested in activating the South Asian Association for Regional Co-operation—SAARC—for it is only through joint efforts of the countries of South Asia that common problems can be solved in the spirit of friendship, trust and mutual understanding. This also is the only way by which interference by big powers in the mutual relations of the countries of this region can be blocked. But, at present, Pakistan has assigned itself the role of launching pad for Washington's so-called strategic interests. From whatever angle you look at, India's security problems and peace in South Asia are getting more and more intertwined.[9]

---

8. V.D. Chopra. Peace in South Asia and Washington. *Patriot*, 21 July, 1986, p. 4.
9. *Ibid.*

Chapter Two

THE CONCEPT

FOR MANY YEARS, problems facing Asia and the Pacific were resolved through confrontation, show of force and the refusal to discuss them at the negotiating table. That is why the July 28, 1986 speech of the Soviet leader Mikhail Gorbachev in Vladivostok is of special interest to all interested in the issues of peace, security and stability in the region. Restraint rather than confrontation is the essence of the peaceful appeal addressed by the Soviet Union to the international community.

The USSR has demonstrated a new approach to the settlement of outstanding issues. The decision to return home six regiments from Afghanistan from October 15, 1986, is a practical contribution to resolving the complex questions of settling the situation in Asia.

There still exist two different approaches to the solution of vital international problems. The line to which the Soviet Union adheres is that of honest efforts for an end to the arms race and to confrontation, of transition to disarmament and broad international co-operation on the basis of the recognition of the legitimate interests and rights of all peoples, and of a realistic assessment of the prospects for development of civilisation in the nuclear weapons age. The other approach is that of power methods in resolving world problems without taking into consideration the possible consequences of their use, the unrestrained arms race, its spread into outer space, and the continuation of the confrontation.

This applies also to the Asia-Pacific region. This region is turning into an independent centre of world politics. The integration processes there are hindered by the policies of strengthening the confrontation hostility and militarisation of that region. This line is embodied in the US policy and actions. President Reagan's principle of force as the only road to peace lies at the core of the US policies and 'security' concept. It pushes to the fore the military component which envisages a drastic increase in the US military potential on the Hawaian islands and at the American bases in Japan, South Korea and the Philippines, the strenghening of military political relations with Tokyo and Seoul and more active attempts to set up a tri-partite alliance with them and military co-operation with the allies during the regular large-scale military manoeuvers like the 'Rimpac", and "Team Spirit" (jointly with South Korea).

The Washington concept of "security" in Asia and the Pacific and the policies based on it destabilise the situation in the region, boost the arms race, increase antagonisms between States, and aggravate contradictions in small and medium-size countries.

The Soviet policies and security concept rule out military or other power methods on the international scene. Taking into account the region's specifics, the USSR advances well-elaborated proposals guaranteeing security and peace which are equally important for the Soviet Union. Concern over the situation in the region was voiced in the April 23, 1986 statement by the Soviet Government, and in the July 28, 1986 speech delivered in Vladivostok by Mikhail Gorbachev. Both the statement and the speech contained a set of proposals which when implemented could substantially strengthen international security and peaceful co-operation in the region.

The proposals are aimed at a regional settlement and at slowing down the region's militarisation. The steps include the lowering of the nuclear armaments, the reduction of the naval activity in the Pacific and of the conventional weapons in Asia, the dissolution of the military blocs, and the drafting of confidence-building steps and measures to rule out the use of force in the region. The USSR has proposed to convene a conference of all the countries of the region to solve all the issues.

As for economic security, the Soviet Union has expressed its interest in the idea of the "Pacific economic co-operation", advanced by several countries of Asia and Pacific including Japan. The USSR is prepared to join a vast exchange of opinion among all the interested countries in that part of the world regarding an equal, mutually beneficial and steady commercial, economic, technological, scientific and cultural co-operation.

The Soviet Union, which is a major Asian power, said Mikhail Gorbachev, is far from being indifferent to ways of the future development of events on the Asian continent. That is why the USSR has exerted so much effort to see Asian become a zone of peace, good-neighbourliness and co-operation. The Soviet Union has more than once taken initiatives for cardinally improving the political situation in the Asian-Pacific region, he recalled. Concern for establishing a durable a peace in the region keynotes the Soviet Government's statement of April 23, 1986, which reaffirms the set of Soviet proposals on seeking ways to peace and security in Asia jointly, through pooling the efforts of all nations. The interests of Asian nationg are, undoubtedly, met by the positive Soviet proposals—the programme for the elimination of nuclear and other types of weapons of mass destruction before the end of this century and by other peaceful initiatives.

It is peace and good-neighbourliness, not the arms race and confrontation, that meet the aspirations of the peoples of Asia. An ever large number of Asian states are joining in the struggle for preserving Asian unity in an integrated world, the Soviet leader Mikhail Gorbachev observed.

The cause of strengthening peace in Asia is, undoubtedly, served by the initiatives of India and Sri Lanka supported by many other countries of the region for the Indian Ocean as a zone of peace. The three states of Indochina, the Democratic Korea and the Democratic Afghanistan have lately made important proposals on a settlement of crisis situations and on improvement of the situation in various regions of the continent. The proposal of the Mongolian People's Republic to conclude a Convention on the non-use of force in relations between Asian states has met with a response in Asia. The proposals of States in the South Pacific to proclaim the region a nuclear-free zone are an important contribution to the cause of detente in Asia.

The Soviet Union, which outlined at the 27th CPSU's Congress a magnificent programme of construction, in which an important place in held by the accelerated socio-economic development of the USSR's Asian part, including the Soviet Far East, fully supports these proposals and keeps on taking new peaceful initiatives. The Soviet Government proceeds from the premise that the tasks of ensuring peace in Asia—where a wealth of experience of collectively solving difficult problems has been accumulated, where the principles of Bandung were worked out—challenging as they are, can perfectly well be fulfilled.

The vast majority of the nations and peoples as well as politicians and governments of the Asian and Pacific region feel the imperative need for Asia to work out and adopt some fundamental principles of inter-state relations and create a new situation where confrontation will give way to dialogue and closer relationships while the feelings of uncertainty and suspicion will give way to confidence, and isolationism and animosity to broad political, economic and cultural co-operation. Although there are considerable difficulties still in the way of a safer peace in the Asian Pacific region, they are surmountable due to a number of factors : the historica gains of the world-wide national liberation movement which has produced over a score of independent nations ; the rising tide of anti-war and anti-nuclear movements ; the growing international prestige and positive role of the non-aligned movement in world affairs; a certain shift towards normalcy in Soviet-Chinese relations; and the mounting pressure of Asian countries for a reshaping of international economic relations and for a new information order.[1]

The Soviet leadership have made a series a workable proposals in the last few years for overcoming the obstacles in the way of a safar peace and closer peaceful co-operation between the nations of Asia. A number of important constructive initiatives concerning some aspects of the security of the Asian continent and its various regions have been put forward by other Socialist nations of Asia as well as by members of the non-aligned movement in recent years.

---

1. George Kim. Peace and Security for Asia. New Delhi, Allied, 1986, pp. 43-56.

"The question now is: isn't it worthwhile considering a general, package approach to security problems in Asia, taking into account all those initiatives as well as, to some extent, the experience of Europe, and a possible pooling of the efforts of Asian States in that direction?" Mikhail Gorbachev said when conferring with Prime Minister Rajiv Gandhi in Moscow on May 21, 1985. "Of course", the Soviet leaders stressed, "there is a hard road to travel. But neither was the road to Helsinki smooth and plain."

The essential point in the Soviet proposal for framing a general package approach to security problems in Asia is to have all the Asian States, whatever their social system, join forces with a view to assuring peace and stability, naturally, taking into account the Helsinki experience.

It was over ten years ago, on August 1, 1975, that 33 European nations plus the US and Canada, meeting in Helsinki, signed a historic document summing up, as it were, all that the peoples understood by the pregnant word "detente."

Unquestionably, the European Conference has been one of great importance. There is much in the experience it produced that could be borrowed by Asian nations. The main thing was that its participants found a way of getting down at one table and exploring and discovering solutions that proved to be acceptable to all the parties concerned.

"It would be possible", says the statement of the Soviet Government on April 23, 1986, "appropriately to prepare and hold a separate meeting of the countries of the Pacific Ocean area to consider matters of security, including those that are economic ones. Considering the potential of the countries of the Pacific Ocean area in the political and economic fields, the holding of such a meeting—and one should see to it that it ends with important decisions – would become a major event for the region and would have a fruitful effect on the situation in the world as a whole."

One cannot, of course, overlook the particular aspects of the present situation on the Asian continent. It is clear that Asia cannot just imitate the forms that the preparations for, and the holding of the European Conference assumed. In Asia, there can, evidently, be different ways to follow—bilateral negotiations and multilateral consultations, to the extent of eventually staging a kind of Pan-Asian forum for an exchange of views and for a joint search for constructive solutions.

Asia can, beyond question, apply the basic principles of the Helsinki Final Act, such as respect for sovereignty and non-intervention in internal affairs, refraining from the use of force, peaceful settlement of disputes, the right of nations to decide their own destinies, promotion of co-operation on terms of equality and mutual benefit. One has to take into account, besides, the fact that the Helsinki principles are consonant with the well-known ten principles of Bandung.

What does the Soviet concept of Asian security follow from and rest on ? First, it rest on the realisation that the peoples of Asia are linked together by the community of their vital interests and that they have to resolve what are in many ways similar problems which arise from the past or which may yet arise in the future. And that makes it imperative for them to promote co-operation and good-neighbourly relations based on a broad system of security that would meet the interests of all and every one of the nations of the region.

In the opinion of the Soviet leadership, such a system could incorporate the entire experience that has been gained and the entire positive peace potential that has been built up by the Asian countries, and the peace proposals and initiatives that have been put forward by individual nations or groups of nations.

The record of the post-war decades provides conclusive evidence to show that it is American intervention that has been the major hindrance to quick, fair and peaceful settlement of the regional conflicts that have erupted in Asia. In these circumstances it is perfectly logical for many prominent Asian politicians and statesmen to be calling for action to safeguard the continent from foreign intervention. This is, incidentelly, the specific object behind the proposal put forward by the USSR during the Soviet-Indian negotiations in May, 1985. Its essential point is that each permanent member of the Security Council (that is, the Great Powers) should undertake to refrain from interfering in the affairs of the countries of Asia, Africa and Latin America, from threatening to use force against them or drawing them into was blocs. For its part, the USSR has expressed its readiness to assume such a commitment.

Over four years ago the USSR suggested holding concrete negotiations about confidence-building measures in the Far East. Any nation could make its contribution towards drafting such measures, taking into account the specific circumstances of the Asian and pacific region. In the context of the present strained situation in the Far East and the Pacific area, the said Soviet proposals are of added relevance.

From the Soviet point of view, it would be advisable to extend confidence-building measures to the seas and oceans, particularly the regions of the busiest sea traffic. That applies, first and foremost, to the Indian and Pacific Oceans.

A point of fundamental importance to peace and security in Asia is to spare it the nuclear threat.

". . . We are for scaling down the confrontation in terms of medium-range nuclear capability", Mikhail Gorbachev pointed out in the course of the Soviet-Vietnamese talks in June, 1985. We would agree ". . . to have our missile holdings frozen in the Asian part of the Soviet Union, provided, of course, the American side takes no action that would tend to change the strategic situation in the region. The Soviet Union would not be averse to discussing this problem with the nations of Asia and the Pacific having similar capability with a view to limiting and subsequently reducing this capability, naturally, on mutual terms."

Way back at the time of the Special United Nations Session on Disarmament, in 1982, the USSR pledged itself, unilaterally by the way, not to be the first to use nuclear weapons. Such a pledge was assumed by the People's Rupublic of China (PRC) as well. A growing number of Asian nations have been proposing that not only the Soviet Union and the PRC, but other nations having nuclear weapons as well should undertake to refrain from using nuclear weapons first, in Asia in this particular case.

"The total ending of nuclear weapon tests by the nuclear powers everywhere, including Asia, the Pacific and Indian Oceans, and the refusal by the nations of the region to have anything to do with the plans to militarise space would certainly serve to promote Asian security," Mikhail Gorbachev stressed at the Kremlin banquet in honour of Mongolian leader Jambyn Batmunh on August 29, 1985.

Of all the nations in possession of nuclear weapons, the Soviet Union was the first to speak out (in 1955) for all nuclear tests to stop, and to make that a point of its disarmament programme. The Soviet leadership have since been putting forward more and more constructive initiatives at major international fora to reduce the threat of nuclear war. These proposals have quite logically led to the latest set of Soviet initiatives aimed at scrapping nuclear arms and all other weapons of wholesale annihilation by 2000, preventing space from being militarised, and making greater headway at the negotiations concerned with disarmament and limitation of every kind of military activity.

This wide-ranging programme is entirely in tune with the interests of Asian nations too. Given an accord for total elimination of nuclear weapons by the end of the century, it would be far easier to come to an agreement on other moves to strengthen security in the Asian and Pacific region and, in particular, to freeze and scale down military activity in the region. It was the American ambition to pose a nuclear threat against the Soviet Union from the southerly direction that led to the US unilaterally breaking off the Soviet-American talks on the limitation and reduction of naval activity in the Indian Ocean area and stepping up its militarisation.

Should a nuclear-free world become a common political goal, there would be no more bid to cobble together any new military blocks in the region or enlarge those already in existence. There would be favourable conditions for the foreign military bases on the territories of the nations of Asia and in the Pacific and Indian Oceans to be dismentled. Isn't that one reason behind the United States refusal to stop the testing of nuclearwe apons and to join the Soviet Union's unilateral moratorium on all nuclear explosions announced on the 40th anniversary of the stom-bombing of the Asian cities of Hiroshima and Nagasaki ?

For an Asian security system to be really dependable, it must take into account all of the experience gained in various parts of the world in the effort to reduce international tensions and promote detente.

In the opinion of the Soviet leadership, proper attention should be given to the many constructive proposals of Asian countries calling for a pledge to renounce the use of force, respect the sovereignty and territorial integrity of all the nations of the region, carry through confidence-building measures in the military and political fields and a number of other steps.

Among them, one should note the Mongolian proposal for drafting and concluding a convention on mutual non-aggression and non-use of force in relations between the States of Asia and the Pacific, as put forward for the first time in June, 1981.

Also notworthy are the peace initiatives of the Democratic People's Republic of Korea (DPRK) for easing tensions in Korea and throughout the Far East. The proposal made at the session of the Supreme People's Assembly of the DPRK in April, 1985 laid good ground for a positive dialogue between Pyongyang and Seoul. To establish national concord and confidence, the Government of people's Korea believes, it is necessary for representatives of the parliaments of the North and the South to enter into direct negotiations.

As a practical measure of primary importance in the course of that dialogue the sides could discuss the question of the adoption of a bilateral declaration of non-aggression, which would certainly help ease tension, improve relations and create an atmosphere of trust and mutual understanding between the two countries.

Showing concern about the future of peace in the region, the DPRK has expressed its readiness to hold a preliminary meeting of representatives of the North and the South in order to examine the initiatives proposed and all other propositions serving the joint search for ways of settling the existing problems.

The initiatives of Pyongyang are an appreciable contribution to the materialization of the DPRK's consistent peace-loving course in the Far East. Their practical implementation would play a positive role in the attenuation of the political climate and in the consolidation of peace not only on the Korean peninsula, but also in the Asian Pacific region as a whole.

The Asian and world public values the constructive position of Vietnam, Laos and Kampuchea, which are working to make Southeast Asia a zone of peace and stability. They have suggested holding a regional conference between two groups of states : the three Indochina nations and the ASEAN members, and signing a relevant treaty. That would help remove the burden of the past and the alienation and mistrust which have accumulated in Southeast Asia over the years as a result of plots and scheming by outside forces.

On February 22, 1981 the USSR made an appeal to the governments of ASEAN states to display political realism and to give due consideration to the proposals put before them. The Soviet Union has expressed readiness to take part, alongside the other permanent members of the UN Security Council, in an international conference aimed at securing a treaty of peace and stability among the countries of the region.

Another issue of growing urgency today is guaranteeing peace and security in the Indian Ocean. The proposal to declare that crucial oceanic basin a zone of peace was put forward by a group of non-aligned nations at their summit in Lusaka in 1970. Their initiative was supported by the UN General Assembly which went on to adopt, in 1971, the Declaration of the Indian Ocean as a Zone of Peace and which decided to convene an international conference in Colombo as a first step towards demilitarization of the region.

Together with the non-aligned states and all progressive mankind the USSR is campaigning for the most rigid restrictions possible on foreign military presence in the Indian Ocean. In May 1985 the Soviet leadership reiterated its proposals to all the states whose ships were plying the waters of the Indian Ocean that they refrain from any steps which might exacerbate the situation in the region without waiting for the convocation of the international conference. This implies not sending large naval formations to holding military exercises there, and not expanding or modernizing the military bases of the noncoastal states which do have such bases.

It should be repeated here that the five principles of peaceful coexistence (Panchsheel) and the ten Bandung principles which were worked out by the Asian states and which have played a positive role more than once in settling various regional conflicts have retained their relevance and importance to the present day. They could just as easily be taken into consideration by the participants in the broad discussion on Asian security.

The Soviet Union would welcome the establishment of nuclear-free zones in the Asia-Pacific region. The decision of the Southern Pacific countries to declare the area a nuclear-free zone has met with the most positive response in the Soviet Union.

An important instrument in the settlement of the problems of Asian security is the development of good-neighbourly co-operation among states with both similar and different social systems, based on the principles of equality and mutual benefit, without any discrimination.

The development of economic cooperation among Asian states on the regional basis is dictated by the objective needs of the development of productive forces there, since joint economic efforts and the advantages of the division of labour give the only opportunity for many Asian states to gain real economic independence. Needless to say, this course would stabilize the political climate in Asia, too.

In the statement of the Soviet Government of April 23, 1986 the following is said in this connection:

"The Soviet Union is proposing to start a wide exchange of views between all interested countries of that part of the world on matters aimed at establishing equitable, mutually beneficial and steady trade-and-economic, technological, scientific and cultural co-operation. The following could become spheres of such co-operation: the development of productive forces, the training of personnel, the use of new sources of energy, including nuclear one, the upgrading of means of transportation, communication, the revelation of new forms of trade-and-economic, and financial co-operation with due regard for the interests of the developing countries of the region, exchanges of scientific and scientific-technical information, the development of measures for the protection of the environment and for rational utilisation of biological and mineral resources of seas and oceans, the conduct of peaceful space research for common benefit, joint work in the field of medicine and health-care, efforts to combat natural calamities and to eliminate their aftermath, and so on".

The Asian states have already accumulated certain co-operation experience on the sub-regional level—notably, within the framework of the ASEAN and of the Regional Co-operation for Development Organization. Positive experience in this field has been stored up, too, by the UN Economic and Social Commission for Asia and the Pacific (ESCAP). The recent establishment of a new sub-regional organization called the South Asian Regional Co-operation Organisation, whose members have spoken up for the development of good neighbourliness and trade and economic links in the region on the basis of equality and mutual benefit, is yet another advantageous factor to be considered here.

The Soviet Union is positive that it is a vital task for all states to promote fruitful co-operation in the name of accomplishing the peaceful constructive tasks faced by each nation and by all mankind. In the name of such fruitful co-operation the USSR invariably campaigns for strong and truly good-neighbourly relations with Asian states.

For more than a quarter-century now the Soviet Union has been developing friendly and diversified co-operation with India. "Soviet-Indian friendship is not just an asset of our peoples alone. It is an important factor of peace and stability in the current strained international situation and an example of how countries with different systems can fruitfully co-operate if they are guided by the ideals of peace and by the principles of mutual respect and equitable co-operation," said Mikhail Gorbachev in his interview to the Press Trust of India news agency.

Stability of Soviet-Indian relations in the political field is complemented with the broad scope and diverse forms of our co-operation in the economic, trade, scientific, technical and other spheres.

The result of the official friendly visit to the USSR by Prime Minister Rajiv Gandhi in May 1985 have again demonstrated that the development and consolidation of friendly Soviet-Indian links go far beyond the framework of bilateral relations in terms of their importance and are a major factor in the efforts to strengthen peace and security in the world.

These friendly links rest on the firm foundation of the Treaty of Peace, Friendship and Co-operation between the two countries, signed in August 1971. They are not aimed against any third countries. Their basic principles in respect for the sovereignty of independent states and non-interference in the latter's internal affairs.

There has been changes in Soviet-Chinese relations too. As was noted in the Political Report of the CPSU Central Committee to the 27th Party Congress (1986), despite the remaining differences in the two countries' approach to a number of international problems, there are also opportunities for joint efforts and interaction on an equitable and principled basis, not to the deteriment of any third countries.

Another important point is the continuation of Soviet-Japanese meetings and consultations at various levels. Improvement in the relations between the USSR and Japan would certainly have a positive effect on the situation in the Asian Pacific region and would contribute to the general trends of the return to detente which were given momentum by the Soviet-American summit in Geneva.

It should be pointed out in conclusion that the numerous responses to the Soviet proposal for the development of general, comprehensive approach to the problems of security in Asia and for a probable unification of efforts of the Asian states in this direction attest to the existence of a widespread drive for exchange of opinions on the problems of peace and security in Asia.

There are some new inspiring trends in Asia, too. Here one must mention such a positive factor as the growth of anti-war and anti-nuclear sentiments on the continent. The governments, parliaments and the public in the countries of the Asian Pacific region are coming to see the validity of the argument of the indivisibility of peace and of the need for most active participation in the construction of inter-state relations so as to decide the future of the planet together with the whole international community. Peace marches, political discussions and seminars, scientific conferences and symposiums dealing with the problems of peace and security are being held throughout the vast Asian continent. It is indicative that even some of the US allies no longer want to follow in the wake of Washington's aggressive militariest course. This follows from the position of New Zealand which, despite massive political pressure, has refused to allow American warships with nuclear arms on board into its ports. Even so, the contribution of the developing Asian states to the struggle for peace and for the cessation of nuclear weapon tests could be greater.

Indeed, the adoption of the concept of security in Asia and the Pacific is not a transient cause but a long-term task which is to be accomplished stage by stage, by moving from simple things to more complex problems. The important thing is that the states of the region join in the common quest for mutually acceptable agreements. This is the main point in the Soviet proposal for a comprehensive approach to the security problems in Asia. The Soviet programme of nuclear disarmament, whose implementation would help mankind enter the 21st century without fear for its very survival, opens up fundamentally new opportunities for the development of a reliable system of Asian security. For its own part, the conversion of Asia into a continent of good-neighbourliness and co-operation would cement the common human potential of peace, reason and goodwill.

Bruce Cronyn, Co-ordinator of the mass US public organisation "Mobilization for Survival", said on July 31, 1986, in New York that American peace campaigners take great interest in the Soviet proposal to start negotiations for reducing the activity of navies in the Pacific contained in the speech by Mikhail Gorbachev in Vlaidvostok. The need for decisive actions in this field had long become urgent, he stressed.

Reducing the level of military confrontation would contribute to improving the situation both in the Pacific and in the whole world. The removal of US military bases from the territories of several Pacific states would also contribute to the cause of peace and security of the nations, Bruce Cronyn said.

Concern has been mounting among peace-longing Asian and pacific nations over increasing militarisation of that vast area of the world.

Pinning hopes of US military superiority and ability to rule the seas in Asia and the Pacific, the Washington strategists have developed a rather unhealthy interest toward this part of the world, constantly escalating US military presence in the area.

Since the second half of the 70s the US has been steadily building up its Pacific force, beefing it up with new types of aircraft, cruise missiles, etc.

At the same time it has gone a long way to knock together a bellicose triangle Washington-Seoul-Tokyo. The Pentagon has deployed nuclear-capable vehicles and warheads in the south of the Korean peninsula and some nuclear carriers in Japan.

All this gives enough ground to state that militarisation and the whipping up of the military threat in Asia and the Pacific is becoming increasingly dangerous, while the Pacific Ocean is being rapidly turned into an area of military and political confrontation, something that cannot help causing anxiety of all the nations of the region, including the Soviet Union, both a European and Asian and Pacific power.

To curb this pernicious process and reverse it the Soviet Union has proposed an array of urgent measures to be implemented by a concerted effort of all countries involved. These were presented by the Soviet leader Mikail Gorbachev in his speech in Vladivostok on July 28.

First the settlement of regional issues to be urgently dealt with in the interests of particular countries (Kampuchea, Korea, Afghanistan) and Asian security as a whole.

Second. It is necessary to put up a barrier to proliferation and build-up of nuclear weapons in Asia and the Pacific. The USSR supports proclaiming the southern part of the Pacific a nuclear-free zone and urges all nuclear powers to guarantee its status.

The Soviet Union proposes starting talks on reducing the activity of fleets in the Pacific, nuclear-armed ships above all, and refraining from anti-submarine activity in certain zones of the Pacific. The Soviet Union remains strongly in favour of resuming the talks on turning the Indian Ocean into a zone of peace.

Fourth, the USSR attaches much important to radical reduction in armed forces and conventional armaments in Asia to the limits of reasonable sufficiency.

Fifth, the USSR remains strongly committed to the idea that the time has long come to which to the practical plane the discussion of confidence-building measures and non-use of force in the region.

Fitting in the concept of a comprehensive international security system proposed by the 27th Congress of the CPSU, a reliable Asian and Pacific security is to be a cornerstone of that system.

Chapter Three

THE MAIN OBJECTIVES

THE MAIN OBJECTIVE of Soviet foreign policy is to ward off the threat of nuclear war, halt the arms race and safeguard and strengthen universal peace. No task is more important today that that of preserving peace. There is no alternative to a foreign policy whose aim is to ensure that all countries and peoples be able to use on an equal basis the benefits of civilization and progress without fear, mutual suspicion and military confrontation. This is a political axiom, which holds true particularly when international tension escalates. The situation in the world was never as explosive as it became in the first half of the 1980s. In the early 1980s the present US administration, which furthers the interests of the military-industrial complex, and the United States major allies in *Nato* and Japan made a sharp turn from detente to a policy based on the old, ill-fated principles of strength. They adopted doctrines which rejected good-neighbourly relations and co-operation as the principles guiding international relations.[1]

Having made an in-depth analysis of the international situation, the Soviet Union put forward a comprehensive programme for the complete elimination of weapons of mass destruction. Announcing the programme in his January 15, 1986 statement, the Soviet leader Mikhail Gorbachev said that the USSR proposed a gradual reduction of the nuclear weapons by the end of the century. The Soviet programme did not come out of the blue, so to speak. It resulted from the fundamental principles of Soviet foreign policy of peace formulated by Lenin and incorporated all the experience

1. George Kim. *Peace and Security for Asia*, New Delhi, Allied, 1986.

gained by the world in working for peace. Therefore, the Soviet Union not only used the traditional diplomatic channels but also addressed its proposal directly to the world's public. It did so because it was convinced that an appeal for peace and peaceful cooperation met the interests of all nations.

The 27th Soviet Communist Party Congress (1986) formulated a number of key ideas in the problem of war and peace. This is of special importance now that mankind has made spectacular progress in science and engineering and, at the same time, created an immense potential of self-destruction. The world must no longer look at its past and present from the viewpoint of the balance of forces and abandon the militaries mentality.

International security is a political problem which can only be solved by political means. It would be no exaggeration to say that the world is now divided between those who regard security as a strictly military problem and therefore, are pinning hopes for its solution on the size of military arsenals and those who consider security mainly as a flexible and complex form of political relations.

In working out the principles that should govern security policy now and in the foreseeable future, the Soviet leadership has come to a number of conclusions of great importance. These conclusions are essential for understanding the Soviet viewpoint on the international situation as a whole and on the situation in individual regions of the world.

The most important thesis formulated in the Political Report of the CPSU Central Committee to the 27th Party Congress is that modern weaponry leaves no state a chance to defend itself by military technology alone, even by building the most powerful defence.

Another important conclusion is that if the arms race continues on Earth and spreads into space, the already critical peace of modernization of the nuclear weapons will accelerate to such an extent that East-West parity will no longer ensure any deterrence. Consequently, even military parity will no longer guarantee security.

This provides further proof that only peaceful co-existence and detente, not military confrontation, are the only effective means of ensuring international security.

It is clear that further escalation of the arms race by rhe United States may create a situation which no political leaders or governments will be able to control. Political leaders will become prisoners of technology. The Pentagon not only wants to computerise the American war machine but, as one American political scientist said, spread the arms race to the farthest reaches of the Soviet System. The idea is to create a potential for waging "a war without men'" or, to be more exact, a potential for mass destruction of people by machines based on computer technology, microelectronics, robotics and artificial intellect. People who will create these machines will eventually be killed by them.

Does mankind deserve such a future ? Reality makes us choose between self-destruction and survival. We have no other choice. "Our world is too small and fragile for war and power politics," the Soviet Communist Party's Central Committee said in its Political Report to the 27th Congress. "We shall not be able to save or preserve it unless we give up once and for all the way of thinking and acting which have been based for ages on the view that wars and armed conflicts are possible and acceptable."

It is absolutely necessary to make a break with outdated political mentality. People must come to realise that the arms race and nuclear war cannot be won. When they realise this, they will see that no country can be secure if there is no universal security.

There is no alternative to a comprehensive system of international security, now and in the foreseeable future. It is time to abandon the traditional practice when one country or group of countries tried to ensure its security at the expense of others. All sorts of "force balance", "strategic triangles" and "axes" and other similar military and political modes always hinged upon confrontation, conflict, fear and mutual distrust.

The only construction approach to the problem of our time is that which guarantees equal security for all and precludes the use of force. It is a new approach based on the understanding of security as a complex phenomenon, which embraces all forms of relationship between states : political military, economic and humanitarian. Such an approach lies at the base of the guidelines for the creation of a comprehensive system of international security, formulated by the 27th Soviet Communist Party Congress. The Soviet plan provides for the renunciation by states, especially nuclear powers, of the use of force against one another or against third countries, non-militarization of outer space, a varifiable reduction of military potential, the dissolution of military alliance and a mutual and balanced reduction of defence budgets.

No wonder the programme for the elimination of weapons of mass destruction by the end of the century, formulated by Mikhail Gorbachev in his January 15, 1986 Statement, was met with universal interest and enthusiasm. This is only natural, because the Soviet peace proposals meet the vital interests and aspirations of all nations, big and small. Even the first steps that would be taken to implement these proposals might bring about a radical improvement in the political situation in the regions where tension is high and where "local wars" and conflicts exist. Peace is indivisible and people who realize this are stepping up their efforts to that the arms race and rid the world from nuclear weapons by the end of the century.

Indivisibility of peace also means that the more vigorous the fight for peace and against militarism and reaction, the better the chances for settling disputes and regional conflicts and solving the global problems of ridding mankind of all weapons of mass-destruction and averting war, which in our time could only mean an end to human civilization. All this fully applies to the situation in Asia and the Pacific.

Meanwhile, the developments in Asia and in the Pacific and Indian Oceans are causing concern. Moreover, they may have a negative effect on the situation in other regions and on the international situation as a whole.

CHAPTER FOUR

FASCISM AND MILITARISM

THE DEEFAT OF German fascism and Japanese militarism more than forty years ago by the states of the anti-Hitler coalition (with the Soviet Union making the decisive contribution), gave a powerful impetus to the struggle of the Asian peoples for their independence and enabled Asia once and for all to choose the path of peace and national independence. But this choice basically contradicted what the imperialists had in mind for the peoples of that region. The number of victims of more than 120 wars and military conflicts unleashed by imperialism in various regions of the planet since the end of the Second World War runs into the millions. And the mojority of these wars and conflicts have left traces of blood on the Asian continent. The flames of the Second World War had no sooner been extinguished when US imperialism, resorting now to political means, now to economic and financial measures, now to military diktat, begun to fill the power vacuum in various parts of Asia, to impose on the peoples of the continent a system similar to "Pax Americana". In the early 1950s the United States embarked on direct aggression against the People's Republic of China and Korea, and gave full backing to the dirty war of the French colonialists in Indo-China. To increase its pressure on the peoples of Asia, in the 1950s imperialism knocked together aggression blocs of states (SEATO, CENTO, ANZUS), and imposed on the developing Asian countries military pacts.[1]

As mentioned earlier, as nazi Germany and militarist Japan defeat in the Second World War, the aggressive Axis ceased to

1, Mikhail Isayev. *op. cit.*

exist as imperialist reaction's shock force. The positions of world imperialism were damaged, and the global correlation of forces was changed in favour of peace, democracy and socialism.

The Asian situation, too underwent a crucial change : many former colonies and dependencies won their independence and sovereignty, and some embarked on the way of socialist development. This state of things, naturally, did not suit imperialism, primarily that in the United States. It promptly retaliated with a cold war, which had an immediate bearing on Asia.

American strategists meant ANZUS as the start for a Pacific pact to comprise all Asia and the Pacific—an idea long cherished in Washington D.C. The US defence line, as conceived by American diplomats, was to cross the Aleutian Islands, Japan, Okinawa, the Philippines, Australia and New Zealand.

Pursuing their military-bloc policy, the imperialist powers next set up SEATO, a broader military-political organization, often referred to as the Manila Pact because its founding treaty was signed in Manila in September 1954. At the time, it consisted of the US, Great Britain, France, Australia, New Zealand, the Philippines, Thailand and Pakistan—with only three Asian member countries, and the most influential members far beyond Asia.

The West, the US in the first place, realized fully well that military-political alliances in Asia would look particularly bad without Asian participation, and spared no effort to lure India, Burma, Indonesia, Sri Lanka and other non-socialist countries in South and Southeast Asia into their blocs.

India was pressurized the most, as the United States assigned a particularly important regional role to it. That was seen in the concept cited below and reflecting well the imperialist political mentality :

1. Eurasia from Britain and its colonies to Indonesia shall present a united front to oppose the Soviet Union and its Asian allies around it ;
2. The United States wanted India's assistance to strengthen its naval ring around the Soviet Union and China ;

3. With its victory in China, communism presents an ever greater threat to Southeast Asia. Hence India's special importance as a "democratic stronghold in the East."

India and some other Asian countries resolutely rejected the American attempts to draw them into military blocs to be used as instruments in the Gold War with socialist countries. As he addressed the joint session of the US Congress during his 1949 visit to the United States, Jawaharlal Nehru made it clear that India's foreign policy as before would be based on an active approach to topical international issues. "Where liberty and justice are threatened, where an aggression takes place, we cannot, and shall not be neutral", he stressed.

India's flat refusal to take part in US-sponsored blocs and be a tool of adventurist American policies made it a target of US attacks and provocations. Jawaharlal Nehru, the first Prime Minister of independent India, was viciously insulted. The *The New York Times* wrote in those days that history was bound to condemn Nehru's course as short-sighted, irresponsible, and destructive to the cause of freedonm. Asian nationalism and justice. American politicians and the mass media accused Nehru of "Asian intrigues", and branded him as one of their country's bitterest enemies.

Abuse went hand in hand with military, political and economic blackmail. The United States made an attempt to play its Kashmir trump card, and expanded its military-political contracts with Pakistan. To substantiate his country's refusal to give India a grain loan, Tom Conolly, then president of the Senate Foreign Affairs Commission, said that the whole complex of US-India relations had to be taken into account in considering the request.

Other Asian states refusing to be US puppets and take part in Washington's crusade against the Soviet Union and other socialist countries, against all forces of national liberation and democracy, were also subjected to arm-twisting and blackmail.

Pressure from the United States and other imperialist powers on Asian countries achieved exactly the opposite results. As the national liberation moment gained momentum and independence of newly-free countries was strengthened in Asia, their collective security became ever more topical. Asia was to achieve it by pooling the efforts of all the liberated nations to withstand and oppose pressure and provocations by imperialism and reaction,

Asia had a long record of solidarity and joint effort, manifested many times previously in the liberation struggle against imperialism and colonialism, and now serving the security cause. Its nations stored valuable experience of work for peaceful co-operation in that part of the world, based on new principles which laid the foundation for a new Asia free of the imperialist yoke.

Asia and the whole world enthusiastically greeted the *Panchsheel*, the five principles, as declared in April 1954 by India and China in the preamble to their agreement on trade and other contacts between the Tibetan China and India. These envisaged :

—mutual respect for territorial integrity and sovereignty ;
—mutual non-aggression ;
—non-interference into each other's home affairs ;
—equality and mutual benefit ;
—peaceful co-existence.

The five principles of peaceful co-existence were instrumental in improving international co-operation and in re-structuring relations between states on a new basis. All progressive forces and peace-loving nations in the world declared their support for those principles.

The Soviet Union was among the first to support the *Panchsheel* principles, as they fully correspond to Lenin's idea of peaceful co-existence and co-operation between countries with different social systems, and to the policy pursued steadfastly by the CPSU since the day the Soviet state was founded. In February 1955, the USSR Supreme Soviet addressed an appeal to all parliaments of the world, calling on all countries to base their relations on those five principles.

The Asian security idea emerged concurrently with the premises which prompted the non-aligned movement concept to be elaborated, the movement subsequently taking shape. Both sets of principles enriched and complemented eath other. This is easy to notice as one analyses the history of the drive to set up a dependable system providing stable peace and security in Asia. The emergence of the non-alignment idea in Asia was as natural as its parallelism with the security concept. Non-alignment was an answer to the Western efforts to draw newly-free countries into military-political blocs, and the early postwar years saw Asia as the object of the most concerted work to that end.

Their desire to remain outside the military blocs inevitably made newly-free states confront imperialism, the system that was imposing on them participation in such blocs. Hence from the very outset the non-alignment policy acquired an anti-imperialist content. Formally, a refusal to join both military-political camps, non-alignment really meant the newly-free countries' opposition to the military bloc policies imperialist countries pursued. On the one hand, the Soviet Union and other countries in the socialist community never attempted to draw young independent states into military-political blocs. On the other, the Warsaw Treaty member countries were consistently coming out for disbanding all military-political blocs. They time and again declared that they would willingly enter into such negotiations with NATO members. From the day they were declared, the Soviet Union supported the ideas of peace and security in Asia as well as the idea of setting up the non-aligned movement, seeing them as beneficial for the entire peace drive.

In the 1960s the imperialists blatantly manifested their aggressiveness in Asia by kindling the biggest military conflicts in Indo-China and the Middle East. In an attempt to justify and "legalize" the American presence in the region, Washingtan advanced many military-political doctrines and concepts—"deterrence", "retribution", "containment of socialism", "local wars", the "Guam Docrine", etc. But the course of events again and again frustrated imperialism's designs, demonstrating in the face of the peoples' liberation struggles, the total bankruptcy of such connections. One of the most glaring examples of this was the fiasco of the US aggression in Indo-China. There, Washington had intended to prove that American military and economic might was capable of suppressing any national liberation movement and hampering the growth of national progressive forces.

Nevertheless, the imperialists have not given up their attempts to take revenge for their defeats and to disrupt the process of detente (which was gaining momentum in Asia in the 1970s) in order to retain their positions by all means. This course became particularly conspicuous in US policy beginning in the early 1980s.

Seeking to slow down the progress of Asian history and to make the development of the situation there conformable to its strategic objectives, imperialism gambled on increasing all types of American armed forces in the area equipped with nuclear-missile weapons, on implanting in relations between the states and peoples of Asia elements of alienation and confrontation, and on inflaming the hotbeds of tensions. The US administration for all intents and purposes, is out to impose on the international community its "right" to interfere in the internal affairs of other states, to "encourage" or "punish" sovereign countries and peoples, to declare whole regions of the world, including those in Asia, zones of its "vital interests".

According to official Washington's concept of "balanced containment", the three centres of imperialism—the United States Western Europe and Japan—must co-ordinate their efforts in such a way as to compel the Soviet Union, as it were, to divide its forces between three flanks: European, Eastern (Pacific) and Southern. Washington makes no secret of its schemes to set up a multilateral military-political structure similar to NATO to the east and south of the USSR, and to make the Indian and Pacific Oceans, along with South and East Asia, into advance positions deploying nuclear weapons, just as it has done in Western Europe and the adjoining Atlantic area. A direct consequence of this course has been the growing threat of unclear war and a complication of the general political situation on the Asian continent.

The formation of the Eastern (Pacific) flank designed for an aggressive structure of "containment" is in fullswing. The USA and its allies have built there an enormous war machine targeting socialist countries, the non-aligned states and the national liberation organizations.

The second most significant grouping (after the European one) of American general-purpose forces is deployed in the Pacific zone. Of particular importance is the US Seventh Eleet, on whose aircraft carriers there are more than 400 nuclear warheads.

More than 300 American military bases and installations—bastions of aggression – from a dense network covering the vast region of East Asia. Many of them have nuclear weapons within whose range is the territory of the socialist and non-agligned countries of Asia and the Pacific area. Preparations are being made for the deployment of hundreds of sea-based Tomahawk cruise missiles in the Asia-Pacific region.

In building a new multilateral military-political structure in that region under its aegis, the United States assigns a special role to Japan, which is being drawn deeper and deeper into Washinton's global strategy. Under US pressure, the Armed Forces of Japan have started patrolling sea routes that are more than 1,000 miles away from the Japanese islands. The United States is speeding up the formation of the Washington-Tokyo-Seoul military alliance.

Washington and Tokyo are planning to set up what they call a "Pacific Community". The Pacific states now account for more than half of the foreign-trade turnover of the United States and for more than two-thirds of that of Japan. But it is not so much commercial and economic interests that make Washington find the plan to form an exclusive grouping in the Asia-Pacific region so attractive as reasons of a military and political nature.

The Soviet Government's Statement of April 24, 1986 notes: "Being highly selecting in choosing the potential members of a 'Pacific Community', its initiators are obviously not interested in making the planned organization a truly representative forum for discussing and solving the long-standing urgent economic problems of the region; nor do they want an organization that aims at changing the region's inequitable structure of interstate commercial-economic relations." In coming out for the creation of such a "Community" the United States intends to eventually transform it into a closed regional grouping, another militarist bloc, and to become a "co-ordinator" of sorts of the military and economic policies of the states in that vast region.

Tensions in the boundless regions of Asia and Africa that face the Indian Ocean are not subsiding either. Washington's policy of turning this area into the southern flank of its infamous "containment" structure, and the corresponding US military build-up there, provide the reasons for this.

In the Indian Ocean zone there is a major US military grouping and about 30 US military bases, including, in the centre of the Ocean, the main one on Diego Garcia Island.

The Pentagon keeps watch on virtually the whole area. On January 1, 1983 it set up a new regional Central Command (CENTCOM), which arbitrarily covers 19 states of South-West Asia, North-East Africa, and also those surrounding the Persian Gulf, and the Arabian and Red Seas. The Rapid Deployment Forces make up CENTCOM's strike unit. Their strength, at the minimum, is to be brought to 400,000 men.

The United States has formed three strategic lines of naval and air-force bases and strong points in the region. One of them runs along the east coast of Africa though the American strongholds in Kenya and Somalia. Another passes through countries of the West Asia (Egypt, Turkey, Saudi Arabia, Oman). And the third line of US bases supports the actions of the US Armed Forces in the eastern part of the Indian Ocean, the biggest of which are the Clark Field and Sublic Bay bases on the territory of the Philippines, and the bases in Australia.

The Pentagon's plans to include the Indian and Pacific Oceans into its "Star Wars" orbit pose a particularly serious threat to the peoples in the region. Some of these dangerous plans are aleady in the stage of realization. For instance, a ground station is being installed on Diego Garcia Island for electronic-optical surveillance of near-terrestrial space and for dislocating artificial Earth satellites. It is planned to build facilitics that will form part of the "Stars Wars" system in other areas of the Indian Ocean as well. The Americans are also in the process of adapting their control and surveillance centres for these purposes, along with their centres for receiving information from spy satellites situation on Mahe Island (Seychelles) and in Alice Springs (Australia).

The dangerous hotbed of tensions in the West Asian region has now been active for nearly four decades. The chief cause of this protracted conflict is American imperialism, looking at this oil-rich and strategically important region through the prism of its claims to world domination. In close co-operation with Israel, its "strategic partner", the United States puts all kinds of obstacles in the way of achieving a just and comprehensive settlement in the Middle East, imposes separatist deals on the Arab nations, and resorts to military force. One need only recall the US travel bombardment of Beirut in 1984 and the barbarous US air raids on the non-aligned movement's member state Libya in 1986, which shocked the whole world.

Meanwhile, the Arab people of Palestine have been struggling for their inalienable national rights for forty years. Their valiant and just struggle takes place in difficult, often even cruel conditions. In the 1970's and early 1980's, the Palestinians and their sole legitimate representatative—the Palestine Liberation Organization (PLO)—achieved significant successes on the international forum, which made the Israeli Zionists quite nervous.

Two factors contributed to the considerable growth of the prestige of the PLO and its cause. First, the world has come to realize ever more that the violence committed against the Palestinian nation is an intolerable and unpardonable barbarity and there is no room for it on our planet just as there is no room for apartheid. Secondly, the Israeli-Arab conflict, the core of which is the unresolved Palestinian question, constitutes a permanent and potentially ever more dangerous hotbed of tension. At a time when local conflicts contain serious risks even of global dimensions more often than in the past, this aspect arouses particularly great concern.

One of the objectives of the Israeli invasion of Lebanon in 1982—just as of its aggression in 1967—was to liquidate the Palestinian resistance movement, but it failed. In the following period, however, under the pressure of imperialist and reactionary Arab circles, this movement developed in an undesirable direction which weakened its unity. Taken from wider viewpoint, this happened at a time when the U.S. Administration stepped up its aggressive pressure against progressive forces throughout the world including the national liberation movement.

When we ask who could have and did have the greatest profit from that *status quo*, the answer is evident. The Israeli coalition government of Shimon Peras (which, by the way, behaves worse than the preceding Likud government on the occupied territories) in very close co-operation with the United States as its strategic partner tried to eliminate the PLO out of the political scene by way of separate negotiations which would truncate the PLO tree to become a powerless stump. Last year (1985), the imperialist and Zionist forces in particular started their separate game, which was to be conducive to an absolute capitulation of the Palestinian leadership and crucifixion of the Palestinian rights, with such incredible cynicism and contempt for the fundamental rights of the Palestinian people that it was bound to end in a failure.

Let us say right off that an opportunity for such action emerged for them on the conclusion of the so-called Amman agreement of February 1985 which violated two principles of the Palestinian struggle inviolable thus far : that the PLO is the sole legitimate representative of the Palestinian people and that the aim of this struggle is self-determination, including the creation of an independent Palestinian state. This, after all, is well known, just as the fact that the readiness to join in obviously unequal separate negotiations with a stone ball of grave one-aided concessions faced the unity of the Palestinian ranks with new hard trials.

It turned out, however, that the so-called peace process, so loudly propagated by the Western bourgeois press until recently and with which Zionist propaganda stultified the Israeli public, is but a great fraud. For Israel, supported by the United States as usual, gave up nothing at all of its totally negativistic attitude to the Palestinian rights and the rights of other Arab countries. Capitulation, which Peres and his people have in mind, cannot be naturally called a peace process. Conservative Arab regimes argued that now it was allegedly the last chance of achieving something.

But what ? That is the question. The objective of the United States and Israel was to drive the whole Palestinian movement by this planned separate development in the abyss of despair. How will the argument that it is necessary to save what can be saved of the western bank of Jordan from the existing stealthy Zionistic annexation hold out in a concrete analysis of facts ? Indeed, neither the incumbent Israeli government nor any other showed willingness to give up the occupied territories. Thus a separate road would mean that only the Palestinian movement would give up something, namely its position, prestige and legitimate demands recognized by the overwhelming majority of the world as lawful. Only disparate fragments of small weight and influence would thus remain of the internationally recognised platform of the PLO.

The experience of the Middle East developments in more than ten years shows quite convincingly that separate negotiations lead only to a blind alley and new complications. It is characteristic that they always weaken the positions of the Arab side and particularly the Palestinian resistance movement. Their attendant phenomenon and consequence is the weakening and undermining of the unity of the Arab world. Egypt's separate negotiations in 1975 further seriously impaired the country's relationship with Syria. The Camp David talks caused a serious breach in the Arab ranks when imperialism and Zionism succeeded in breaking such an important country as Egypt out of the Arab front. Shocks caused by a separate agreement between Israel and Lebanon—fortunately rejected later—are still within living memory.

It was always only Israel and its U.S. ally that profited from separate negotiations, while the Arab world as a whole, and particularly the Palestinian resistance movement and Arab countries standing in the front ranks of the struggle against the imperialist-Zionist expansive aggressiveness and hegemonistic course suffered losses. For example, why neither Israel nor the United States wants the Middle East conflict to be solved at a broad and representative international conference ? The reason is that in contrast to separate negotiations, all participating parties would act as equal partners at such a conference. Israel could not blackmail so shamelessly as it did with obvious cynicism during the Camp David talks, when it tried to make the Labanese government accept humiliating conditions in 1983, or when it "selected" allegedly suitable Palestinian candidates for "talks" in 1985.

Attempts to impose a capitulationist policy on the Arab and the Palestinian resistance movement through separate agreements, to undermine the national cause of the Arab people of Palestine and to split the Arab liberation movement can, of course be countered. A way to this is waging an organized and goal-oriented political and armed struggle of the people, relying on the concept of a global situation of the Middle East conflict on a broad international base.

This concept is represented by proposals of the Arab summit conference in Fez (Morocco) in 1982 and Soviet proposals, very close to them, submitted in the same year. Despite the complex situation in the PLO prospects of its national struggle are very favourable. The Palestinian people are determined to continue their struggle until they achieve their legitimate rights.

These prospects were aptly expressed by General Secretary of the Popular Front for the Liberation of Palestine George Habash when he said that the struggle of the Palestinian people is inseparable from the all-Arab and world revolutionary process. We live in the period of transition from capitalism to socialism, in the period of victories of nations struggling for freedom, independence and social progress. The Palestinians are firmly convinced that they will definitely win their struggle for the just cause.

What is the main thing in the present situation ? For the Palestinian and a successful development of their just combat effort it is obviously the unity of their ranks on a highly principled anti-imperialist base and the co-ordination of their actions with the activities of all progressive and patriotic forces of the Arab world. The PLO will continue to play a significant role in this struggle. Nobody shall disrespect the rights of the Palestinian people. However, separate negotiations could compromise and seriously endanger the prospect of their achievement. It is necessary to resolutely counter and reject such negotiations in the interest of the real national interests of the Palestinian people.

Having recently adopted the doctrine of a "new globalism", Washington continues to whip up international tensions. The essence of the new doctrine, as the Soviet leader Mikhail Gorbachev has emphasized in March, 1986, is "complete disregard for the generally accepted norms of international relations ; it is encroachment upon the sovereignty of states, the same vain attempt to deprive the peoples of the right to build their life according to their own will." The murderous attack on Grenada, the endless attempts to overthrow the legitimate Sandinista Government in Nicaragua, the open support for the dushman murderers in Afghanistan and for the UNITA cut-throats in Angola, the aforementioned crimes of the American military in West Asia these are conspicuous manifestations of the anything-goes principle being preached in Washington.

Military pressure is accompanied by economic enslavement. Imperialism has managed to create and adjust the most subtle system of neo-colonialist exploitation, by which it has tied to itself a large number of developing countries, including those in Asia. The consequences have been tragic. The developing countries are inhabited by more than 2,000 million people, and practically all of them live below the poverty line. This is a region of illiteracy and darkness, of chronic malnutrition and starvation, horrifying child mortality, and epidemics which affect hundreds of millions of children. Such a situation is an infamy of civilized mankind, and imperialism is to be blamed for it. The destitution of the developing nations has become a major world problem. And this, too, is one of the sources of conflicts in Asia.

By ruthlessly exploiting the developing states, imperialism grows richer and richer and makes barrels of money. It finances the arms race largely at the expense of the developing countries. We in India know the outcome of such a policy : on the one hand, there is the trillion dollars debt of the developing nations ; on the other, the super profits of the transnational corporations and banks. The developing countries of Asia as well have endured the imperialist policy of plunder.

The complex and in many respects contradictory political situation that has emerged as a consequence of imperialism's intrigues in the 1980s in Asia, the continuing instability in a number of regions of the continent and in the adjoining areas of the Indian and Pacific Oceans, make it imperative that greater efforts be made to improve the political climate there.

Although the social systems, national interests and tasks of the Asian nations differ, the realities of the nuclear age necessitate the search for mutually acceptable solutions to the problems of ensuring peace on the Asian continent. This can be achieved only through the joint efforts of the Asian states ; there is no other way. Only joint efforts can bring them closer to the solution of the task of ensuring security in Asia and in the seas and oceans which wash its shores—a task which affects the vital interests of each individual country in Asia as well as those of all the states in this immense region.

Obviously, with growing outside interference in the domestic affairs of the Asian nations and considering the complexity and multifaceted nature of political, socio-economic and other realities of present day Asia, the problem of consolidating peace and stability there, though extremely urgent, is a difficult task requiring a long-term solution.

The task, however, is solvable. Asia can and must become a continent of peace and good-neighbourliness. Only in conditions of reliable security will the Asian nations be able to cope successfully with the complex socio-economic tasks facing them, and to march confidently ahead on the road of national and social progress.

CHAPTER FIVE

NATO OR HELSINKI

WE WOULD SUGGEST even if not as an immediate objective, a Helsinki-type Pacific conference to be attended by all the countries gravitating towards the Pacific Ocean. When (and, of course, if) we suggested in agreeing on its convocetion, we shall also be able to decide on its venue. One possible candidate is Hiroshima. Why should not this city—the first victim of the atomic evil—become a sort of 'Helsinki' of Asia and the Pacific ?" Mikhail Gorbachev said in Vladivostok on July 28, 1986.

Putting big initiatives into practice is no easy matter, especially if they stem from new, unconventional political thinking. This makes it all the more significant that the idea of "holding a Helsinki-type Pacific conference to be attended by all the countries gravitating towards the ocean," put forward by Mikhail Gorbachev in his Vladivostok speech, attracted universal attention. Let us face it, this attention is not of a uniform character. Steadfast peace champions have expressed resolute support for the idea, but there are also those who say that a "Pacific Helsinki" is a good idea, but quite unrealistic. This opinion is to be heard not only, say, in Japan or Australia but also in some of the non-aligned Asian states. And what about the United States ? According to *Washingtcn Post*, "State Department officials said the U.S. does not favour such a meeting under present circumstances."[1]

"Under present circumstances..." But is the Soviet Union so naive as to think that the time for such a meeting is ripe ? A Pacific conference is a long term objective. Carrying it out would require

1. D. Volsky. NATO or Helsinki; *New Times* (Moscow) (32) 18 August, 1986.

tremendous effort and, above all, will. To believe Washington Post, the U.S. Administration prefers an attitude of skeptical disapproval to action.

Well, life will always take its course whether anyone likes it or not. Once the idea of holding a European conference also met with a skeptical, not to say hostile attitude on the part of Washington. An entirely different—anti-Soviet, anti-socialist—approach to European affairs came to predominate there back in the forties and found its embodiment in the NATO bloc. And now Washington would like to re-enact the NATO story in the vast Pacific region. It has even suggested a name for the NATO equivalent there—"the Pacific community." It is to include not only the USA, Japan and Australia, but also the developing countries that are members of ASEAN and possibly some other big Asian countries. This conglomerate of states is to oppose the Soviet Union and its Asian friends, to establish a legal mechanism whereby the United States' partners in the Pacific could be drawn into the Pentagon's war preparations and the positions of imperialism there strengthened generally.

"Almost all the countries to be included in the 'community', a publication issued by an Indonesian university this summer says, "maintain bilateral co-operation with the United States both in the defence sphere and in the sphere of military aid. What's more important, all of them are within range of the U.S. Seventh Fleet which covers a zone stretching from the Hawaii through Subic Bay (a U.S. base in the Philippines) and the South China. See all the way to Diego Garcia. Therefore the creation of the 'Pacific community' will mean an actual recognition of U.S. military superiority and U.S. control over the Pacific and Indian ocean routes outside the member states' territorial waters."

The resemblance of the proposed bloc to NATO is striking indeed. This is no mere coincidence: the "community" is supposed to complete the "encirclement" of the U.S.S.R. from the west and the east. The difference between the two is also much in evidence, and it lies not only in "East being East, and West being West", to paraphrase Rudyard Kipling. The root of the matter lies elsewhere. Most of the Western states in the North Atlantic have similar socio-political systems and approximately the same level of development, and share many customs and traditions. The East, on the other hand, the Pacific region in particular, is marked by striking contrasts arising from the uneven peace of historical development of the countries in the area and for the most part inherited from colonialism and neo-colonialism exploitation. Washington and Tokyo now intend to perpetuate this system of exploitation by creating a local NATO equivalent.

Are not they expecting too much of a frangile idea even before it is carried out ? It is not for nothing that Washington is now talking about "a system of co-operation" rather than a "community," although both names have the same meaning. All this is idle talk anyway which evokes no positive response in the developing countries of Asia. It is quite safe to predict that the "Eastern NATO" project will remain on paper—or rather on geographical maps. But besides geography, history also has a part to pay here; it is much harder to do in the eighties what could have been done in the forties.

Over the past decades the peoples have acquired a wealth of political experience—both negative and positive—which is not confined to any one state but knows no frontiers. The record of these decades shows, with utmost clarity, that it is not the aggressive North Atlantic doctrine which puls the world in jeopardy that has stood the test of time, but an entirely different political concept based on the common interests of different countries seeking to strengthen international security and promote equal co-operation. In Europe, it manifested itself in the Helsinki process which, despite all setbacks, lessens tension and ensures a certain degree of stability. And this is what the Asian and Pacific nations now need most. That is why the Helsinki experience is so valuable to them. An objective analysis of this experience shows the realism of the new thinking, as Moscow's example proves.

Monopoly position in economy, extraction of superpofits at the expense of other nations are not the only goals of international imperialism in the Asian-Pacific region. Its policy is increasingly dominated by another super goal related to the sphere of global strategy : geopolitical domination. The aggressive nature of this strategy is today revealed in a concentrated form in Asia and in the

Pacific. Washington does not make a secret of its "special" attitude towards this region. At the turn of this century it predicted that the Pacific was an ocean of the future. But in our days the White House and the Pentagon have a much more selfish interest in that region. Michael Mansfield, US Ambassador in Japan, forecasts that the next century will go down in history as the age of the Pacific. How does he explain his forecast ? States in this region are going through their rebirth and the main potentialities are hidden exactly here, the US diplomat says. From his point of view this region determines everything and the future of the United States lies in it. The US has come here to stay.[2]

High-ranking officials of the Washington administration, as well as the President himself, on every occasion speak about "increased attention to Asia" about "the transfer of the centre of gravity from the Atlantic to the Pacific", anticipate the advent of the "era of Asia and the Pacific" by which they explain the "increased significance of the Asian factor" in the foreign policy of the White House.

Of late the United States has noticeably intensified its military preparations. Washington is seeking to involve the countries of the region in the implementation of its global military strategic plans, including the notorious Pacific Doctrine. It is interfering in the affairs of sovereign nations and hampering the solution of problems through negotiations. Following its disgraceful "position of strength" policy that has no future and counting on the world domination, the US administration thinks in military and strategic categories and notions of the pre-nuclear age. It is doing this while possessing a powerful nuclear arsenal. "Theatre of war", "limited war", "local military conflict"—this is the vocabulary of the White House and Pentagon bosses. They keep on saying that all their strategic plans are directed only against the Soviet Union and other socialist countries of Asia. An attempt is thus made to camouflage the danger to which the imperialist military preparations expose the young countries of the region. But if the substance of virtually all conflicts in Asia is looked into deeper, it will be easy to find

2. See Vladimir Godyna. *Asia : Economics, Politics, Security*. New Delhi, Allied, 1986, pp. 27-32.

that they are either caused by imperialism or are deliberately whipped up by it.

The efforts of the Pentagon and its allies increasingly make Asia look like a European theatre of war. The true reason behind the growing attention of Washington and Pentagon strategists to the Asian-Pacific region is to turn East Asia and the Pacific and Indian oceans into a kind of NATO and to fill this region, like Western Europe, with forward-based nuclear weapons.

The nuclear aircraft carriers *Carl Vinson* and *Midway*, the *New Jersey*, modernised battleship armed with Tomahawk cruise missiles, the *Enterprise* nuclear aircraft carrier, nuclear submarines of the Ohio and Michigan class, carrying nuclear missiles, are ploughing the Pacific Ocean. About 140 US warships and over 800 warplanes are operating in the Pacific.

In one of his recent statements Caspar Weinberger, US Secretary of Defence, disclosed some of the important principles of the US Pacific policy today. First, he noted the predominant significance of US security relations with Japan; second, US adherence to ensuring stable security in the Korean Peninsula; third, US efforts aimed at establishing close relations with the People's Republic of China; fourth, US support to ASEAN members with a view to ensuring their political and economic stability, and, fifth, US long-standing partnership with Australia and New Zealand within the ANZUS framework.

If one listens to the Pentagon's boss and his peace rhetorics he seems to be a veritable champion of peace. But in fact there is no need to be particularly shrewd to understand hat that United States has assumed and is zealously playing the role of the world policeman and not the guardian of peace and security of nations.

The US ruling circles are busily engaged in setting up a new political-military structure to bring to life the NATO's double in the Asian-Pacific region. According to this design, Japan become the key link in the "Eastern front" which is anti-Soviet, anti-socialist and targeted against independence of many Asian countries. The bilateral military agreements between Washington and

Tokyo and Seoul to make the Japanese Islands and the South of the Korean Peninsula the Pentagon's nuclear springboard are being transformed into the tripartite Washington-Tokyo-Seoul alliance. Washington still keeps on its agenda the formation of a "Pacific community" in which it seeks to involve the six countries which make ASEAN.

Let us deal with these questions in the above sequence.

Japan. Forty years have passed since militarist Japan surrendered. It is written in the Preamble and Article 9 of the postwar, peacetime Constitution of that country that Japan forever renounces war as a means of settling international disputes. That fundamental document says that Japan will never maintain land, sea, and air forces, as well as other war potential.

What do we see today?

The Liberal-Democratic Party (LDP) which has ruled Japan for the past 30 years openly intends to revise the Constitution. In November 1985 the LDP adopted a new programme which announced that revision of the Constitution was the political course of the Party. The goal of the conservatives is to revoke the anti-military provisions of the Japanese Constitution, and above all, its Article 9.

It does not follow at all that remilitarisation of Japan is a matter of the distant future. The anti-military provisions have long since been violated. The so-called forces of self-defence created in the early 1950s have become a modern army whose combat power is comparable to that of the armed forces of some leading imperialist states. But to be more precise, as regards the combat power, the Japanese armed forces are fifth or six among armies of capitalist countries. According to Yomiuri Shimbun, if comparison is made between Japan and NATO countries it is fourth in its naval tonnage and sixth in the size of its air force. The National Defence Agency (NDA) of Japan is planning to buy soon several dozen US F-15 fighter-bombers with the view of becoming second, after the United States, in the capitalist world in the number of these warplanes. The NDA, according to its chief, Koichi Kato, plans to equip the "forces of self-defence" with modern warships and planes, missiles, and sophisticated tracking and detecting systems.

Militarist ambitions of the Japanese right-wingers have a powerful financial backing. The regular five-year programme for building up the Japanese armed forces (1986-1990) recently approved by the Nakasone government will cost over 76,000 million dollars; it provides for an annual 5.4 per cent growth in real terms for the whole duration of the five-year period.

Thus allocations for military purposes are over one per cent of the GNP, that is the official limit on military spending. The ceiling was introduced in 1976, which was a forced reaction of the then government to sharp criticism in the country with regard to growing military spending. And now the limit has been exceeded.

We are thus witnesses of the process about which NBC said that now when due to their worldwide obligations the US armed forces are deployed in many parts of the world the United States wants Japan to assume greater responsibility in the western Pacific. In other words, it means that a part of the US police functions in the region would be passed on to Japan.

No wonder Washington officials welcomed this decision by the Nakasone government. Washington wants to shift a part of the "burden of military responsibility" for the situation in the region to Japan. In other words, to force upon her the military functions which the Washington administration wants to get rid of for some reason.

The United States naturally welcomes this success for this is a very positive step, Casper Weinberger was quick to state in connection with Tokyo's new decision in the field of armaments.

There was different reactions from the progressives in Japan and in other countries. These decisions by the Nakasone government made the Socialist Party of Japan, the largest opposition party, can on the Japanese people to prevent the sliding of the country on to a dangerous path of militarism and aggression. Concerning the military programme the appeal said that the adoption of that programme actually annulled the existing principle of, limiting military spending to one per cent of the GNP. The arms buildup undermined the constitutional provisions and contradicted the wish of the Japanese people for peace and friendship with other nations.

On the basis of a public opinion poll, *Yomiuri Shimbun* came to a conclusion that the Japanese people most negatively regard the course aimed at the feature arms buildup going beyond the present framework of the country's defence capability.

If the militarist preparations cause alarm among honest people in Japan, apprehensions of the people of South East Asia who had fallen victim to the Japanese occupation during the Second World War are all the more understandable. They still remember the years of the brutal rule of Japanese colonialists. They remember and do not want a repetition of anything of that kind. One can often find conclusions in the Western press to the effect that the Japanese wartime aggression her relations with other countries today. But in fact these relations are darkened not only by the aggression of those years but by the reluctance of Japanese leaders to learn lessons of history, and by their remilitarisation of the country.

The apprehensions in the region on account of the rapidly growing war potential of Japan can be confirmed by questions asked by reporters of television companies of the Philippines, South Korea and Thailand at several recent press conferences given by Weinberger. The US Defense Secretary's reply to the effect that "Japan's neighbours have nothing to be afraid of" can allay the anxiety of credulous people only. The growing activity of militarist and revenge-seeking forces in Japan, the latter's readiness to become a wheel in the Pentagon's war chariot are there for all to see. As distinct from the recent past when Japan was assigned by Washington to the "second line of fire", it is being transferred to the first echelon of the Asian strategy of the United States. To turn the Japanese islands into a stronghold of their thermonuclear strategy in the Asian-Pacific region, to involve her in NATO's integration plans and operations, in fact to make her a military ally of the United States like NATO countries—this is the present-day goal of the

Pentagon's strategists. Among approximately 120 US installations on the Japanese islands there are some where nuclear weapons are stored and where new components of nuclear weapons are brought to. The latest nuclear-capable fighter-bombers have been deployed at the Misawa air base on the Honshu island. Washington seeks to make Japan a powder keg which spells danger for many Asian countries.

The "three non-nuclear principles" (not to manufacture, not to acquire and not to deploy nuclear weapons) which allegedly the Japanese government adhers to have in fact become a mere declaration. But the words do not differ from the deeds when the "forces of self-defense" are blocking the international La Perouse, Tsugaru and Korea straits, patrolling a 1,000 mile zone around the Japanese archipelago, and escorting US warships of the US 7th Fleet which are known to base in Japanese ports. The same Carl Vinson and Enterprise are guests in the ports of Sasebo and Yokosuka, the Air Force uses the bases in Misawa, Yokota and Kadena, and Okinawa has long since become a military island.

As to the ruling circles in Tokyo, they appear to be eager to see the 21st century as the "era of Japan's leadership", at least in the Asian Pacific region. Isn't it attested to by the fact that Nakasone is so much tempted to get involved in the implementation of the SDI plans, for which he has been nicknamed as "Star Wars vendor"? This is proved by the installation in Japan of relay and control facilities necessary for the operation of US space-based weapons.

South Korea. It is another side of the militarist Washington-Tokyo-Seoul triangle created under the US auspices. Obsessed with imperial ideas, the White House in its urge to lay its hands on the countries of the region and to make the Pacific an "American lake" pins great hopes on South Korea as well. In this connection, George Schultz, US Secretary of State, stressed that in such a key region as the Pacific the accent is made on the consolidation of South Korea's war potential.

The Pentagon's star strategists regard the South of the Korean Peninsula, where a 42-thousand-strong US occupationist corps is deployed, as a trump card in their geopolitical game. South Korea has been turned into a major US springboard not only in the Far East but in the whole of the Asian continent. Thanks to Washington's "care" South Korea has become a huge base, or rather a network of nuclear weapon bases. It is literally stuffed with 38 bases. They are located in Sosan, Kunsan, Taegu, Kwangchu, Seoul, Pusan, even in camps along the demarcation line. The US troops in South Korea, the Western press reports, have about 1,000 nuclear bombs, mines, shells, and missile warheads, and recently nuclear kits have been added to them.

According to reports in the US press, the United States is planning to deploy in South Korea the latest types of nuclcar weapons. The Aviation Week and Space Technology reported that the Pentagon intended to dispatch there the latest types of cruise missiles fitted with nuclear warheads. The Washington Post wrote that the neutron weapons would also be deployed in South Korea. The US troops have lately been rearming at a fast pace. A squadron of assault planes was flown there as well as the sophisticated F-16 fighter-bombers which are capable of carrying nuclear weapons.

The total number of F-16 fighter-bombers deployed is South Korea has reached 150. US warships with nuclear weapons aboard are frequent "guests" in Chinhae and Pusan ports.

Militarisation of South Korea stepped up by the United States assumed a threatening scope. US generals count on 600,000 South Korean troops as cannon fodder for the operations in the region they plan. US General Roberts said openly that in Korea a US taxpayer has an army which is a perfect watchdog guarding investments in that country, and a force which gives maximum results at minimum cost.

As to US military aid to Seoul, it has a tendency to grow permanently. It 1983 it amounted to 210 million dollars, in 1984, 230 million, and in 1985 US Congress allocated 240 million dollars.

Within the framework of this "aid" the US administration approved arms supplies, including M55-1 tanks and Stinger guided missile. With US assistance the South Korean munitions industry is developing at a fast rate. F-5G fighters are built under US license. South Korean shipyards turn out warships of different classes,

South Korea is being militarised not only through US aid.

Seoul allocated almost 40 per cent of its budget for military purposes. And this is 292 times higher than in 1960. According to foreign information services, a sizeable part of these funds is spent on the purchase of US arms—first of all the offensive ones—and other war equipment, in particular, F-16 fighter-bombers, missile-carryingdestroyers, Thor and Hawk missiles, and so on. Altogether Seoul inends to buy 8,000 million dollars' worth of military hardware.

The south of the Korean Peninsula is infected with militarist fever. And it is not the only intention of the Reagan administration "to restore America's strong role in the Pacific and Asia". The US administration also deliberately turns South Korea, its forward-based nuclear springboard, into the same theatre of war or nuclear battlefield as it is turning Western Europe. It is no accident that the Pantagon intends to deploy there the kind of mass destruction weapons which have been developed for the European theatre of war.

In this connection no one either in Seoul, Tokyo, or anywhere else should have illusions about the fact that by accommodating in their territory US military bases the "hospitable hosts" thus invite a potential retaliatory blow. The Pentagon, on the other hand, locaing its bases in as many countries as possible, hopes to divert in this way from US territory a possibly larger part of the massive retaliatory blow and direct it against the states which have US bases on their territory.

The major strategic line of US military policy in the region is also attested to by the persistent efforts detailed above to set up in the Far East an aggressive military alliance, a kind of Far Eastern NATO. The United States regards the bilateral agreements of "Mutual Defence" with South Korea and "Security Treaty" with Japan as a basis for such an alliance.

The Soviets are far from suggesting that the diplomatic methods used in Europe be mechanically transferred to the Pacific region which has specific features of its own that need to be taken into account Instead of looking for some non-existent traps, it is necessary to show respect for the legitimate interests of all nations and to refrain from bringing pressure to bear on them from the outside. Neither should anyone think that everything will be plain sailing. This is a complicated matter. The important thing is to make a start—and it has actually been made. The discussion that has begun, to which the impulre has come from Gorbachev's speech in Vladivostok on July 28, 1986, is convincing evidence of this.

CHAPTER SIX

THE HELSINKI SPIRIT

The Soviet Union stands for the Asian-Pacific region to be included in the general process of creating a comprehensive system of international security. Issues of regional settlement are particularly important. Mikhail Gorbachev has expressed the firm view that there are no insurmountable obstacles to establishing mutually acceptable relations between the Indochinese and ASEAN countries. To attain this end, goodwill must be shown and efforts made to settle disputable questions without outside interference.

The Soviet leader has stated that to promote Asian and Pacific security, nuclear weapons should be jointly prevented from being spread and accumulated. The USSR has pledge itself not to increase medium-range missiles in its Asian part. Moreover, it has proposed that the nuclear weapons and their arsenals be destroyed altogether by the end of this century, which, without doubt, also concerns Asia and the Pacific. That is the reason why the Soviet Union is in favour of turning the southern Pacific into an nuclear-free zone. In the words of the Soviet leader, the idea of creating such a zone in South-East Asia has also attracted great attention.

Mikhail Gorbachev has stated thst reducing the armed forces and conventional armaments in Asia to reasonable amount would help normalise and stabilise the situation. He has put forward the idea of step-by-step measure.

The Soviet Government calls on all Asian-Pacific nations to strengthen co-operation for the sake of peace and security because it wants peace for its own country and security for all Asian-Pacific nations. Therefore, it has set the aims of holding a Helsinki-style conference on the Pacific with the participation of all nations concerned.

Why is it that now, 12 years after the Helsinki Conference (1975), the people in many countries are still calling for support of the Helsinki spirit, emphasising the need to further implement the programme of action adopted by the Conference on Security and Co-operation in Europea and to share the Helsinki experience with other continents ?[1]

The answer is simple. The Helsinki Conference in 1975 pinpointed (and outlined solutions to) problems which are still facing not only Europe, but other continents as well.

What are these problems and how do they affect the interests of the Asian peoples.

The Helsinki Conference culminated in the signing of the Final Act by the leaders of 33 European countries, as well as the United States and Canada. For these countries the Final Act has become a platform of uniteral, bilateral and multilateral action for many years to come. It stressed that responsible representatives of the participating states were "motivated by the political will, in the interest of peoples, to improve and intensify their relations and to contribute in Europe to peace, security, justice and co-operation as well as to approachment among with themselves and the other states of the world."

The heart of tbe Final Act is the Declaration on Principles Guilding Relations between Participating States, irrespective of their political, econmic and social systems, their size, geographical location or level of economic development. These principles, dubbed by the world press a "Code of Peace and Security for Europe", govern international relations at the present stage. The countries of Asia are in no less need of such a code than are

1. Lev Bausin. *For Helsinki Spirit in Asia*. New Delhi, Allied, 1986, pp. 3-48.

those of Europe. Therefore, many influential statesmen and public figures in Asia are calling for an extension of the "Helsinki spirit" to other continents.

Asia is, by no means, politically or economically homogeneous. Capitalist and socialist states, monarchies and republics, industrially advanced and developing countries that have just begun to restructure their lives on a modern patter—all of them are objectively interested not only in peaceful co-exitence, but also in mutual co-operation and assistance. Of course, an employee of the Japanese Mitsubishi corporation faces quite different problems than an Arab bedouin, but both of them, and millions of other Asians, share the common desire to live better tomorrow than yesterday and to do so in peace and tranquillity.

Asia plays an important role in the world today, and the voice of the Asian peoples is being heeded in thc international arena. At the same time, the continent faces a host of acute economic, politicl and social problems. Some of them have been inherited from the colonial past, others are connected with the constant interference of imperialists in the affairs of independent states, and still others are the result of internal contradictions and difficulties. The immediate and distant future of billions of people depends on the solution of these problems. The "Code of peace and Security for Europe" elaborated in Helsinki is aimed at solving such basic problems, which also include those facing Asia.

What, according to the Helsinki Conference participants, are the principles that should guide nations and that could be useful in tackling Asian problems?

Take such a basic principle as the sovereign equality of states, which includes the right to legal equality, territorial integrity, freedom and political independence. The participant states in the Helsinki Conference have pledged to respect each other's right to choose freely and develop their political, social, economic and cultural systems. This principle is essential to all states in Asia.

Another concept is territorial integrity. For several years now Washington and Islamabad have been persistently seeking to dismember India, openly discussing plans to carve out of India an independent state called "Khalistan". A ramified network of Sikh separatist centres have been functioning in the United States, Britain, Canada and the Federal Republic of Germany. The Sikh separatists received broad support from Pakistani authorities, and camps for training subvessive agents are operating in that country. Arms and money to be used for purposes of sabotage and murder pour in from Pakistan.

Meanwhile, in the Middle East, the Tel Aviv authorities, flagrantly violating the rights of the region's states to territorial integrity, have annexed art of Syrian territory—the Golan Heights. Israel has also seized lands in the south of Lebanon. Work is under way there to divert the waters of the Litani river to Israel's territory, although water is badly needed by Lebanon for the irrigation of its own land. "It seems the day is not far off", wrote the Lebanese newspaper *al-Liwa*, "when Israel will begin to build its settlements in the region." While overtly violating the principle of territorial integrity, Israel is seeking to perpetuate the division of Lebanon by providing the Israeli-financed puppet army of General Antoine Lahad, which is operating in the south of Lebanon, to indulge in armed provocations against the UN forces and the national-patriotic Lebanese formations. Tel Aviv also incites the Lebanese right-wing Christian forces to foil all attempts to resolve the internal political conflict through peaceful means.

Now let's take a look at yet another region of Asia—the Pacific, where an archipelago of small islands known as Micronesia is situated. Micronesia is administered by the United States under the UN Security Council's mandate. In an effort to strengthen its domination there, Washington has virtually divided the archipelago into four parts, forceing on two of them shackling commitments under which they are granted only "internal self-government" while the United States retains "all rights and responsibilities with regard to defence and security". This in fact enables Washington to maintain there powerful military bases and missile and nuclear weapons testing grounds.

These few examples of violation of the right to territorial integrity with regard to Asian peoples convincingly show how important it is that the countries of Asia undertake joint efforts in order to implement on their continent as well the underlying basic principles of the Helsinki Final Act.

Another principle of the Final Act is the non-use of force or threat of force. That is force should not be employed as a means of settling disputes, and no circumstances may justify resorting to the use or threat of force.

There is no need to elaborate on the importance of this principle as regards Asia. In recent years military hostilities between Iraq and Iran have been sharply exacerbated. A million people killed and wounded from both sides and thousands of prisoners—such was the war toll by the spring of 1986. Material damage has climbed upto tens of billions of dollars.

Using threats of force as a means of bringing pressure to bear on Asian countries has become altogether commonplace. American fleets cruising in the Pacific and Indian oceans constitute a permament threat to peace. Suffice is to recall the period of extreme aggravation in US-Iranian relations. In 1980 the number of US warships at the Iranian border in the Gulf reached 97. It was from these ships that the abortive attempt at a raid of American commandos on Teheran took place. On February 7, 1986, on the eve of the Presidential elections in the Philippines, a squadron of US warships headed towards the islands—to serve as a "weighty factor" of influence on that country's internal affairs. As regards Israel, partial mobilisation, troup formations in combat readiness deployed near the borders of Arab states, and bellicose statements by Israeli generals have become a constant instrument of political pressure on its neighbours.

In January 1986 Syria was again compelled to send to the US Secretary General a message pointing to Israel's threat to use military force against Lebanon and Syria. This was the eleventh time Israeli leaders had threatened to use force against Syria since January 1982.

The situation on the Thai-Kampuchean border has, of late, been used constantly by American imperialists to put pressure on the people of Kampuchea. The Reagan administration has openly declared that it will finance and supply units of the "non-Communist rebels" with arms. In actual fact, these "rebels" are none other than the followers of Pol Pot who mercilessly exterminated more than three million of their fellow-countrymen. By using the units of these cut-throats stationed in camps on Thai territory near the Kampuchean border, Washington intends to make Kampuchea agree to concessions infringing on its sovereing rights.

Hum Sen, Chairman of the Council of Ministers and Minister of Foreign Affairs of the People's Republic of Kampuchea, noted that the main cause of tension on the Kampuchean-Thai frontier was the all-round support rendered by the forces of imperialism headed by the United States to Pol Pot and other Khmer reactionaries who had entrenched themselves in Thailand.

A direct threat to Asian states can be found in Japanese Prime Minister Nakasone's statement in which he expressed the desire to "take under Japanese control" interntional straits around Japan and create a one-thousand-mile "zone of defence" of its sea communications right up to the Island of Guam and the Formosa Strait. By mentally drawing a line around the Japan islands at a one-thousand mile radius, one can easily see that such strategic plans pose a threat to seven Asian countries.

The threat to use force sometimes assumes a sinister character in the Asian region. Pakistan continues to build up its nuclear preparations with Washington's help. It is common knowledge that the United States has decided not to apply to Pakistan the Symington-Glenn Amendment, which prohibits military supplies to states developing nuclear weapons. Pakistan is using this opportunity to obtain certain components necessary for producing warheads as well as missiles and their nuclcar delivery vehicles.

They even do not deny in Islamabed that these weapons are planned to be used primarily against India. Hints of this kind are readily dropped by American diplomacy. Washington makes it clear to Indian representatives that the US administration might possibly agree to checking Pakistan's nuclear programme, but only in exchange for political concessions, a bargain India is absolutely unwilling to accept. The USA wants Delhi to recognise the "legality" of the US Navy's presence in the Indian Ocean, agree to let Diego Garcia Island be turned into the Pentagon's stronghold, and to renounce the demand that Pakistan should not allow its territory to be used for foreign military bases. In short, using the Pakistani nuclear threat the United States would like to make of India, if not an obedient ally, then at least a passive on-looker while the former undermines Asian security.

Many Asian countries are for peaceful settlement of conflicts. The League of Arab States for instance, is now working for putting an end to the Iran-Iraq war and the establishment of normal relations between the two warring Muslim countries. The League's actions are actively supported by the governments of the Yemen Arab Republic, Saudi Arabia and Egypt. India, as chairman of the non-aligned movement, has been showing commendable initiatives aimed at ending the military conflict between Iran and Iraq.

With Syria's mediation, an agreement was signed in Damascus early this year between the main politico-military groups of Lebanon on normalising the situation there and restoring unity in the country. Despite numerous violations of the agreement, work towards a peaceful settlement of Lebanese disputes is continuing.

The Communique of the 12th Conference of Foreign Ministers of Kampuchea, Loas and Vietnam held in the Loatian capital, in February 1986 contained a programme for the peaceful political solution of the problems facing South-East Asia, including a settlement in Kampuchean-Thai relations.

The communique stressed that Kampuchea's domestic problems should be settled by the Kampuchean people themselves, without anyoutside interference. This echoes the guiding principles of the Helsinki Final Act, which prohibits all forms of interference—direct or indirect, individual or collective—in the internal affairs of states. "Accordingly" the Final Act, says, "they will, *inter alia*, refrain from direct or indirect assistance to terrorist activities, or to subversive or other activities directed towards the violent overthrow of the regime of another participating state." It seems that a document of this nature could be signed by the vast majority of Asian states. especially because interference in their internal affairs, and terrorist activities against their political leaders, governments and parties have become particularly widespread, of late.

Thus last year when the government of New Zealand (incidentally, a US ally in the ANZUS bloc) approved the bill prohibiting foreign atomic-powered warships or those with nuclear weapons on board from calling at the country's ports (one would agree that this measure is entirely within the competence of the government of any country), Washington served several "stern warnings" to the government in Wellington. The New Zealand public has justly regarded these warnings as flagrant interference in the country's domestic affairs. And if the United States can so overtly interfere even in the internal affairs of its allies, then its attitude towards non-aligned countries in Asia is simply outrageous. The roots of the plan to murder Indira Gandhi, Prime Minister of India and Chairperson of the Non-Aligned Movement, can be traced—this has become quite obvious today—to terrorist camps and headquarters stationed in North America. The Sikh terrorists enjoy support there. In August 1985, the US administration told India that there were no "legal grounds" for closing one such camp in the State of Alabama, where Sikh territorists were being trained. Meanwhile, it was the territorists who distroyed an Indian plans with 329 passengers on board over the Atlantic and killed several political leaders in India.

The United States and its partners have been stepping up their interference in the internal affairs of Afghanistan and intensifying the training of terrorists in Pakistan to be sent into Afghan territory. One billion two hundred thousand dollars have already been spent on the arming, training and upkeep of numerous counter-revolutionary gangs perpetrating atrocities on Afghan land. They are killing innocent people and inflicting colossal damage on the country's economy. Support is also being rendered to the bloody Pol Pot bands operating on the Indochina Peninsula.

Acts of state terrorism are being committed by the United States against the Palestinians in Western Asia. In late 1985

American fighter planes intercepted an Egyptian Boeing-737 passenger liner in order to arrest persons active in the Palestinian movement who were not to Washington's liking. A present, American high-ranking officials are vociferously advocating the adoption of measures to combat "international terrorism". But such words can be assessed only as hypocrisy and cynicism in the light of the above-mentioned facts.

The White House has brought international terrorism to the level of government policy. Recently it initiated the creation of a special group within its apparatus designed to co-ordinate aid to bandit formations all over the world. The Reagan administration is thoughtlessly trampling upon the right of nations to free and independent development and is blatantly violating international law. It is not surprising that countries following in the wake of US policy act on its example. The Israelis seized the Libyan plane and committed numerous acts of violence on the Palestinian territories they have occupied. In Lebanon, using terrorists from among right-wing Christian groups, the Zionists have massacred Palestinians in the Sabra and Shatile refugee camps, which caused a wave of indignation the world over. So the ban on all forms of interference in internal affairs and aid to terrorists activities proclaimed at Helsinki is even more important to Asia.

A look at other political principles approved at Helsinki the inviolability of frontiers and the refraining from any violation of these frontiers; the territorial integrity of states; respect for the rights and freedoms of man; equality and the right of nations to be the masters of their destinies—will suffice to show the universally applicable character of the standards of behaviour among states worked out there. In this way, the success of the Helsinki Conference has not only advanced the European countries in the direction of strengthening their own security, but also provided a vivid example of building inter-state relations on the entire continent on tthe basis of peace and co-operation.

The Asian public and quite a few statesmen and political figures are coming to realise that a successful solution to the problems facing them will not be possible until the security of the continent is ensured. Certain steps have been taken recently in this direction. However, many people in Asia believe that it is time to approach the problem of security from a broader angle. It could include the five principles (panchsheel) elaborated at one time by Asian countries, the Ten Principles of Bandung, and a number of initiatives put forward by the Soviet Union, the Mongolian People's Republic, the People's Democratic Republic of Korea, the countries of Indochina, India and other countries of the region all concerned with Asian security and turning the Indian Ocean into a zone of peace.

"The significance of the Asian and Pacific direction is growing," emphasizes the Political Report of the CPSU Central Committee to the 27th Congress of the Communist Party of the Soviet Union. "In that vast region there are many tangled knots of contradictions and, besides, the political situation in some places is unstable. Here it is necessary, without postponement, to search for the relevant solutions and paths. Evidently, it is expedient to begin with the co-ordination and then the pooling of efforts in the interests of a political settlement of painful problems so as, in parallel, on that basis at least to take the edge off the military confrontation in various parts of Asia and stabilise the situation there."

The Soviet Union's constructive approach to the problems of ensuring peace in Asia meets with broad public approval and the support of realistically-minded government and political, figures in Asia.

Of special importance for strengthening peace and international security in the Asian and Pacific region in the present complicated situation is the proposal put forward by Mikhail Gorbachev in his statement of May 21, 1985, to approach the problem of security in Asia in a comprehensive manner. He suggested that a pan-Asiatic forum be held some time in the future to exchange views and jointly search for constructive solutions. This idea was further developed by Mikhail Gorbachev in if his speech in Vladivostok on July 28, 1986 : "The Soviet state alls upon all Asian and Pacific nations to co-operate for the sake of peace and security. Everyone who strives tawards these goals and who hopes for a better future for one's people, will find that we are willing to talk and are honest partners," the Soviet leader stressed. The Soviet Union has demonstrated once again its striving to build new, fair relations in Asia and in the Pacific, to develop co-operation with full respect for the right of every people to live according to its own choice and to solve its problems independently under conditions of peace. Moscow has shown the whole world that the Soviet Union is a devoted adherent of the idea of disbanding military groups, of renouncing military bases in Asia and in the Pacific, and withdrawing troops from other countries' territory. "For an objective, however remote, we would like to propose a conference, in the mould of the Helsinki conference, to be attended by all countries gravitating towards the ocean. When an agreement is reached on its convocation (If an agreement is reached at all, of course) it will be possible to establish the place for this conference. Hiroshima is a possible option. Why should that city, the first victim of nuclear evil, not become a "Helsinki" for Asia and the Pacific Ocean ?" Mikhail Gorbachev said.

The proposals advanced in Vladivostok (if they are implemented) would help overcome confrontation for the sake of co-operation among all peoples of this region with due account of the Helsinki experience. The *Nation Review*, a Bangkok newspaper, notes that the Soviet Union displays great diplomatic flexibility in relations with non-communist countries in Southeast Asia. Thepaper points out that Moscow's proposals on holding an all-Asian forum are timely.

In connection with the fact that Hiroshima was suggested as the venue of a forum on the security of the Asian-Pacific region, Mayor Takeshi Araki states that this is a great honour for the city.

As pointed out by Mikhail Gorbachev in Vladivostok, "our views on security in the Asian-Pacific region did not come out of thin air. They take into account the experience of the past and of today." The accumulated experience of relations of goodneighbourliness and co-operation shows that all peoples without any exception will only gain if they jointly work for the elimination of mistrust, for the attainment of mutual understanding in the sphere of inter-state ties. One should not underestimate the difficulties lying on the way to the conference. But the idea of convening the conference on security and co-operation in Europe initially also seemed to be a chimera. And yet the idea was implemented and yielded tangible positive results. "The longest road also beings with the frist step" goes an old saying. Time is calling upon all of us to take this step. Asia which since the ancient past has done much for humankind's progress can and should contribute to the creation of a world without nuclear and conventional, wars without bloodsheads.

Moscow regards the Asia-Pacific region as part of a general process of establishing a comprehensive system of international security, the basic principles of which in the military, political, economic and humanitarian spheres were put forth at the 27th CPSU Congress.

Specifically, these concern primarily the issues of regional settlement. There are many issues of such kind. First, the problems facing South-East Asia and Kampuchea, and the situation around Afghanistan and in the Korean peninsula must be settled. Second, the USSR is for blocking the proliferation and build-up of nuclear weapons in Asia and Pacific Ocean. Third, the Soviet Union proposes that talks be held on the reduction of the activity of naval forces in the Pacific, in particular, nuclear-armed ships. It remains strongly in favour of resuming the talks on proclaiming the Indian Ocean a zone of peace. Fourth, the Soviet Union attaches great importance to the radical reduction of armed forces a conventional armaments in Asia to limits of reasonable sufficiency. Fifth, the Soviet Union believes that it is high time to switch to practical discussions on confidence-building measures and on the non-use of force in this region.

Other socialist countries of the region are also actively socialist countries of the region are also actively seeking to strengthen peace and security in Asia and the Pacific basin. In 1981, the Mongolian People's Republic put forward a proposal to conclude a convention on mutual non-aggression and non-use of force in relations between states in Asia and the Pacific. In January 1985, the Sovialist Republic of Vietnam, the Laotian People's Democratic Republic and the People's Republic of Kampuchea jointly advocated the creation of a zone of peace, co-operation and stability in South-East Asia, the holding of a regional conference between the countries of Indochina, ASEAN and other interested countries of the region for the purpose, as well as the signing of bilateral or multilateral treaties on the peaceful co-existence of Vietnam, Laos and Kampuchea with the People's Republic of China. At a meeting of the foreign ministers of Vietnam, Laos and Kampuchea in Phnom Penh in 1985 new initiatives were put forward : a deadline for the withdrawal of the Vietnamese volunteers from Kampuchea was set and Kampuchea announced its readiness to begin negotiations with representatives of Khmer groupings abroad with a view to discuss the question of national reconciliation on the basis of outsting the Pol Pot followers and holding general elections after the complete withdrawal of the Vietnamese volunteers. The three countries expressed their readiness to normalise relations with the United States and the People's Republic of China.

A peaceful settlement in Korea was discussed in January 1986, during a visit to the Democratic Korea by Eduard Shevardnadze. the USSR Foreign Minister. In a Joint Soviet-Korean Communique the Soviet representative "confirmed the USSR's solidarity with the policy of the government of the Democratic People's Republic of Korea aimed at the withdrawal of American troops from South Korea and the Korea's unification on a peaceful democratic basis without outside interference. The communique also supported DPRK's ideas to form a democratic confederative republic through a dialogue and negotiations between the parties concerned; to replace the armistic agreement by a peace agreement in Korea; to elaborate a declaration on non-aggression between North and South Korea, as well as to take constructive steps for the development of a broad peaceful dialogue between them. The government of the DPRK has put forth an important proposition on the establishment on the Korean peninsula of a nuclear-free zone.

The war danger looming over mankind has never been so grave. But never before have the possibilities to preserve and consolidate peace been so real. The increased aggressiveness of imperialism is countered by the growing potential of the forces of peace. This is above all the socialist states and their increasing economic and defence capacities. The emergence of the world socialist system and the strengthening of the socialist community have led to a radical shift in the correlation of forces in the international arena. This is manifested in the fact that a majority of Asian, African and Latin American countries, which are members of the non-aligned movement, are vitally interested in preserving peace and halting the arms race, and are actively pursuing anti-imperialist policies; it is manifested also in the upsurge of anti-war movements on all continents.

"The forces of peace and progress all over the world", says the Resolution of the 27th CPSU Congress on the Political Report of the CPSU Central Comittee (1986) "can neutralise the threat emanating from imperialism, halt the world's slide towards the brink of the nuclear abyss, and prevent outer space from becoming a battlefield. Human life, the possibilities of its all-round development, the interests of the advance of society, rank uppermost."

Now, 12 years after the successful conclusion of the Conference on Security and Co-operation in Eruope, we refer back to the ten principles of the Final Act which heralded the end of cold war and became the symbol of true humanitarian ideals. The achievements at Helsinki were, above all, a result of the consistent peace-loving policy of the Soviet Union and other socialist states. This policy has been supported by all progressive minded people the world over, by noted statesmen and political figures, as well as by outstanding scientists and cultural figures.[3]

At the same time, the past eleven years have revealed the true intentions of imperialism. Soon after the signing of the Final Act, political leaders in the United States and in some Western countries shelved this document and turned their attention to the arms race, following the road of the aggravation of world tension. Instead of

3. *Ibid.*

fulfilling the hopes and responding to the wishes of millions upon millions of people of goodwill by strengthening security and broadening co-operation, the United States has begun deploying new nuclear first-strike weapons in Europe and elsewhere.

Washington is exerting tremendous efforts to draw its NATO and other allies into the implementation of the Star Wars programme. The West is spending astronomical sums for military purposes.

The main reason for the retardation in the early 1980s of the multilateral process begun in Helsinki was the actual refusal of the United States and NATO to recognize one of the conclusions drawn by the All-European Conference and defined in the Final Act, namely, the need to complement political detente with military detente. Washington's policy of arms build-up aggravates the situation in Europe and Asia and considerably heightens the danger of a nuclear conflict. Moreover, NATO member-states blatantly ignore the important and entirely feasible peace initiatives of the Soviet Union and other Warsaw Treaty countries, as well as proposals put forward by non-aligned states, particularly those in Asia. They thereby undermine the possibility of solving the problems of the limitation and reduction of nuclear and conventional arms and the non-militarisation of outer space.

But the ideas of peace, security and co-operation are gaining ever firmer ground. The principles laid down in the Final Act are still vital. The successful conclusion of the Belgrade and Madrid meetings has proved their vitality. This is also demonstrated by the growing anti-nuclear and anti-war movement. The efforts aimed at turning Northern Europe, the Balkans and many regions of the Asian continent into nuclear-free zones, refusing sea-going vessels with nuclear weapon on board access to the ports of many countries, and the mass movement against the deployment of American nuclear weapons in various parts of the world and against SDI are fully in keeping with the principles of the Final Act. It can safely be said that the ideas of Helsinki are being put into practice in regions many thousands of miles away from Europe,

The conference in Helsinki has shown that meetings of such kind constitute an important form of co-operation between nations, and that their successful outcome depends on the same factors—as do international relations as a whole.

A process begun by a well-prepared conference can in itself have a considerable impact on the international situation.

The signing of the Final Act in Helsinki has paved the way for expanding and strengthening bilateral and multilateral co-operation between the peoples of Europe, Asia and other regions. The conference participants declared their desire to build up confidence between the peoples and governments, complement political detents with military detente, and guarantee all nations a peaceful future. The past decade has proved that this task is a difficult but feasible one. Goodwill and concerted efforts are required for its implementation.

The favourable conditions created during the 1970s promoted economic and trade ties, cultural exchanges, and political contacts among European states, and showed the peoples of other countries and continents a realistic road towards achieving this aim. The socialist countries have been, and remain, in the vanguard of those forces which are sincerely striving to implement the principles of the Final Act. There are now ever greater opportunities for rallying the world nations in the struggle to liberate humanity from war altogether and strengthen peace and security. This aim has been pursued by numerous initiatives of the socialist and non-aligned countries.

The Helsinki Conference has convincingly confirmed that differences in the political systems of states do not prevent them from co-operating in the search for joint solutions in the interests of universal security.

The majority of the world's population is concentrated in Asia. The voice of Asian states acting jointly can play a decisive role in solving the most crucial issues facing humanity.

The process of detente should be universal and embrace also the Middle East, the Pacific and Indian ocean regions, the Far East,

Central America and Africa. The task of continuing the process begun eleven years ago at the Helsinki Conference is complex and enormous, but to it there is no alternative but war. The spirit of Helsinki means hope which should not be allowed to die.

A halt in the preparation for Star Wars is a necessary step. The arms race in outer space in any form should be banned without delay. The peoples of Asia should demand this too, for the testing and improvement of space weapons can lead to an irrevocable situation.

Rather than stepping up the arms race, which will have fatal consequences, the peoples of the world must come out against all military preparations in outer space, for keeping it only as a field of international co-operation for peaceful purposes.

Measures for stabilising peace must be carried out immediately. The most important among them is to put an end to the arm race. Positive shifts in the reduction of armaments and ultimately the complete elimination of nuclear weapons will facilitate the solving of other pressing tasks and improve international climate.

The present strained situation in the world requires urgent concerted efforts drastically to improve the political climate in Europe and Asia. The entire potential of the Helsinki Final Act should be geared towards achieving this purpose.

The concerted actions can have far-reaching results. This has been demonstrated by the Helsinki Conference. It provided an excellent example to follow and charted the best course for the struggle for peace and co-operation among nations.

The call of Mikhail Gorbachev for an Asia-Pacific "Helsinki" is a proposition that should be actively convassed by the peace constituencies, solidarity organisations and supporters of the non-aligned movement, because Soviet policy and the aspirations of the peoples of the Asian-Pacific regions coincide. It is urgent need that a conference of this nature should be convened because neo-colonialist penetration must be halted and the US plans for the region's militarisation must be stopped.

The Soviet peace initiatives, especially after the 27th CPSU Congress, have received acceptance both in the West and the Third World. However, while Mikhail Gorbachev call for Helsinkis, the US President Ronald Reagan is insisting on Nevadas nuclear tests and more Nevadas. This brings out more clearly than anything else the commitment of the two countries to peace or the lack of it. Gorbachev has rightly pointed out : "Mobilisation of the potential of common sense existing in the world, the partnership of reason are now more important than ever to arrest the sliding to catastrophe."

CHAPTER SEVEN

WHITHER ASEAN ?

AT THE END of June 1986, the capital of the Philippines, played host to the 19th annual meeting of ASEAN foreign ministers. This forum was followed by talks, which are also held on a regular basis between ASEAN leaders and heads of the U.S., Japanese, Australian, New Zealand and Canadian foreign policy departments, as well as Common Market representatives.

The six association members are going through a difficult period. The rather high economic growth rates of the 1970's have given way to a profound and protracted crisis. The plummeting of world prices of oil, rubber, tin, and palm oil—their main export items—has adversely affected these countries' economies. Currency earnings have dropped sharply. Thus, sales of oil and gas netted Indonesia \$19 billion in the 1981-82 fiscal year, as against \$12 billion in 1985-86. Indonesian experts expect the figure to be another \$4 billion less this fiscal year. Things are no better in this respect in the Philippines, Malaysia, Thailand and even Singapore, until recently considered a capitalist show case in the region. The situation is further exacerbated by U.S. and Japanese protectionism, and the huge debts run up by some of the members. (Indonesia and the Philippines owe \$ 26 billion each, whole Malaysia owes \$13 billion.) That is why ASEAN members have to slash national construction programmes, seek new loans, and fighten their belts at the bidding of transnational banks and monopolies. All this brings living standards down and aggravates social tensions.[1]

1. Valery Andreyev. "Southeast Asia : Will the Noose be Loosened?" *New Times* (Moscow) 4 August, 1986, pp. 12-13.

Aware of the direct connection between self-seeking Western policies and their own economic difficulties, ASEAN members tried to obtain some concessions, in particular from the U.S., which is largely responsible for the present situation. When President Reagan made a stopover in the Indonesian island of Bali on his way to the Tokyo Big Seven summit, ASEAN ministers handed him a memorandum setting out their claims. However, the Tokyo meeting failed to live up to their expectations. As Indonesian Minister Mochtar Kusumaatmadja put it, the meeting did not alter the approach to the problems facing the developing countries. And Malaysian Premier Mahathir Mohamad stated, not without bitterness, that the industrialized Western countries and Japan not only reject a new international economic order based on a fair and democratic foundation, but are working to establish a diametrically different order of things.

The ASEAN countries intend to tackle their economic problems along two lines.

Firstly, promotion of regional economic co-operation in order reduce their dependence on the imperialist states and the fluctuations of the world capitalist market. The President or the Philippines, Corazon Aquino, attaches special significance to this. She criticized the association for failing, in the nearly two decades of its existence, to build up really strong regional ties. She urged it to pass from words to deeds in this matter, and her call found a ready response: the June conference endorsed two documents, on inter-ASEAN co-operation in the power industry and no oil sales. The latter provides for deliveries of oil-rich Brunei, Indonesia and Malaysia to their partners in the association—the Philippines, Singapore and Thailand.

Secondly, ASEAN will press for the abolition of Western protectionist barriers, the stabilization of world industrial commodity prices and free acess to high technology. But their efforts have failed to bear tangible fruit. As has already been mentioned, the hopes pinned on the Big Seven's magnanimity were not realized. U.S. Secretary of State George Shultz did not even bother to hide his reluctance to make economic concessions. The Japanese displayed greater flexibility. Foreign Minister Shintaro Abe brought to

Manila a "new doctrine," prompted by sharper criticism of Japan's economic and military policies. He said that the lessons of the past had not been lost on Japan and it was not going to become a major military power again; instead it wanted to base its relations with the Southeast Asian countries on mutual understanding, cordial friendship, and equitable economic co-operation.

Yet his promises to increase aid and galvanize a friendly exchange of opinions were so vague that they can hardly be regarded as serious concrete commitments. It is believed in ASEAN that the "new doctrine" is aimed not at solving the problems that have built up in Japanese-ASEAN relations, but at taking the edge off them and impressing the public favourably. In general, Kyodo Tsushin reports from Manila, the talks with the U.S. and Japan were disappointing for the ASEAN ministers—all they had got were promises and not concrete measures.

For his part, George Shultz tried to move economic questions to the background, bringing political ones to the fore and trotting out the bogey of the "Soviet threat" again and again. He did not manage to hide Washington's irritation at the failure of the ASEAN states to appreciate the validity of its thesis that a "growing Soviet presence,' in Southeast Asia is the main cause of tension in the region. Indications of this, observers note, are the recent pronouncements of Indonesian and Malaysian leaders, who have in fact rejected the U.S. allegations.

Furthermore, the fact ASEAN members are pressing ever more actively for a nuclear-free zone in Southeast Asia also goes against Washington's grain. The implementation of this idea, along with the already proclaimed nuclear-free zone in the South Pacific, does not square with U.S. military strategic plans for the Asian-Pacific region, nor, for that matter, with its global strategy as a whole. In this connection the Indonesian Merdeka wrote that the Secretary of State was again out to impose the U.S. concept of nuclear weapons, opposing it to the idea of a nuclear-free zone. However, the paper went on, ASEAN would not allow Southeast Asia to become a common grave for victims of a nuclear holocaust as humanity had more than its share of U.S. atomic genocide in Hiroshima and Nagasaki forty years ago.[2]

Some other statements in the final communique are also characterized by anti-war feeling. The foreign ministers censured the nuclear arms race and called for strict observance of the SALT-2 treaty. They urged the United States and Soviet Union to abide by the treaties concluded and understandings reached, and not to reject them. Clearly, the ASEAN countries are seriously concerned about Washington's policy of reneging on its commitments under the Soviet-U.S. treaties on arms limitation and disarmament.

For all that, there are still issues on which the ASEAN counries toe the West's line. This inconsistency may be attributed to the varying degrees of their political military and economic dependence on the United States (including their status as debtor countries) and to some other factors, both internal and external. All this made itself felt at the Manila meeting. Some participants tried to inflate the "Kampuchea question." Calling for a comprehensive political settlement in Kampuchea, they reiterated the "eight-point programme" which the Kampucheans had resolutely rejected. Attempts to present the "problems of Kampuchea" as an obstacle to making Southeast Asia a nuclear-free zone and a zone of peace, freedom and neutrality exposed the unconstructive, patently anti-Vietnamese character of this approach which is incompatible with the course at dialogue with Vietnam pursued by Indonesia, a course that objectively lays the groundwork for a settlement. Analyzing this section of the Manila communique, the Hanoi Nhan Dan wrote : "Slander, falsification and pressure on the Indo-China states is no way to work for a settlement in Kampuchea. They can only raise new obstacles to it."

The significance of the conference, however, lies elsewhere. It clearly demonstrated—and most observers agree here—that the ASEAN countries are striving for a more independent policy and greater interaction in tackling the complex problems that face them. The meeting has also shown the association's growing realization of the grave consequences of the unbridled arms race

2. *Ibid.*

Washington seeks to impose on them, and their reluctance to play the role it allots them in its militaristic scenario.

It is noteworthy that in their coverage of the Manila conference many ASEAN journalists stressed the importance of promoting good and more active relations with the Soviet Union and other socialist countries.

The Soviet Union has always displayed readiness to broaden all-round co-operation with individual ASEAN countries and with the association as a whole—not out of some ulterior motives, but in the full conviction that such co-operation is in the interests of the nations concerned and contributes to greater security in Southeast Asia and throughout the world. As hitherto, the Soviet Union intends to back this principled stand with practical action.

Meanwhile, the Pentagon usually tries to keep secret where its nuclear weapons are sited outside the United States. But all of a sudden the U.S. Department of Defence published the list of 20 air bases in Europe and Asia, where U.S. fighter-bombers equipped with nuclear weapons are kept in combat readiness. The list includes such Asian countries as Turkey and South Korea.

Along with other documentation, the list was tabled by the Pentagon at the recent hearings at the Congress Sub-Committee on Military Construction. The Pentagon had to publish it in a bid to convince the Sub-Committee that secret U.S. air force nuclear weapons depots had to be built in close proximity to the bases.

The aircraft in these bases remain in combat readiness round the clock and are capable of taking off within 15 minutes of being ordered to do so. When some of the planes are in the air, the nuclear bombs for those still at the base are brought there from nuclear weapon depots located some distance away from the airfields for safety reasons.

Now the Pentagon wants to build these depots near the take-off strip itself so as to reduce the time of their delivery. This means that nuclear weapons in future will be based together with the strike fighter-bombers.

As far as Japan is concerned, the news agency Kyodo Tsushin reports that a total of 360 underground nuclear depots are to be built in that country. Another 36 are to be built in South Korea. As for Turkey, the newspaper Cumhuriyet says the existing nuclear warhead depots at four military airfields (Malatya, Murted, Balikesir and Eskisehir) and at the Incirli U.S. air base are to be modernised. Squadrons of F-4's and F-104's are based there. They carry nuclear weapons on their endless combat patrol duty.

The obviously means that the Pentagon intends to build up its nuclear potential outside the U.S. within the framework of its military strategy directed not only against the Soviet Union but also against many independent states in the Asia-Pacific region. It is no mere coincidence that Admiral Ronald Hays. Commander-in-Chief of the U.S. Pacific and Indian Ocean forces, has called the "U.S. military forces" a key to peace and stability in Asia. Washington is bending over backwards to turn Asia and the Pacific and Indian Oceans into lines for forward-based nuclear weapons, as it has done with Western Europe and the Atlantic.

Apart from plans to build the new nuclear depots, the U.S. is also reported to have been amassing nuclear arms for a long time at its military bases on Okinawa. Diego Garcia, in the Philippines and elsewhere. Missiles with nuclear charges are carried by dozens of U.S. warships in the Pacific and Indian Oceans, and by hundreds of warplanes, whose number in the region keeps increasing. Such a concentration of U.S. nuclear forces on the Asian continent constitutes a serious threat to its peoples.

It is not by chance that the movement for nuclear-free zones is growing in Asia. The initiative of 13 States of the region is typical in this respect. They signed the South Pacific Nuclear-Free Zone Treaty banning forever the deployment, manufacturing and testing of nuclear weapons on their territories, as well as the dumping of radioactive wastes into the ocean. Meanwhile the ASEAN member-States have proposed to declare South-East Asia a nuclear-free zone. Recently the Democratic Korean Government issued a statement proposing to turn the Korean Peninsula into a nuclear-free zone, a zone of peace.

CHAPTER EIGHT

INDIAN OCEAN PEACE

THE INDIAN OCEAN has become a dangerous flashpoint of international tension. Crudely ignoring the desire of the peoples to have this region demilitarised, the USA has converted the ocean into an arena of unprecedented military preparations. The USA has dumped there hundreds of combat planes, dozens of ships and a large contingent of interventionist 'rapid deployment force' (RDF). The Ocean is plied by nuclear submarines and strike aircraft carriers. Regularly overflying it are strategic B-52 bombers loaded with lethal cargo.[1]

Central to the Pentagon's military plans in the Indian Ocean is the island of Diego Garcia, which has become a US naval and air base. The Pentagon is keeping in its gunsights many countries of the region and also more remote territories Diego Garcia has been turned into a large link in the chain of US strong points in the Indian Ocean. American emissaries are now pressing for spring boards on the territories of Sri Lanka, Pakistan and other countries of the region. They are now nurturing plans to deploy first-strike Pershing-2 missiles in the region. In effect, the Indian Ocean is being turned into new area of US forward-based strategic forces in addition to Western Europe and the Far East.

People are particularly alarmed by Washington's plans to use the bases in the Indian Ocean in the 'star wars' programme. The specially set-up Central Command (CENTCOM). which is charged with planning and guiding punitive operations of the American

---

1. Attar Chand. U.S. Military design and Indian Ocean Security. *Indian Nation* (Patna) 3 September, 1986, p. 6.

military in the Indian Ocean and the Persian Gulf area, is at present drawing up measures to implement the American space militarisation programme in the region.

The unrestrained military expansion of the United States is causing grave alarm not only among the littoral states, but also among most of the UN members. In 1971, the international community of nations adopted the Declaration on Turning the Indian Ocean into a Zone of Peace. Its underlying principles are : to eliminate the foreign military bases in the area, to end the arms, to ban deployment of nuclear weapons, to renounce the threat and use of force against the sovereignty, territorial integrity and independence of the developing countries situated there. But these principles do not suit the ruling quarters in the United States, which, under Reagan's doctrine of new-globalim seek to establish in this vast region with one-third of the world's population, their military-political domination.

Historically the Indian Ocean is the most "ancient". Shipping here dates back to the Egyptian Pharaohs, almost 2,500 years B.C. Geographically, of all the Earth's oceans, it is the "smallest", but the "richest". About half the world's oil reserves are concentrated in the Persian Gulf alone. The Gulf countries account for about a third of world oil production and around two-thirds of capitalist-world oil exports. Besides that, as much as 80 percent of world gold production, over a half of tin and about a third of maganese are concentrated in the Indian Ocean countries. Other resources include natural rubber, bauxite, lead, nickel, iron ore and zinc. The United States, for example, imports 40 types of raw materials from here.[2]

The Indian Ocean is also strategically important. Sea and air routes run across it linking Europe, East Africa, the Middle East, South and Southeast Asia, the Far East, Australia and Oceania, The Indian Ocean, "connecting" the Atlantic and Pacific Oceans, is a major hub of sea communications (third place in the world in the volume of sea shipping). The net work of water ways is denser here than anywhere else in the World Ocean.

---

2. See Yevgeni Rumyantsev, *Indian Ocean and Asian Security*. New Delhi, Allied, 1986, pp. 3-18.

Air lines stretching over the Indian Ocean have also become significant. Their total length exceeds one million kilometers. Of the world's 240 airports serving inter-continental air routes, about a third are in the Indian Ocean countries.

As to Russia, it used the Indian Ocean from ancient times. In 1466 the Russian merchant Afanasii Nikitin, after going down the Volga and then across the Caspian, crossed Iran and via the Indian Ocean reached India where he spent almost three years, leaving mankind his diary "A Journey Beyond Three Seas." Having come across the diary in the middle of the 19th century, the great Russian historian N.M. Karamzin wrote: "Up until now geographers have not known that the credit of one of the most ancient record of European travels to Indian belongs to Russia... While Vasco de Gama only thought of finding a possible route from Africa to Hindustan, our man from Tyer (Afanasii Nikitin was born there; the city is now Kalinin) was already travelling on the Malabar Coast..." Nikitin's mission was commercial and peaceful. In short, Russians sailed in the Indian Ocean even before the discovery of America. Such are historical facts.

About a third of mankind lives in the Indian Ocean basin: Hindus and Moslems, Buddhists and Christians, the followers of many other religions—peoples speaking hundreds of languages and dialects, each with its own historical traditions, customs and practices. And yet, for all the diversity of political, socio-economic and religious features, most of these peoples have many things in common that unites them: an identical historical destiny, their striving to become the true masters of their present and future and play a worthy role in the world community. National liberation from colonial oppression, which was commenced by India's gaining of independence, is the highway of development for the peoples of this region.

The determination by new national states to play an ever more active role in world politics and to withstand imperialism's designs together gave rise to one of the biggest positive movements in contemporary history—the movement of non-alignment, now incorporating over 100 countries with a total population of 1.5 billion. It was the Indian Ocean countries that were in the majority among the founders of this movement. Having grown literally from the depths of the Indian Ocean, the non-aligned movement, which possesses a great peace potential, pays high attention to this region. This is reflected in the documents adopted by the movement. Their keynote is the desire to see the Indian Ocean as a zone of peace, security and co-operation.

Thus, in the Political Declaration adopted by the 7th Conference of Heads of State and Government of Non-Aligned Nations in New Delhi in 1983 it was noted that "ever since the Lusaka Summit Conference first called upon all States to consider and respect the Indian Ocean as a zone of peace, non-aligned States have consistently extended their unanimous support to the Declaration of the Indian Ocean as a zone of peace... The non-aligned countries are determined to work for the success of the Conference on the Indian Ocean... They urged the United Nations Ad Hoc Committee to complete its preparations for the Conference strictly in accordance with its mandate."

The leaders of non-aligned countries, gathered in New Delhi, expressed their "full support for Mauritian sovereignty over the Chagos archipelago including Diego Garcia which was detached from the territory of Mauritius by the former colonial power in 1965 in contravention of United Nations General Assembly Resolutions 1514 (XV) and 2066 (XX). The establishment and strengthening of the military base of Diego Garica has endangered the sovereignty, territorial integrity and peaceful development of Mauritius and other States. They called for the early return of Diego Garcia to Mauritius.

The forthcoming Conference of Heads of States and Government of Non-Aligned Nations in Harare is a major opportunity for the non-aligned movement to raise its voice in the struggle for peaceful waters of the Indian Ocean.

Characteristically, it was in the Indian Ocean that the United States and other Western countries faced a resolute attempt by newly-free states to liquidate the existing system of imperialist exploitation based on uncontrolled domination on the part of Western monopolies. At the beginning of the seventies oil-rich Indian Ocean states united into an Organisation of Petroleum Exporting Countries (OPEC). Having nationalised oil and expanded in a number cases co-operation with the socialist states, they turned from being an object of the oil policy of imperialism into a force actively resisting it.

This experience has shown that developing countries can take a vigorous and effective stand against the system of economic neo-colonialism, for a review of the relations existing in the world capitalist economy, for their restructuring on a just and democratic basis and for the establishment of a new international economic order.

The conflict between the interests of the former colonial powers and their former colonies and between the Western countries and the states dependent on them economically and politically remains the main conflict in the Indian Ocean region. Only the tactics of the latter-day colonialists have become more flexible.

Typical in this sense is the behaviour of Britain, and in particular the policy it proclaimed in 1968 of withdrawing from the area "east of Suez." In this connection the imperialists began talking of the formation of a "vacuum" which supposedly needed to be filled to prevent a "Soviet menace to coastal states" (this thesis has since been actively used by the USA as an explanation for its military aspirations in the region).

The British "withdrawal" showed a change of tactics by the former colonial giant which was no longer able to retain power by force, but which was still anxious to keep its influence. The British withdrew from the mainland in order to settle up in the ocean's islands where militant national movements could not threaten them,

Moreover, the British had prepared for withdrawal from the area "east of Suez" before hand. In 1964 they surveyed, together with the Americans, the Indian Ocean with the aim of selecting islands for military bases. At the end of 1965 the British government announced a decision to establish a new colony in the ocean's western part to be known as British Indian Ocean Territory, and already a year later the British gave it to the Americans for use for a period of 50 years. This is how the USA got the Diego Garcia island which had been wrested by the British from Mauritius for three million pounds sterling.

Despite its statement about "withdrawal", Britain in the early seventies was still connected with the Indian Ocean militarily. It was a member of CENTO and SEATO and had military agreements with a number of states (Mauritius, Oman, Malaysia, Kenya) and had a number of military bases including the strategically important base at Simonstown. South Africa, Australia and New Zealand as the closest allies; the shift to an "island strategy"; and most important, the sharing of dominance in the Indian Ocean with a new neo-colonialist plunderer, the USA (then not yet placing this area at the top of its list of priorities)—such was Britain's "withdrawal."[3]

The withdrawal was neo-colonialist in spirit. Whereas there was much of assiduous farewell bidding, the real intention was to stay. Is this not a proof that the thesis about a "vacuum" after Britain's withdrawal from the "east of Suez" area needing to be filled to prevent a "menace to coastal states from the USSR" was false? In the postwar years, especially after the out break of the Cold War, the United States intensified its attempts to expand its penetration into this region. The US imperialists were then driven not only by economic, but also by strategic interests and, more specifically, by a search for places for locating US military bases.

As Emilson Randriamihasinoro, Secretary of the World Peace Council for East Africa and the Indian Ocean, points out, "during the Second World War, and especially afterwards, the United States set up a whole system of military bases, both naval and air force, in the Indian Ocean basin. These bases form a great 'belt of security and a strategic arc' extending from the Australian coast to the Gulf of Oman and to Southern Africa" ("Indian Ocean and Great Powers" by Saral Patra. Sterling Publishers Pvt, Ltd., New Delhi, 1979, p. 77).

In the fifties, the years of the Cold War unleashed by Washington, there appeared the doctrines of "containment," "deterrence" and "rolling back communism." The USA began to surround the countries of socialism, above all the Soviet Union,

3. *Ibid.*

with a network of military blocs and bases and to create pro-American regimes in developing states in Asia and Africa, including Indian Ocean countries.

During this time the USA established the following military-political blocs: in 1951 ANZUS (Australia, New Zealand, USA); in 1954 SEATO with the participation of Pakistan, Australia and New Zealand; in 1955 the Baghdad Pact (from 1959 CENTO), which included Pakistan and Iran from among Indian Ocean coastal states.

In the sixties the United States continued its military-political drive in the Indian Ocean. Plans arose to link its and other NATO countries' bases there from Southern Africa to Australia together, to connect NATO and SEATO and to link the US Sixth (Mediterranean) Fleet with the Seventh (Pacific), to "clamp the jaws of a giant crocodile," to quote an American general.

US economic penetration in the Indian Ocean basin also grew. The availability of cheap manpower in the Afro-Asian countries led to much faster growth of US capital investments here than in Western Europe. As the profits grew, so did the appetites.

And yet, before the start of the seventies, the Indian Ocean zone yielded in US policy to such "vital" oceans as the Atlantic, which lies in the sphere of action of NATO, and the Pacific where a whole series of Washington's allies in Asian blocs and Japan, the US mainstay in Asia, are located.

But in the middle of the seventies the US setback in Vietnam, the temporary closure of US military bases in Greece and Turkey and later the fall of the pro-American regime in Iran induced the Pentagon strategists to think of the Indian Ocean zone already as a separate politico-geographical and strategic area. The Indian Ocean, Elmo Zumwalt, former US Chief of Naval Operations, said in 1974 at hearings in the US Congress, had become an area where shifts in the global balance of forces might occur within the next decade. This he saw as necessitating the United States to exert its influence on developments in this area adding that capacity to deploy US military strength there was a substantial element of such influence. In the middle of the seventies such statements became ever more frequent circles of the USA.

However, in spite of the limited US military presence in the Indian Ocean till the mid-seventies and even later, it would be wrong to think that there was none of it at all. As early as 1948 US warships were stationed at the British militaiy base Manama in Bahrein. From the sixties on, visits by US naval units to the Indian Ocean became increasingly frequent. They almost annually participated in manoeuvres there. But not just that. In 1962, for example, a unit of the US Seventh Fleet was ordered into the Bay of Bengal during the Indian-Chinese border conflict. And in 1964 a US Indian Ocean naval task force, Concord, was set up. In the same year a joint US-Iranian training exercise involving US ships took place; it was to fine-tune offensive operations.

From the early seventies such manoeuvres became more formidable. Aircraft carriers began to participate in them. In December 1971 the largest of such ships the carrier Enterprise, escorted by a whole group of naval vessels, entered the Bay of Bengal, threatening India, which gave support to the just struggle of the people of the future Bangladesh.

In 1972 the Indian Ocean was included in the "zone of responsibility" of the US Pacific Fleet.

In 1974 the US Navy participated in CENTO's biggest manoeuvres "Middlelink" involving up to 50 combat ships, including atomic submarines. During this exercise the US aircraft carrier Constellation paid a visit to the Persian Gulf, in a threatening show of force to the Arabs following their oil embargo of 1973. There was a similar incident in 1975 when a group of US Seventh Fleet ships led by the carrier Enterprise again appeared in the Indian Ocean with the aim of pressuring countries of the region. The earlier-begun construction of US military bases and the search for new ones intensively continued at the time.

And yet, in the second half of the seventies and even at the end of this decade the situation in the Indian Ocean was not yet relatively tense. The military presence of non-coastal states was comparatively limited. It then seemed that the process of detente could be extended to this area as well. In this context the Soviet Union, desirous of cutting short the tendency towards an escalation of the arms race in the Indian Ocean, started negotiations with the USA on limiting and subsequently reducing the military activity here.

In its approach to this part of the world, the Soviet Union has proceeded from the general peace-loving course of its policy. The USSR has always said frankly that in the Indian Ocean it had, has and will have its lawful interest which impinge on no one. From the times of Afanasaii Nikitin the commercial peaceful waterway of Russia to the Asian countries lay across the Indian Ocean. Today via the Indian Ocean the USSR is linked by trade and economic ties with dozens of Afro-Asian states, which is mutually advantageous. For the Soviet Union the Indian Ocean is the only sea route that remain unfrozen the year round and which links the western and the eastern parts of the country. In the Indian Ocean the USSR is also conducting a significant amount of scientific research and work, *inter alia* connected with outer space. When the Indo-Soviet space crew worked in orbit in 1984, contact with them was maintained by Soviet research vessels stationed in the waters of the Indian Ocean.

Though Soviet ships are present in the Indian Ocean, there is no "Soviet military threat" here. It is enough to look at the geographical map to see that the Indian Ocean is only hundreds of kilometres from Soviet territory, not thousands of miles as it is from American; and that the territory of the USSR is within the range of ships, planes and bases in the Indian Ocean for a nuclear strike. All these clearly show that the USSR cannot remain indifferent to the development in the Indian Ocean. It directly tells on the security of the USSR.

Yes, it is security interests that make the USSR keep its ships in the Indian Ocean. But the USSR does not introduce its strategic force here. It did not and does not intend to have its bases here. Since 1971 the presence of Soviet naval vessels in the area has been minimal and invariable : 4-6 destroyers, escort ships, sea mine-sweepers (also 5-6 ships). The overall tonnage of all these ships does not exceed half the displacement of a US aircraft carrier. And, most importantly, in tactical and technical characteristics they are designed to fulfil purely defensive functions but cannot launch offensive operations, that is, against shore. They can only defend themselves; they can't attack and they threaten nobody.

When the Soviet Union started negotiations with the USA, it was guided exclusively by the aims of its peace-loving policy. Four rounds of the talks took place from June 1977 to February 1978. The talks proceeded encouragingly. The sides agreed to approach the question of reducing military activity in the Indian Ocean on a step-by-step basis; first not to increase their military presence, and then go over to its curtailments. They agreed on some points of a future cut and, what was more, reached on understanding that new military bases would not be created in the area and that the US bases at Diego Garcia and in Berbera, Somalia, would be dismantled.

One might think that the sides had very little left to—just seal on paper the agreements reached. The USSR was ready to do it. And the USA ? It was at the time of negotiations that it allocated 3 billion dollars for a new expansion of the Diego Garcia base, the very same base which during the talks it promised to dismantle. And in February 1979 it unilaterally broke off the talks and then, in spite of the repeated proposals of the Soviet Union, never came back to the negotiating table again.

By then the USA had already completed a plan for its strategic uses of the Indian Ocean, allocating for these purposes 30 billion dollars for 1981-85. The talks on reducing military activity in the Indian Ocean proved to be an obstacle—the Pentagon and Washington had been thinking and planning its increase.

It turned out that Washington needed the talks just as a smokescreen or a diversion for its military buildup in the Indian Ocean.

Diversions of this kind include the various historical forgeries which allege a Russian striving almost centuries ago "towards the warm seas," that is, the Indian Ocean. In particular, much is being made of a "will of Peter the Great" which did not exist. There was a 1723 decree signed by Peter on sending an expedition of several ships with a mission to cross the Indian Ocean. The decree read : "When with God's help you arrive at your destination in East India, then appear there before the All-Powerful Mogol and try in every way to persuade him to allow Russia to do commerce and have a treaty with him." That is, the aim was commerce and peaceful co-operation, not a conquest of Asian countries.

Back in 1928 Jawaharlal Nehru wrote, characterising as myth the so-called "Russian threat" to Indian security, the alleged attempts by Russia to reach the Indian Ocean, a myth assiduously spread by the British at the turn of the century. He wrote that scarecrow of a Russian invasion had, for a long time, been used to frighten India and provide a justification for the huge burden of arms expenditures. As the time of Tsarism, he noted, the Indians had been told that Russian imperialism had always been striving towards the south, anxious to get an outlet to the sea and perhaps to India, itself; the Tsar was no longer there, and now the Indians were being told that the Soviet government was threatening India.

The myth about a "Soviet military threat" is now again in currency. Its variant is the thesis about a "rivalry of the two super powers" in the Indian Ocean. It is as false and harmful as the myth about a "Soviet menance." The data on the military presence of the USSR are incomparable. The USA's is an immeasurably larger presence. The USSR has no bases in the region. Nor can there be any talk of Soviet attempts to establish its "control" over the Persian Gulf, let alone the entire Indian Ocean. Not once during the time of the presence of Soviet naval forces in the Indian Ocean have they held any manoeuvres or any demonstration of strength; they have never posed a threat to the security of the coastal states.

There are really no Soviet military bases in the Indian Ocean, despite the numerous attempts by the West to assert the contrary. What a hullabaloo was raised by US propaganda over "the existence of Soviet bases in Somalia". However, the United States, having acquired in Somalia a partner after that country's swing to the right, discovered no Soviet bases there. But in August 1980 the USA itself signed an agreement with the local authorities envisaging the granting to US armed forces of the right to use the Somalia port at Berbera, the port and the airfield at Mogadishu and some other facilities. US military specialists are stationed there, tens of millions of dollars go into military construction and a regional headquarters for the US Rapid Development Force is being created there.

The Soviet Union has never participated and does not intend to participate in any military-political alliances with the Indian Ocean countries. And its treaty obligations with some of them are dictated only by the interests of peace and co-operation; they're not aimed against any third states.

Yet the myth about a "Soviet threat", through time-worn, has not been removed from the propaganda armoury of the apostles of the US aggressive line. To justify the growth of the US military presence in the Indian Ocean, they have found an "argument"—the stay of a limited contingent of Soviet troops in Afghanistan. But in adducing it they somehow "forget" that the United States had broken off the talks with the USSR on limiting military activity in the Indian Ocean much before the induction of Soviet forces into the DRA at the request of the lawful Afghan government in accordance with the 1978 Treaty of Friendship between the USSR and the DRA, and in full conformity with Article 51 of the Charter of the United Nations.

What great gains Western propagandist took to present the events around Afghanistan as "Soviet expansion seeking an outlet to the Indian Ocean" and as a "threat" to the oil-rich Persian Gulf! Suffice it to recall how many "secret" documents about a depletion of oil resources threatening the USSR were published in the West at that time. In spite of the fact that experts questioned and then altogether rejected these "documents", Washington kept trumpeting that the Soviet Union "covets Arab oil"; that the Soviet Union "is on a drive towards the warm seas".

The Soviet forces are in Afghanistan only because an undeclared was is being waged against the young republic, a war funded, inspired, encouraged and guided by the same United States of America. Could the dushmans, who have entrenched themselves in numerous camps on Pakistani territory, wage this war without American and other Western money, arms and propaganda poison? Could the Pakistani military regime offer them protection to such an extent were it not materially, morally and in every other way backed by Washington and other Western governments? Whenever the Pakistani regime does attempt to react somehow to the repeated peace initiatives of the DRA government, its overseas patrons hold it back by the coat-tails, as it were.

"...Counter-revolution and imperialism have turned Afghanistan into a bleeding wound," it was noted in the CPSU Central Committee Political Report of the 27th Congress of the Party. "The USSR supports that country's efforts to defend its sovereignty. We should like, in the nearest future, to withdraw the Soviet troops stationed in Afghanistan at the request of its government. Moreover, we have agreed with the Afghan side on the schedule for their phased withdrawal as soon as a political settlement is rached that will ensure an actual cessation and dependably guarantee the non-resumption of foreign armed interference in the internal affairs of the Democratic Republic of Afghanistan."

It is the United States that needs the atmosphere of tension around the DRA, in particular for the purpose of having yet another argument to justify its military presence in the Indian Ocean. From the writings of US strategists it is absolutely clear that the US effort for the establishment of control over the Indian Ocean will continue even after the Afghan question has been solved. The Afghan events are only a pretext for the development of the U.S. policy of militarising the Indian Ocean. The mythical "Soviet threat" was needed to cover up the real, US threat to the peoples of the area.

The Soviet Union has no aspirations for control over the Indian Ocean. Consequently, there is no "great-power rivalry" in this area. In particular, the rivalry thesis was needed to equate the USSR and the USA and oppose the Soviet Union to the developing countries of the region. And, of course, to justify imperialism's policy of escalating its military-political and economic dominance in this part of the world.

Naturally, all this is camouflaged with propaganda rhetoric, "Stabilising factor", 'stability', 'world peace', 'security', 'economic matters',—these police phrases and words are, of course, familiar to all. These seemingly innocent terms cannot and do not conceal the fact that what is involved are the economic and strategic interests of the US and its Western allies, writes a leading Sri Lankan journalist and public figure, Mervyn de Silva. "Peace does not mean peace for the people of these countries (i.e. the Indian Ocean countries—Y. R.) but the security and stability of these entrenched vested interests, the exploitation of the natural resources of the area, and the use of regimes and the rulers to 'protect' such interests. The defence of these interests is only necessary for the prosperity and stability of the US and its allies, but for the perpetuation of American dominance in the world".

Imperialism does not want to give up resources and markets in the Indian Ocean. It wants to see this basin as a preserve of neo-colonialism. It would like to retard or stop the growth of the national liberation movement here and to suppress the desire of the young newly-independent states for genuine independence. In recent years, along with this, the geopolitical aspirations of US imperialism are also becoming ever more prevalent in this area. Militarising the Indian Ocean is today a part of the overall US strategy, with world domination as its ultimate aim.[4]

A giant US aircraft carrier is advancing on the Asian continent. The phrase aptly reveals the dynamics, essence and cause of tension in the Indian Ocean, from where the "US aircraft carrier" is threateningly advancing on the peoples of Asia. That is, the entire military structure of the USA in the Indian Ocean, including ships, bases, submarines, planes, the Rapid Deployment Force and war games. In other words, the instrument of violence and diktat.

In fact, in February 1978, the USA unilaterally interrupted the USSR initiated Soviet-American talks on the limitation and then reduction of military activity in the Indian Ocean. The US repeatedly wrecked the holding of an international conference on the Indian Ocean which was to have been held in Colombo as early as 1981. The international community condems this obstructionist US line. The 40th session of the UN General Assembly instructed the Ad Hoc Committee to complete preparatory work in the current year so that the conference in Colombo should open as soon as possible at least not later than 1988.

---

4. *Ibid.*

The Soviet Union takes a firm and consistent stand for peace and security in Asia. It has supported the proposal of the non-aligned states to turn the Indian Ocean into a zone of peace. The Soviet Union believes that the convocation of an international conference at the present moment has become the pivot of the struggle for establishing a zone of peace in the Indian Ocean. Much could be done now, without waiting for such a conference. The non-littoral states could refrain, for example, front sending large naval squadrons there, not conduct exercises and manoeuvres and not set up new military bases and strong-points there. The Soviet Union has repeadly declared that it has no intention of building military bases there and calls upon the US to assume the same stand so as to ensure stability and peace in the region.

In his book 'Indian Ocean and Asian Security' (New Delhi, Allied, 1986). Mr. Yevgeni Rumyantsev has rightly stated : "Safe guarding Indian Ocean security is to no small extent, the key to security in Asia as a whole. And the situation in Asia, occupying a third of the Ear this land mass and having three fifths of the world's population, considerably influences the political climate in the world. The Soviet Union is not indifferent to the turn of events in the Indian Ocean and the adjacent areas. A great Asian power, the USSR is sincerely interested in stabilising the political situation here and, together with other states, it is looking for ways to undo the complex knots of contradictions. The security interests of the Soviet Union, its social and economic tasks and its steadily growing economic, trade, scientific and cultural co-operation with the Indian Ocean states require this."

The United States and a number of its allies have refused to discuss the working document on preparations for an international conference on the Indian Ocean drawn up by the group of the developing countries. This happened recently at the meeting of the UN Ad Hoc Committee, which concluded in New York. Moreover Washington has even proposed that the work of the Ad Hoc Committee be suspended.[5]

Throughout its quarter-century history, the Non-alignment Movement has advanced quite a few constructive proposals,

---

5. Attar Chand. *op. cit.*

including the major initiative of turning the Indian Ocean into a zone of peace, elimination of foreign military bases in the region, a halt to the arms race, ban on the deploymeut of nuclear weapons, renunciation of the use or threat of force against the sovereignty, territorial integrity and independence of the developing countries situated in the region.

The US military preparations in the Indian Ocean cause a serious alarm among the NAM members. In the past years there preparations reached an unprecedented scale. The Pentagon has concentrated in the region hundreds of warplanes, dozens of ships and a large contingent of the interventionist 'rapid deployment force'. Its waters are plied by submarines and strike aircraft carriers. To support its militaristic strivings Washington set up in 1983 the Central Command (CENT COM), whose sphere of action includes 19 non-aligned countries in Asia and Africa. The Pentagon also has plans of using the Indian Ocean for the militarisation of space.

The military base on Diego Garcia plays an important role in the realization of Washington's plans. The Indian Ocean is now being turned into a new forward-based area for the US strategic forces in addition to those in Western Europe and in the Far East.

This course is resolutely censured by all peace-loving forces, including the Non-alignment Movement. The 40th session of the UN General Assembly adopted a resolution, proposed by the non-aligned countries, instructing the Special Committee to complete the preparatory work in the current year for the Colombo conference to begin its work not later than 1988. But the US administration and its allies have been blocking the holding of the Colombo conference.

The Soviet Union firmly supports the non-aligned countries' proposal on turning the Indian Ocean into a zone of peace. It is convinced that the convocation of an international conference has at present become pivotal in the struggle for the establishment of a zone of peace in the Indian Ocean. The Indian Ocean must be turned from an area of confrontation and rivalry into a region of peace, good-neighbourliness and mutually advantageous co-operation.

The Indian Ocean as a zone of peace would certainly enhance security throughout Asia. The Policy Report by the CPSU Central Committee to the 57th CPSU Congress mentioned, among the necessary and useful steps made last year, the Soviet-Indian summit in Moscow. Its participants stressed the importance the two countries attach to converting the Indian Ocean into a zone of peace, the joint Soviet-Indian statement said : "The Soviet Union and Indian express concern over the further complication of the situation in the Indian Ocean and call for closing all foreign military bases in the region and not allowing the establishment of new bases. They are also against any attempts to increase the foreign military presence in the Indian Ocean. The Sides stand for early implementation of the UN Declaration on turning the Indian Ocean into a zone of peace and support the decision by the UN General Assembly to immediately call a conference on the Indian Ocean for the purpose. The Soviet Union decisively backs the striving of India and other non-aligned countries to reach this objective."[6]

The Soviet Union and India realise that this objective is part and parcel of the security issue for Asia. That was why during the Soviet-Indian summit, Mikhail Gorbachev advanced the idea of a comprehensive approach to Asian security and of pooling the efforts of Asian nations towards this end.

What was it that motivated the Soviet Union in putting forward this important proposal ? To began with, on the assets side of the international agenda are quite a few specific proposals and ideas formulated by socialist countries and non-aligned Asian states.

Along with the idea of a peace zone for the Indian Ocean, a whole number of constructive initiatives on other aspects of Asian security have been advanced in recent years. In 1981 the Soviet Union proposed discussing confidence-building measures for the Far East, similar to those which are being implemented in Europe on the basis of the 1975 Helsinki agreements. The Mongolian People's Republic suggested concluding a convention on mutual non-aggression and non-use of force by countries in Asia and the Pacific. The states of Indochina are steadily working to make South-East Asia a zone of peace, stability and co-operation. A better situation in the Far

6. Yevgeni Rumyantsev. *op. cit.*, pp. 45-53.

East would be promoted by implementing the proposals of the Democratic People's Republic of Korea to withdraw American troops from South Korea and to reunite the country on the basis of peaceful and democratic principles without outside interference.

Outside intereference is the main reason for the growth of tension in Asia, interfering with trust and co-operation in the region. However, the interest is growing everywhere in fostering trust and protecting Asia from external interference, as there are apprehensions that the region can become the scene of global confrontation. Anti-war and anti-nuclear sentiments are on the rise. This is evidenced, in particular, by the decision countries in the South Pacific adopted to de-nuclearise the area and by New Zealand's decision prohibiting nuclear-equipped warships to call at its posts. This decision by New Zealand has promoted a major crack in the ANZUS bloc.

Of the utmost importance is to protect Asia, which accommodates five out of the world's even most populous countries, from foreign inteference. Accordingly, while advocating a comprehensive approach to Asian security, the Soviet Union has proposed that every member of the UN Security Council should undertake not to interfere in the affairs of countries in Asia, Africa and Latin America, not to theaten them with force, and not draw them into military blocs. The USSR is ready to assume such a commitment. Imperialist intrigues in Asia and the conflicts and wars ravaging there highlight the need for joint efforts to promote Asian security.

In favouring an overall approach to asian affairs, the Soviet Union stands by firm principles. The USSR bases its concept on the key Leninist principles of foreign policy. In the USSR's opinion, a code for Asian security could provide for all nuclear countries refusing to be the first to use nuclear weapons in Asia. Significantly, both nuclear countries in asia, *i.e.* the USSR and China, have pledged to act so. These principles could cover the non-use of nuclear weapons against non-nuclear countries and areas in that part of the world; adoption by the nuclear-free countries of the three non-nuclear principles, *i.e.* not to have, not to produce and not to bring in such weapons; accession to the non-prolifera tion treaty of those Asian countries which have not yet signed it.[7]

7. *Ibid.*

This issue is as important for Asia as it is for Europe. In Asia and the Pacific, the Pentagon is aiming to upset the balance of strategic forces, establish nuclear springboards to threaten the USSR and countries in the Indian Ocean and the Pacific. It is reported that nuclear delivery systems have been deployed at US bases in Japan, South Korea and the Philippines and that South Korea, Taiwan and Pakistan are near-nuclear countries.

Asian security could be effectively promoted also by a complete ban on nuclear tests in Asia, the Pacific and the Indian Ocean; a military activity freeze; refusal by Asian countries to participate in space militarisation, non-admission of new or enlarged military blocs in the region; and the renouncement of outside support for separatists and terrorists. The panchsheel principles and the principles of Bandung, formulated by Asian nations, are a major contribution to the practical aspect of international relations. These principles have helped settle conflicts and they remain effective. They could also be included in the code of principles of Asian security.

The Soviet Union sees a comprehensive approach to security in Asia as a first step on a long road. The USSR is against cut-and-dried formulas being enforced upon nations. The Soviet Union holds that security and a lasting peace in Asia can be secured not through regional military, political and economic divisions, but by mustering every effort against the threat of war. Said Mikhail Gorbachev : "It is extremely important to ensure that this region is not a source of tension or a sphere of military confronation. *We want the political dialogue among all the states here grow in the interests of peace, good-neighbourliness, mutual trust and co-operation.*" This dialogue, the USSR believes, could be conducted in different forms, such as bilateral talks, multilateral consultations and an all-Asia forum to jointly seek constructive solutions.

The idea of a comprehensive approach or, as it was evaluated in the region, the idea of a Helsinki-type conference for Asia, has met with a lot of favourable comment in the continent.

The Soviet Union's search for peace, security and co-operation in Asia is part of its effort for peace and security on a planet-wide scale. The world is one, indivisible and interdepedent. The sentiments of the peoples of Asia are echoed by the Soviet programme to abolish nuclear and chemical weapons by the end of the century, as outlined by Mikail Gorbachev, General Secretary of the CPSU Central Committee, on January 15, 1986. The issues of peace and security are as pressing in Asia as they are in Europe. Asia, namely Japan's Hiroshima as Nagasaki, was the first victim to nuclear blasts, while Vietnam was exposed to chemical weapons.

The USSR views its programme to free mankind from nuclear weapons as a contribution to all-Asia searches for a common overall approach to creating a continental system of security and a lasting peace. The January 15, 1986 Statement says that implementing the Soviet-proposed programme "would radically change the situation in Asia, deliver the nations in that part of the world from the nuclear and chemical threat and boost regional security."

As the 27th CPSU Congress stated, the CPSU regards the drive to implement the programme to abolish nuclear and other weapons by the end of the century, as set forth in Mikhail Gorbachev's statement, as "the Central direction of its foreign policy for years to come."

As a great Asian power, the Soviet Union sees Vital importance in ensuring security in Asia. Calling for immediate efforts to resolve contradictions in Asia, the 27th CPSU Congress states that "evidently, it is expedient to begin with the co-ordination and then the pooling of efforts in the interests of a political settlement of painful problems so as, in parallel, on that basis to at least take the edge off the military confrontation in various parts of Asia and stabilise the situation there.

"This is made all the more urgent by the fact that in Asia and other continents the flashpoint of military danger are not being extinguished. We are in favour of vitalising collective quests for ways of defusing conflict situation...in all of the planet's turbulent points. This is imperatively demanded by the interests of general security."

The Soviet Government's Statement of April 23, 1986 as regards Asia and the Pacific is a major contribution to implementing the idea of peace and security in Asia by the region's joint efforts, The statement defines a programme, areas and principles for gradual progress towards trust, security and co-operation in this vast region.

What is the Soviet Union calling for ? Moscow says that nowadays all nations should show matual restraint, not to admit actions which can complicate the political atmosphere there or interfere with positive processes, the dialogue and the exploration of ways to improve the situation regionally. The USSR expressed its concern at the plans of the United States and Japan leading to the establishment of a "Pacific community" which can be eventually transformed into another militaristic bloc. In Moscow's opinion, this can result in a dramatic growth of tension in Asia and the Pacific.

Fair co-operation among all nations, not their confrontation, should be the foundations for relationships among countries in this and any other part of the world. The Soviet government believes that the peoples of Asia and the Pacific have common interests and that the resolution of the issues they are facing requires constructive efforts on the part of all the states of the religion, irrespective of their social and political systems.

For this purpose, the USSR proposes the following clear-cut moves.

—bilateral and multilateral consultations to create pre-requisites for an all-Asia forum to jointly explore constructive solutions. At the same time, a Pacific conference could be arranged to deal with security matters, particularly with economic security;

—confidence-building measure and reduction in navel activities in the Pacific;

—nuclear-free zones for Asia and the Pacific;

—extensive exchange of opinion among all countries in the region as regards fair, mutually advantageous and stable trade, economic, technological, scientific and cultural co-operation.

The USSR proposed a wide programme for such co-operation and stated that relevant major long-term projects could be examined within the framework of UN agencies, particularly the Economic and Social Commission for Asia and the Pacific.

The statement expressed the confidence that greater goodneighbourliness and friendship among all the countries in Asia and the Pacific and their joint efforts to find effective solutions to the issue of regional security would favourably affect the situation elsewhere. This is really so, since the proposals incorporated in the statement, a document of long-term importance, have a universal character. In particular, they can be used as a guide for action to settle issues in the Indian Ocean.

The concept of a comprehensive system of international security, formulated by the 27th CPSU Congress, is of tremendous importance for peace and security in Asia and other regions. Now about the essence of this concept. In this nuclear age no weapons, no strategic systems can guarantee anyone's security. Such security is a political target to be attained by political means. As regards the USSR and the US, the world's two leading powers, their security can be only mutual. However, there cannot be security for these two countries alone. Security concerns all in this world populated by tens of states and nations, all of them having specific legitimate interests. These are differing states. A common major task for all of them is, despite their political, social and ideological contradictions, to learn to live in a civilised manner, practising correct contacts and co-operation.

What can such universal security rely on ! In the USSR's opinion, "nowadays it is more important than ever to find ways for closer and more productive co-operation with the governments, political parties, community organisations and movements which are really concerned over world peace, with all nations..."

First, such a system can rely on political accords, global and regional. Important here are joint efforts to resolve regional conflicts and crises wherever hotbeds of military danger exist, be it the Indian Ocean, the Middle East, Central America or Southern Africa.

Second, a comprehensive system of international security can be created not only through military detente, although the prime importance is attached, of course, to specific normalising measures in the military field. As the foundation for a comprehensive system of international security, the Policy Report of the CPSU Committee to the 27th CPSU Congress points, along with efforts in the military field, to political, economic and humanitarian actions,

Third, steps to stabilise peace should be taken without delay. While recognising the importance of all the aspects of the campaign to improve the international situation, the Soviet security concept centres round the efforts to stop the arms race. These efforts, which are to eliminate the main source of threat of peace, should not be set against agreed-upon political settlement of regional conflicts of building confidence among the states belonging to the two social and political system. Cuts and eventual abolition of nuclear weapons would help settle other pressing issues and improve the international situation.

Among these issues is the conversion of the Indian Ocean into a zone of peace. All things are interdependent in the world today. The more vigorous the efforts to resolve a regional issue, the greater their impact on global matters.

Every step towards this goal requires joint efforts, solidarity, the unity of action, and the nations' awareness of common interests It is only by acting together and resolutely that will it be possible to ensure peace and security in the Indian Ocean, Asia and the world as a whole.[8]

The crux of the matter is the role attached to Indian Ocean in the current US leadership's global strategy the role of a gigantic arsenal and base standing on guard of the neoglobalist interests of the USA in that part of the world.

As a result of the Pentagon's strategic development of the Indian Ocean, there are now nearly 30 US military bases located there. Some of them are planned to be used also in the 'star wars' programme. The permanent presence of big US naval and airforce contingents and the naval ships of its allies – Britain, France and the FRG, turns the Indian Ocean into another area of forward basing of the NATO forces.[9]

The government and public of the littoral countries favour an immediate holding of an international conference on the Indian Ocean, which would contribute to turning it into a zone of peace and co-operation. Yet, the USA and the other NATO countries are out to prevent its convocation. A further evidence of that is their stand at the latest session of the UN Ad Hoc Committee.

---

8. *Ibid.*
9. Attar Chand, *op. cit.*

CHAPTER NINE

NEOGLOBALISM

US NEOGLOBALISM, which is the new doctrine announced by President Ronald Reagan in the beginning of February this year, is a new threat to the Asian and Pacific nations. This is the conclusion to be drawn from the directions of regional policy as out-lined in Pentagon's recent reports to Congress on budgetary issues.[1]

These reports expose one of the concrete forms of US neoglobalism in Asia, which is military aid.

US military aid is already a sufficiently effective method of permanent political and military pressure on the Asian countries, and of their subjugation to American dictates. It is noted in the Pentagon reports that the objective of US policy in Asia is consolidation of links between the US and its friends and allies, including China, on the basis of 'common security interests'. However, as noted in the same reports, in return for its direct or indirect military aid to these friends and allies, the US intends to use them as instruments in securing the strategic interests of the US in the region. This is confirmed by the fact that the lion's share of this aid is being chanelled into areas which the US has declared 'a sphere of vital US interests'. The West Asian and South-West Asian countries account for 11 per cent of this US aid, and the East Asian and Pacific countries for another five per cent.

Using the instrument of military aid, the US has always sought to create a system of relations in the Asian-Pacific region

1, Attar Chand, US Neoglobalism in Asia-Pacific Region, *Patriot*, 11 September, 1986, p. 4.

which would allow it, directly or otherwise, to make maximum use of the manpower and material resources of the local countries and of their territories in pursuing its global military-political line. Some of these countries, which have military agreements with the US, are being forced by Washington to build up in their military potential while others are expected to pool their efforts and take a more co-ordinated part in the US global strategy. The increased military-political co-operation between the US and Israel, Pakistan and Thailand on the basis of military aid has prodded the recipients of this aid into aggressive acts against their neighbours and turned them into a bridgehead for the deployment and use of American armed forces.

US military aid generates arms race in most countries, and its most obvious results are the periodic flare-ups of regional and general tension on the Asian continent. This refers to the persisting conflicts in West Asia and in South and South-East Asia, and to the continuing tension in the central part of the Asian continent around Afghanistan.

Another aspect of US neoglobalism is the efforts to nip in the bud the trend towards the establishment of a climate of trust and mutual understanding among individual Asian states.

In South-West Asia, the bastion of US policy is Pakistan, whose territory is used as a spring-board for aggressive actions against neighbouring states. Islamabad receives lavish military and economic aid from the US. In the period between 1983 and 1987 it will have totalled 3.2 billion dollars. Under this aid programme, Pakistan has already received massive shipments of modern combat hardware, including F-16 fighters and 155-mm Howitzers. In the next fiscal year, the US administration intends to deliver an additional batch of advanced weaponry to Islamabad. Under the new deal, Pakistan will receive sea-launched Harpoon missiles, Orion snooper planes and other combat hardware and material. A considerable share of the fund received by Islamabad is meant for the maintenance, training and armament of the bandit formations of Afghani counter-revolutionary who operate from Pakistani territory.

The nefarious role of the US in the large-scale co-ordinated armed interference by the imperialist forces in the internal affairs of Afghanistan, which results in persisting dangerous tension in the centre of Asia, consists in its extensive support of the Afghan counter-revolution. In recent years, every new White House request for the expansion of subversive operations against Afghanistan has been at least twice the previous sum requested. By 1986 the allocations for this purpose have reached 470 million dollars, while altogether Washington has already spent 1.5 billion dollars on arming, training and maintaining the numerous gangs which are committing crimes on Afghan territory.[2]

According to Washington's decisions, the heavy arms buildup in Pakistan with American assistance is meant to pose a serious threat to India and to strain the situation on the Indo-Pakistani border. The sharply increased activity of Sikh separatists in Punjab and of the extremists in north-eastern Indian States had coincided with massive deliveries of American weapons to Pakistan which began in 1983.

In another part of Asia, US aid is meant to encourage Thailand in its criminal war against Kampuchea. A sizable share of this aid is used for militarisation of the region along the Thai-Kampuchean border and for all-round support of the piractic raids by the Khmer reactionary forces into Kampuchea from Thai territory. In 1985 alone, the US allocated five million dollars for these purposes.[3]

As regards another South-East Asian nation, the Philippines, the US annually grants it 240 million dollars in military and economic aid. After the transition of power in that country to a new President, representatives of the US Administration have announced that Washington will consider an increase in that aid. Beside direct aid, this includes credits for the import of American combat hardware. In the present unstable political situation in that country, this aid is viewed as an important instrument of pressure on the Philippines.

2. *Ibid.*
3. *Ibid.*

Such is one of the aspects of US neoglobalism in Asia which is called US Regional Policy in Asia in the Pentagon reports. High on the list of its means is military aid whose shackles are the cause of the growing military tension and political instability in various parts of the Asian-Pacific region.

The book of "defence of the USA's vital interests" is a favourite argument of Washington designed to justify the feverish military preparations in Asia. This concept is so vague that virtually everything can be included in it. For this reason, we are going to dwell upon just a few of its aspects.

True, the United States has interests in the Asia-Pacific area, and these interests are not small. Suffice to say that such strategically important commodities as oil, zinc, lead, tin and India rubber go to the West by sea routes passing near the Gulf. The United States, and particularly the transnational corporations, has also immense investments in various economic enterprises and projects in the area. These investments guarantee billion-dollar projects.[4]

But it is possible to ensure the security of the sea routes and communications by purely military means? Military experts express different views on this question. But it is abundantly clear that if one resorts to force as a guarantee of security, such a concept would lead to an arms race of truly unprecedented scale in the area. For instance, in the view of a number of experts, to reliably "cover" the Bab el Mandeb strait alone (to cover against a mythical Soviet threat), the Pentagon must additionally spend over 300,000 million dollars and additionally station more than 30 squadrons of the F-16 warplanes, about 2,000 missiles for hitting sea, air and ground targets, and other armaments in close proximity of the Bab el Mandeb strait, namely in the Persian Gulf and Indian Ocean. It is doubtful that even the inflated US military machine can afford such measures in the foreseable future. Even if such plans were translated into reality, there would be counter measures by other states which would rightly view such excessive military preparations as a threat to their security.

---

4. See George Kim, *op. cit.*, pp. 19-31.

As a matter of fact, from whom does the USA intend to defend the straits ? Who threatens Washington thousands of miles off American shores ? As for the international sea lanes, they are used by other states in an equal measure and fully in accordance with the international law of the sea. It is the interest of all countries in security of the vital sea communications and strict observance of the well-known charters and agreements on the law of the sea and not military confrontation that are the best guarantee of security.

The US strategists try to justify the massive military preparations in the Asia-Pacific region by references to a "Soviet military threat." But this book does not bear scrutiny. The US military-strategic concepts in the Asia-Pacific region are distinguished not by a defensive but by a marked offensive spirit. Even today nuclear missiles which can reach the regions of the Soviet Union from the far East to the European heartland can be launched from the US submarines and military bases in Asia, and the Indian and Pacific Ocean zones.

Armadas of surface ships and submarines carrying nuclear weapons ply the waters on the far and near approaches to the Asian continent. The Pentagon keeps thousands of nuclear charges in combat readiness in the area. The USA has embarked on practical preparations for deploying strategic and tactical nuclear weapons in direct proximity of the USSR and other socialist countries of Asia, as well as India and all other states with governments that do not suit the United States.[5]

That is why the US militarists put the cart before the horse when they trumpet about a "Soviet military threat". In fact, the USSR keeps military forces and means in Asia and there are missiles in Asian part of the USSR, but they are stationed there as a forced defensive measure. They are directed not against the Asian states but only against the US military complex which is second in size and might among those deployed beyond America and which threatens the Soviet Union and other Asian peoples from the confines of the Asia-Pacific region. The Soviet leadership

---

5. *Ibid.*

has repeatedly stated that it is prepared to drastically out, for instance, the number of medium-range missiles deployed in the Asian part of the USSR if Washington takes respective steps. But no positive answer has been given to this constructive proposal.

The fact that US strategists do not want to understand that even the most powerful systems of weapons cannot any longer guarantee absolute security graphically manifests itself in the Asia-Pacific region. Illustrative of this is the elaboration of such doctrines as "low-intensity conflicts", "local nuclear wars" and others by the Pentagon military experts. These theories are another emphatic proof of the aggressiveness of the American military doctrine and render invalid claims of it being purely defensive. These concepts have also another distinctive feature—they show that, no matter under what pretexts the American military bases and strong points are set up in Asia and what references to a "Soviet military threat" are used as a camouflage by their builders, they are directed in an equal measure against the Soviet Union and other socialist countries and the forces of national liberation, social progress and democracy, against the states and governments in the area, whose independent foreign policy line does not suit Washington.

The wars in Korea and Vietnam, the overthrow of the Mossadeq progressive regime in Iran in the 1950s, the US intrigues against Afghanistan and Kampuchea, and the encouragement of the separatist and anti-government elements in India and some other states in the region are elements of the same chain which are designed to create an atmosphere of political chaos and instability in the areas suiting the United States.

"Low-intensity conflicts" and "local wars" serve as practical tools for carrying out such a policy and show that Washington has not only arbitrarily assumed the right to impudently interference in the affairs of sovereign states but has also worked out concrete military-strategic schemes for such interference and prepared social troops contingents for such operations—the Rapid Deployment Force.

The arguments in favour of sabre-rattling, alleging that the USSR provokes regional conflicts, collapse like a house of cards. And it is built by Washington itself. It also seeks to put the regional conflicts issue almost on top of all world problems and to link the questions of nuclear disarmament with them.

The White House views regional conflicts or, in a broader outline, all processes taking place in the world in light of Soviet-American confrontation, a struggle between the two systems. We must say in this connection that the Soviet Union offers the United States the chance to transfer this contention into the sphere of peaceful development and to prove the advantage of one or other socio-economic system in peaceful endeavours and not on battlefields.

Since the world is much bigger than the USA and the USSR, it would be a great mistake to see reverberations of relations between these two countries in all trends of the world's development. This fully applies to regional conflicts. Most of them are rooted in history. By intentionally narrowing the regional conflicts issue the geo-politicians from the banks of the Potomac seek to ensure for the USA a more active role in the newly-free countries. This is the aim of the concept of "neo-globalism" which was worked out by the present US Administration and which is designed to give an answer to the so-called "inspiring of conflicts in the Third World by the USSR."[6]

The concept of "neo-globalism" and the US approach to regional conflict clearly show that Washington intends to considerably intensify the struggle against, in Washington's terms, "pro-Communist regimes", from Nicaragua to Angola, from Afghanistan to Kampuchea. In doing so, it characterises virtually all progressive states pursuing an independent foreign policy as "pro-Communist."

Analysing recent history, one sees that the concept of "neo-globalism" and its practical expression ensue from the ill-famed Tonkin Incident. In July 1964 the ships of the US 7th Fleet entered the Gulf of Bakpo (or Tonkin) and thereby violated the

6. *Ibid.*

territorial waters of the Democratic Republic of Vietnam. But the DRV displayed reserve and did not respond to the provocation. Then Washington staged an "attack" by Vietnam against the American Navy. This marked the beginning of the US direct aggression in Vietnam which developed into on of the bloodiest conflicts since the Second World War. The Tonkin Incident most vividly and frankly demonstrated the expansionist aggressive essence of the foreign-policy line of the United States and its readiness to engage in the most impudent provocation for translating its hegemonistic ambitions into reality.

The question of settling regional conflicts is certainly very serious and needs resolution. According to calculations by experts, over 100 so-called "limited wars" have occurred since the Second World War, and this figure increases to 300, taking into account the large-scale conflicts which differ little from the "limited wars." All in all, over 20 million people perished in them. This is double the toll taken by the First World War and makes up 40 per cent of the losses by World War Second. While 38 countries participated in the First World War and the military operations took place on the territories of about 40 states during World War Second, the above-said "minor wars" involved more than 60 states of the Third World.

In principle, the Soviet Union, far from being opposed to discussing regional problems, stands for an active search for ways to settle them. At the same time, it would be wrong to forget that neither the peace-making process, nor peace itself can be of regional character. That is why the Soviet leadership is against resolution of such global problems as disarmament and dismantling of weapons of mass destruction being linked with the problem of conflicts or being dependent on it.

Facts show that the imperialist quarters pay lip service to settlement of conflicts. The USA actively supports apartheid in South Africa and that country's intrigues against the neighbouring African countries and Israel's brigandage in the Middle East. The conflict situations in these and other areas are maintained and, moreover, created by Washington's policy. This is the way things are in case of Nicaragua.

Crises and conflicts very well serve the interests of imperialism which is accustomed to exploit an atmosphere of tension and political instability in its own imperial, selfish interests. This is clearly-visible in the case of the Asia-Pacific region. It is US imperialism and its NATO partners, as well as the US-supported regional reactionary forces that are to blame for the continued bloodshed in Afghanistan and Kampuchea and for the persisting explosive situation in the Korean Peninsula where US-South Korean military exercises are systematically staged. The USA also makes use of the Iran-Iraq conflict in its own interests, sending ever new naval armadas to the Gulf under the pretext of defending its "vital interests."[7]

Thus, the US hackneyed lies about an "arm of Moscow" are, in fact, nothing but a propaganda camouflage for the attempts to turn the US imperial ambitions into reality. The emergent states, especially those of them which follow the road of progressive social and economic change, are not set against Washington automatically and no other state is behind the fact that their attitude to the US policy becomes negative. This is quite natural reaction to the US intrigues against them, to the US efforts to roll back the wheel of history through restoration of reactionary forces, obedient to the USA, in power in them.

"We are in favour of vitalising collective quests for ways of defusing conflict situation in the Middle East, Central America, Southern Africa, in all of the planet's turbulent points. This is imperatively demanded by the interests of general security," Mikhail Gorbachev said from the rostrum of the 27th Congress of the CPSU (1986). Not concepts of policy "from strength" and not imperial "neoglobalism" but recognition of the inalienable right of each people to freedom and independence, to an independent choice of a path for its development must serve as a clue to such settlement. The Soviet Union is against violation of this right by any one, against any attempts at interference from outside, and stands for triumph of freedom.

What can Asia and the Pacific expect of the US doctrine of "neoglobalism" which manifests itself in an unrestrained arms build up, pushing the region to this endless mad race ?

---

7. *Ibid.*

It's hard even to enumerate all the negative aspects of this crippling race. A major point is that the pursuit of illusory security based on tanks and missiles robs the developing countries of their tremendous resources.

The world spends nearly a trillion dollars a year on arms and other military requirements. Nowadays, the developing countries account for 16 per cent of the world's military expenditures. In 1980, the combined military spending of Asia, Africa and Latin America was just above 7 per cent of the figure for the world. Between 1973 and 1983 the military expenditures of the developing countries were growing 4.7 per cent a year as against 2.7 per cent for the industrialized nations. This confirms that the developing countries are spending more and more on military pursuits.[8]

This is extremely dangerous, especially for the developing countries, their economic situation being deplorable as it is. According to the International Bank for Reconstruction and Development, at the end of 1985 the Third World's external debt constituted 980 billion dollars, with interest payments claiming 143 billion dollars a year. In the developing countries, hundreds of millions suffer from hunger or malnutrition, child mortality is twenty times the figure for the industrialized nations and the average longevity is twenty years less than in the latter mentioned group of states. Over 14 million children die of virus disease and hunger in Asia, Africa and Latin America every year.

The developing countries have over 16 million people under in the armed forces, their best men who could promote economic growth. Further, the army requires money and people to maintain it. It is estimated that another 240 million people cater for the army and operate the war industry in these countries. There is an interdependence between the growing military expenses of a country and its worsening economic position, particularly dramatic falls in its living standards. In Asia and the Pacific, this concerns the countries which are major importers of US weapons, notably Pakistan, the Philippines, Thailand, Bangladesh and South Korea. Their economic performance has drastically worsened of late, with the external debt growing and living standards going down.[9]

---

8. *Ibid.*
9. *Ibid.*

Many other emergent countries, even those who were more or less all right economically but recently, also have big external debts. The main reason is the arms race, the American weapons which are being forced upon these states. The external debt of the Philippines makes up some 25 billion dollars, that of Malaysia, 13 billion and that of Thailand, 11 billion. South Korea's debt has nearly doubled over the past five years, with the social infrastructure of that country being one of the least developed in the world.

The Washington-inspired arms race, bleeding these countries, does not make for the security of states involved in the militaristic preparations by US imperialism, as the advocates of power politics allege. The arms race undermines the security of the countries concerned, promoting dangerous regional conflicts.

Understandably, a country which purchases large quantities of US weapons automatically rouses mistrust and suspicions on the part of its neighbours. This triggers a chain reaction, with its neighbours, acting from security considerations, urgently building up their military potentials with the latest weapons. This is confirmed by developments in South Asia. America's militaristic policy in the region, with Washington favouring Islamabad's military regime, has resulted in the steep increase of the armed forces in South Asia. With the numerical strength of the armed forces having grown by 0.3 per cent worldwide in 1983, in the South Asia the corresponding figure rose 12.8 per cent.

Imperialism exploiting strife and mistrust among developing countries and supporting jingoism and chauvinism to promote militarist sentiment lead to Asia, Africa and Latin America getting deeply involved in the global arms race which generates tension and regional conflicts. Developing countries purchase up to 75 percent of the weapons exported by others. Imperialism sees these nations as clients of its war industry. While going broke through the arms race, the Third World countries are adding to the fabulous riches of the West.[10]

In his statement of January 15, 1966, Soviet leader Mikhail Gorbachev stressed direct connection between the arms race and

10. *Ibid.*

the worsening social and economic performance of the developing countries and indicated ways to overcome the situation : "The principle of armament instead of development, enforced upon the world by militarism, should be reversed to disarmament for development."

"We must work vigorously to end the arms race, reduce weapons stocks and discontinue nuclear testing if we are to stop destroying the environment, explore new sources of energy and combat economic backwardness, hunger and disease. The Soviet Union wants every step to limit and reduce armaments and free the world from nuclear weapons, to make for universal security and increase funds to promote living standards. Out to catch up with the industrialized states, emergent countries link freedom from the external debt to imperialism, exhausting them economically, to curbing and abolishing arms, slashing military expenditures and gearing resources to social and economic growth."

Regions, buying large quantities of American weapons, are permanent flash points. The Far East, Southern Africa, the Middle East, South Asia and Central America are the main seats of conflicts.

A number of developing countries, particularly those in Asia. are showing a new and dangerous trend to establish a war industry of their own. It is estimated that 30 developing countries have such industries. They manufacture aircraft, missiles, tanks and other sophisticated weapons, sending tremendous resources and research efforts down the drain. What is even more dangerous is that many developing countries are on the threshold of creating nuclear weapons. Altogether, some 15 countries can start the manufacture of nuclear weapons, with many of them situated in Asia: Israel, Pakistan, South Korea and Taiwan. These and other countries joining the "nuclear club" may have unpredictable consequences regionally and globally. The emergence of "smaller nuclear powers" is exceedingly dangerous also because most of them, particularly those mentioned above, are chained to the Pentagon's war chariot, pursuing aggressive policies with regard to their neighbours and being a source of constant regional tensions.

Oversaturating Asia with nuclear weapons is extremely dangerous for the region even if this means only the storage of such weapons. Like Europe, Asia is a fragile, and over-populated home for mankind.

That is why US attempts to involve Asia and the Pacific in Washington's militaristic strategy are generating legitimate alarm in the region. Nuclear weapons were used for the first time in Asia. Here as well, the imperialists are continuing their intensive nuclear testing, using vast Pacific areas for the purpose. In Asia in Indochina, in particular, the United States employed chemical weapons on a massive scale, the consequences of which have not yet been overcome.[11]

It is only quite natural that the anti-war movement is growing in Asia and the Pacific. The countries of Asia have a great capability to stand for peace. They have a wealth of experience in fighting against the militaristic aspirations of the imperialists. At this moment crucial to world peace, this experience should be effectively used to avert the threat of war.

11. *Ibid.*

CHAPTER TEN

U.S. PACIFIC STRATEGY

THE UNITED STATES of America has recently raised the bogey of the Soviet threat in the South Pacific region. Richard G Lugar, chairman of the Senate Foreign Relations Committee, visited Australia and opposed the sentiment of turning the area into a nuclear-free zone as symbolised by the Avarua Treaty (1985), signed by 10 countries in Fiji and ratified by four countries. US has been joined in its opposition by France, as also Britain. The Japanese 'White Paper' on Defence mentions that it joined US in declaring that the Soviets are engaging in a military build-up in the region. What is the truth ? The US keeps in Asia and the Pacific six carrier battle groups, more than 100 military bases and strongholds and, conducts military exercises in the region as it does in North Europe and the Mediterranean. A part of its presence in the Asia-Pacific, the US has felt the need to deploy F-16 fighter-bombers in Japan at Misawa base and arm Seventh Fleet combat Ships with the Tomahawk cruise missiles. Why does it do this ? Asia-Pacific is part of the US global-meta-global imperialist designs. It believes that in case there is a war in Europe, the force in this region will be necessary. Obviously this is to hedge in on the Soviet Union.[1]

As part of this US and NATO are conducting exercises in the North of Europe, code-named 'Wedding-86', which involves 35,000 soldier 'baraties' from ten countries, including Denmark and Norway, The wedding party will include an impressive armada of 150 surface ships and submarines and several hundred warplanes. They will lead to the operation of landing 10,000 marines headed by

1. Rakesh Gupta, US Concern over Asia-Pacific. *Patriot* (New Delhi) 9 Oct., 1986, p. 4.

US units on the shores of Denmark and Norway. For whom does the bell toll ? The Norwegian press says both for the USSR and North European states. In Pakistan, Prime Minister Junejo had extended the invitation to the US Secretary of Defence Caspar Weinberger, who is gracing the subcontinent by his personal presence in Islamabad (October, 1986), since Pakistan is a conduit to destabilise Afghanistan by supply of arms, including chemical weapons, to the counter-insurgents in Afghanistan. For any 'wedding' religion is necessary and better if it is more fundamental, and so Zia's Pakistan is obliged to provide the orchestration for the wedding. Again, bleed the Soviets in Afghanistan, as the SDI intends to drain their economy. Will the Russian bride be wooed ? History shows it is difficult. West Europeans have tried it and been defeated. Both Napoleon and Hitler must be a reminder to a simple fact that it is not the Russian winter but the Russian mind and mettle that is hard to crack. The nascent Soviet state could not be cracked despite years of encirclement and intervention—Lenin saw to it; as did Stalin.[2]

The US is getting more and more bellicose. Talking about New Zealand's policy of not allowing US ships carrying nuclear cargo, George Shultz said : "We are parting as friends, but we are parting." Mrs Jeane Circkpatric believes that this may mean 'exposing' New Zealand to the Russian menace'. America belied that Pacific and half of Atlantic was its defensive shield. Now it believes Atlantic Mediterranean-Indian Ocean-Pacific is its security belt or soft belly capped by SDI. The US Defence Secretary Caspar Weinberger refuses to delimit US 'vital interest' and so, the Reagan Administration can only view Gorbachev's friendships as 'Provocations' and moratoriums as propaganda ploy'.

Asia, with the adjacent Pacific area, is today a very complex knot of international relations. There appears to be no other part of the world with an array of states so differing in economic development, social system, culture, religion and traditions.[3]

Socialist, developed capitalist and developing nations are in the array. It also includes several great powers. Perhaps no where

2. *Ibid.*
3. George Kim. *op, cit.*, pp. 9-18.

else, except Europe, do their armed forces each other so closely, which alone creates a very precarious and dynamic situation.

So it would be in the interests of all countries, both Asian and non-Asian yet closely linked with the region in trade, economic and other field, to ensure the continent lasting peace and security. Alas, we see instability in Asia, the persisting hotbeds of conflict and the war threat.

This stems mainly from perialist policy, with the USA as the chief destablising factor in Asia, worse even than all the economic, racial, religious and national strife nurtured in the past—the colonial legacy of most Asian states.[4]

The present, as the past, shows Washington's policy to be the main threat to Asian peace. Counting on military force as a means for achieving imperial aims has always been part of the US international stand. But the supremacy drive became particularly intense in the late '70s and the early '80s. This reflected Washington's global ambitions and pretensions to "world leadership." According to S. Hoffman, a leading American political scientist, the idea of a world in which the USA would be just one of the *dramatis personae* is intolerable to some US Administration men. This is borne out by the well known statement of the Pentagon chief C. Weinberger that the Asia-Pacific region is an area where the USA cann't accept "parity" or "equality", and area where it must be militarily superior.

Imperialism is desparate to preserve the old order and seize new ground in the former colonies. Under the pretext of countering the "communist threat", imperialist states pose as defenders of Third World sovereignty and try to install their men there. Such a line on the part of US imperialism means assumption of the role of world policeman. The USA has carried out over 200 acts of open military intervention in sovereign states' home affairs since the end of World War II. In Asia, specifically, it participated in the major, postwar armed conflicts—the wars in Korea and Vietnam.

4. *Ibid.*

As early as in the 50s, the USA started establishing aggressive military blocks and two-way military alliances in this area. It is significant that of the eight US sponsored military blocs, five operated within the geographic boundaries of the Asia-Pacific region, including the South-East Asia Treaty Organisation (SEATO) known also as the Manilla Pact, and the Central Treaty Organisation (CENTO), formerly the Baghdad Pact.

Though there have been many US conceptions vis-a-vis the Asia-Pacific region, American geo-politicians still view this continent through the prism of the Guam Doctrine or the Nixon Doctrine, a US long-range military-political course in Asia. This doctrine, proclaimed on July 25, 1969, by the then US President Richard Nixon, for the first time defined the aims of Washington's post-Vietnam Asian policy. In came down to the following : the expansionist aims of US policy in Asia would remain unchanged, the US military build up in Asia would continue, and nuclear arms would be built up the fastest ; US allies in the region would be tied ever tighter to the Pentagon chariot and strengthen their own forces in line with the theory of "equal partnership." And, most importantly, Asians loyal to the USA would war against those disloyal. The USA is still vigorously pursuing the Guam Doctrine, which advocates a strengthening of the alliance between imperialism and regional reaction in their fight against socialism, democracy and national liberation.[5]

The US forces in the Asia-Pacific region totalled 130,500 men at the beginning of 1985. They include large air and land units in Japan (5,800 men), South Korea (over 40,000) and the Philippines (more than 15,000). In addition, the Seventh Fleet (18,300 men), patrolling the West Pacific, has permanent bases on Guam and other islands of Micronesia. in Japan and the Philippines. Apart from the Seventh Fleet, US submarine based strategic forces are in the West Pacific. Of great importance to the Pentagon are the various communication centres for ship and plane movement control and radar and space tracking stations located in Northeast and Southeast Asian countries, Micronesian islands and Australia.

---

5. *Ibid.*

To attain US supremacy on the sea, the Pentagon has begun updating its naval forces. The Seventh Fleet already represents a powerful strike force, including aircraft carrier units, amphibious assault groups with battalions of marines, multi-purpose nuclear submarines, and escort vessels. A programme to equip ships with cruise missiles that can carry both conventional and nuclear charges is being implemented. The modernised battleship New Jersey, with Tomahawk cruise missiles on board (to be tipped with nuclear warheads), and the latest atomic aircraft carrier Carl Winson are also with the Seventh Fleet.

The strongholds of US "Pacific strategy" are the American was bases in Japan and South Korea. What makes the enlarged triangle Washington-Tokyo-Seoul particularly dangerous is the concentration of a large amount of nuclear weapons there. In South Korea nuclear arms are deployed four times as densely as in some NATO members states. In a published US study "Pacific Command : The Structure and Strategy of American Armed Forces in the Pacific Ocean", it is said that the chief strike force of the US ground forces in South Korea is nuclear mines and the depots across the country with nuclear artillery shells and air bombs. Both in Japan and South Korea, a large number of F-16 fighter-bombers are amassed, and US warships with nuclear weapons aboard regularly call at ports of both countries. US atomic submarines are permanently stationed off the coasts of Japan and South Korea.

US military activity has sharply intensified in the Indian Ocean. Under the current Administration, this entire area, including the Gulf, South and Southeast Asia and the Middle East, has been proclaimed a "third strategic zone" (along with Western Europe and the Far East). As a matter of fact, a bridgehead of US forward based forces is now being created there at an accelerated pace. Its foundation has already been laid : about 30 bases and strongholds of the Pentagon, stretching from the eastern coast of Africa to Australia. Another ingredient is the dozens of ships permanently stationed in the Indian Ocean, including aircraft carriers, missiles cruisers, destroyers and frigates (most of them missile-carrying), atomic submarines, floating bases, transport ships, tankers, auxiliary and warehouse ships. Also permanently stationed here are the weapons of the "strategic tiad," including Trident submarines and B-52 bombers, large contingents of conventional forces, including naval units, are being deployed.

Several strategic lines of Pentagon naval and air facilities are currently being formed in the Indian Ocean zone. One of them extends along the eastern coast of Africa, encompassing American bases in Kenya, Somalia, the Sudan and the port of Djibouti, which the USA uses for its ships. Another is in Middle Eastern countries : Egypt, Turkey, Saudi Arabia and Oman. The third line of bases supports the actions of US forces in the eastern part of the Indian Ocean. It includes the bases in Thailand (Sattahip and Utapao), on Philippine territory (Subio Bay and Clark Field) and in Australia. The Diego Garcia island has been turned into a multi-purpose base.[6]

The Indian Ocean also figures in the Pentagon's star wars scheme. On the same Diego Garcia a ground-based electro-optical space tracking station is being installed to put artificial Earth satellites out of action, and the submarines stationed here will be equipped with vertical launch systems for missiles with nuclear warheads or explosive device whose energy transforms into laser beams capable of destroying enemy missiles directly at their sites.

There have been reports of US intentions to create facilities that would form elements of star wars systems elsewhere in the Indian Ocean. The US centres for control, tracking and information reception from military satellites, located on Island Mahe (the Seychelles) and in Alice Spring (Australia), are being converted for this purpose. Deployment of F-15 planes, from which miniature self-homing systems (MSS) to intercept satellites can be launched, is also planned at US bases along the Indian Ocean's perimeter and on the aircraft carriers stationed there.

On January 1, 1983 the USA announced the establishment of a new regional Central Command (Centcom), the sphere of action of which includes 19 states in Southwest Asia, Northeast Africa and

6. *Ibid.*

the Persian Gulf and the Arabian and Red sea zones. The command has at its disposal regular army and naval units to talling about 300,000 men.

The Rapid Deployment Force is the striking nucleus of Centcom. Higher mobility distinguishes this part of the US war machine from conventional forces as does its designation : to capture territories that are far away from the United States. Britain and France are now also creating their own rapid deployment forces.

The British Falklands adventure, the US aggression against Grenada and Lebanon, France's intervention in the events in Chad and the provocations against Libya convincingly show that NATO's Rapid Deployment Forces have not only been created but also operate beyond this bloc's formal sphere of activity.

All this reveals imperialism's systematic preparation for an imperial "crusade" against socialism and national liberation, against the forces of democracy and progress. Having proclaimed this crusade, the USA and its closest NATO allies are now setting up facilities for military intervention in any region of the world, wherever they might regard their interests as "endangered".

Declaring the Gulf and the rest of the Indian Ocean's a "third strategic zone" of US vital interests has become for the Washington politicians sufficient "justification" for an unprecedented US military buildup in this area. But what "vital interests" can the USA have in the Indian Ocean, thousands of miles from American frontiers ?

It is clear that the United States is anxious, noted the well known Indian journalist Brojendra Nath Banerjee, to establish its military and strategic domination over the Indian Ocean in general and over the Persian Gulf in particular, in order to keep the independent states of the region under its surveillance and control them by means of force or threats of force. This definition appears to apply perfectly to the policy of Washington in the Indian Ocean in the eighties.

Not content with the building up of its own military strength in the Asia-Pacific region, the United States is drawing allies, both from among the NATO states and Asian countries themselves, into its dangerous schemes. In the Pacific area, for example, a particularly important role in this respect is being allotted to Japan and South Korea.

South Korea has been turned into a major birdgehead of the USA by now. It must be stressed again that there are about a thousand tactical nuclear weapons here and the preparations are under way for the erection of launching sites for Pershing and Tomahawk intermediate-range missiles. Apart from the force of about 40,000 officers and men that it has in South Korea, the Pentagon is also constantly pressurising Seoul to enlarge and strengthen its own armed forces. At present, the South Korean army numbers about 700,000 and is one of the biggest armies in the Pacific region.

No less active war preparations are being conducted in Japan, where 127 different US military facilities (out of America's Asia-Pacific total of about 300 war bases and strongholds) are located. Japan has today become, in violation of the well-known international conventions and the provisions of the Japanese constitution, one of the most powerful military states in the world. Though not yet large (270,000 men), the Japanese army is equipped with all types of arms and, according to US experts' estimates, holds 6th-7th place among the armed forces of the capitalist countries in fire-power, mobility and other combat characteristics.

The recent period has seen a major extension of the functions of Japan in the US strategic system. Japan has promised anti-aircraft and anti-submarine operations in the northern part of the Pacific, thus acting as a part of the military-strategic system of the USA. Japan has agreed to participate, if necessary, in mining the straits that lead from the Sea of Japan to the Pacific Ocean. The aim is obvious to block the Soviet fleet and not to allow it into the Pacific Ocean.

A recent Japanese-US meeting in Hawaii further advanced Japan's involvement in the USA's strategic military system. A radar for beyond-the-horizon observation will be installed on two islands of the Ryukyu archipelago. The range of the radar is to be about 3,000 kilometres, and the task is to collect intelligence on Soviet air and naval forces and to pass this information on to the Pentagon.

"Judging from everything," it was underlined in the Statement of the Soviet Government of April 23, 1986, "certain political circles in the USA and Japan do not picture of the Asian-Pacific region in any other way than in the form of confrontation of different countries. On the practical plane, attempts are being made for that purpose to create a structure and mechanism of a so-called 'Pacific Community' which can be transformed in the future into a closed regional grouping, into another militaristic bloc."

Earlier, when observers scrutinised the military efforts of Washington, Tokyo and Seoul, they pointed out that in this triangle a third side, the direct military ties between Japan and South Korea, was virtually lacking. But, under US pressure, an intensification of Japanese-South Korean military co-operation is now taking place.

The military-political alliance between the USA, Japan, and South Korea is acquiring ever new contours and becoming a still more ominous, destablising factor in the Pacific region.

The United States is also out to tie ASEAN to the Pentagon chariot by turning this regional economic grouping into a military-political bloc. Not only is the USA doing everything it can to keep its large military bases in the Philippines and war facilities in Thailand, it is also building up its military presence and putting pressure on the ASEAN countries to increase arms spending and buy American combat equipment.

This far from complete list of facts, showing the truly gigantic scale of war preparations by the USA in the Asia-Pacific region, answers the question of why hotbeds of military tension still persist in Asia, why there is no political stability there and why this vast continent suffers from large and small wars from time to time. In this context it is obvious that the issue of safeguarding peace and security in Asia is no less acute, and in some areas even more acute and painful. than, for example, on the European continent.[7]

7. *Ibid.*

The strategy of imperialism in the Asia-Pacific region poses a danger not only for those against whom it is direct whom it is directly aimed—the USSR, the other socialist countries national-liberation movements—but also seriously threatens the security of the current US allies in the region by allotting to them the role of the Pentagon's "nuclear hostages."

Realising that the whipping up of war hysteria in Asia is causing growing concern among Asian states and evoking protest on the part of the peace-loving forces of the area, the Washington strategists are trying to prove that they "have the right" to be permanently present in Asia and the contiguous Indian and Pacific Ocean basins, and not just to be here. In so doing they put forward their standard politico-ideological set of doctrines and concepts to make a "case" for such presence.

Although the militarization of the Pacific region is not yet equal scale to that in Europe it is proceeding fast enough to have potentially fatal consequences. However, it is not yet too late to prevent the Pacific becoming an arena of military-political confrontation. The pre-requisites exist for the Pacific to become what its name suggests.

One pre-requisite was the decision of 13 states and self-governing territories in the South Pacific to proclaim the region a nuclear free zone. The treaty establishing such a zone was drawn up and approved at the August 1985 session of the South Pacific Forum (SPF) with which these countries are affiliated. The session was held in Avarua (the Cook Islands). Hence the name of the document adopted—the Avarua treaty. Early in August, 1986 the 17th SPF summit was held in Suva, the capital of the island state of Fiji, to discuss the problems involved in formalizing the non-nuclear status of the South Pacific region.

The Avarua treaty binds its signatories to refrain from developing, producing, acquiring and deploying nuclear weapons on their territories and bans nuclear tests and the burial of radioactive waste within the zone the treaty applies to.

The Avarua treaty has now been signed by 10 of the thirteen SPF states—Australia, New Zealand, Western Samoa, Kiribati

Papua New Guinea, Nauru, Fiji, Tuvalu, the Cook Islands and Niue. The four last-mentioned have already ratified it.

Some states in the region consider the treaty inadequate because it does not ban the passage of nuclear-carrying warships and aircraft through the nuclear-free zone, or deny them the use of the zone's ports and airfields. The treaty leaves it to the individual SPF states to make the appropriate decisions. This, incidentally, is why Vanuatu and the Solomon Islands have not signed it.

The South Pacific nuclear-free zone covers an enormous area, 8.5 million square kilometres. It is therefore almost as large as that established in Latin America in 1967 under the Treaty of Tltelolco (so named after the district of Mexico City where it was signed). The confines of the new nuclear-free zone have been established as being the Equator in the north and the 60th Parallel in the south. In the east, it will adjoin the Tltelolco Treaty nuclear-free zone, and in the west, pass between the territorial waters of Australia and Indonesia and along the symbolic borderline between the Pacific and Indian oceans.

The extraordinary importance of the decision to declare the South Pacific a nuclear-free zone is indisputable. It was, after all, in the Pacific that the first atomic and hydrogen bombs were tested. France is still testing its latest nuclear weapons on Mururao atoll.

At the estimate of the regional religious organization, the Pacific Ocean Conference of Churches, the U.S. has no less than 10,000 nuclear warheads on its insular bases ships and submarines in the Pacific.

The Suva conference worked out and adopted the final versions of the protocols extending the principles that underlie the Avarua treaty, and specified the commitments of states signatory to it. The protocols call on all nuclear states to pledge themselves to respect the status of the nuclear zone, not to use, or threaten to use, nuclear weapons against the states signatory to the treaty, and to test no nuclear devices in the zone covered by the treaty. The session demanded that the US stop nuclear testing without delay as a first step towards an agreement on ending tests altogether, and resolutely condemned the policy of France which is continuing to implement its nuclear test programme on Mururoa atoll.

The establishment of nuclear-free zones, like other measures to curb the race in the most dangerous weapons, is meeting with vigorous opposition on the part of aggressive imperialist circles, especially the United States, Washington has always been opposed to nuclear-free zones. During his recent visit to Singapore George Shultz, the U.S. Secretary of State, described the decision of the SPF states as "a mistake," while William Bodde; the former U.S. Ambassador to Fiji, stated that "the movement for a nuclear-free Pacific Ocean was the most serious threat to American interests in the region." Clearly, he meant the interests of US militaristic circles.

Paris has stated it will not abide by the SPF states' treaty and will continue with its nuclear tests on Mururoa atoll. The decision of the Suva session to petition the U.N. committee on decolonization to put France's overseas territory of New Caledonia on the list of the territories subject to decolonization has also caused displeasure in Paris.

The Soviet Union has always regarded the establishment of nuclear-free zones in various parts of the world as an important measure in the struggle to limit the sphere of the nuclear arms race. "We are in favour of putting up a barrier in the way of the proliferation and build up of *nuclear weapons* in Asia and the Pacific," said Mikhail Gorbachev in his Vladivostok speech.

This is why the Soviet Union has from the out set supported the efforts of the South Pacific states to establish a nuclear-free zone in the region.

The People's Republic of China has also voiced its support for a South Pacific nuclear-free zone.

Washington's attempts to build the Pacific Community" with Tokyo's assistance—a community headed by the US and opposed to the USSR and other socialist-community countries—provides a vivid example of an outdated political mentality. The Asian and Pacific region is offered a system similar to that built 40 years ago in the North Atlantic, namely the NATO system. This threatens to turn Asia and the Pacific Ocean into a dangerous arena of confrontation, which may endanger universal peace. A military conflict in the Pacific Ocean may cause a global chain reaction at any movement.

In this context, there is no reasonable and acceptable alternative for the Pacific nations than that of peaceful co-existence and co-operation. In the USSR's opinion, a Pacific forum similar to the All-European Conference in Helsinki will be a landmark on this road.

The wars in Korea and Vietnam, where the Pentagon considered the possibility of using nuclear bombs, demonstrated how important it is for the whole world to lay the firm foundation of security in the Asian and Pacific region. The Helsinki process in Europe revealed the possibility of different countries, joint work for strengthening security and broadening international co-operation. The experience of this process could be used for solving the problems facing the Pacific region. To recognise the objective historical laws and present-day political realities is to open the road to success. The Soviet policy with regards the Pacific Ocean is based on this idea. The USSR stands for a free choice of ways of development by all nations—big and small, This right is as inalienable as the right to economic independence and to utilisation of natural resources in national interests.

The opponents of such rights are well known. The neocolonialist practices inflict damage on Asian countries and on the prospects for Pacific co-operation. The hope for perpetuating neocolonialism, resolutely rejected by the newly free states, is as dangerous at the Pentagon's control over the Pacific zone.

The Pacific nations need to broaden equitable co-operation in the political, economic and ecological spheres, and they have ample opportunities to do so. The economic structures of many of these states largely supplement each other. Moreover, the Pacific Ocean, in our age of fast and powerful means of transportation, can become a giant channel for development and not an obstacle to it. This course can vanquish confrontation and the global system of security can extend to this region.

CHAPTER ELEVEN

POWER POLITICS AND SECURITY

THE MODERN AGE of high technology makes it imperative for the world to devise such rules and standards of international behaviour as to enable it to survive. Soviet leader Mikhail Gorbachev, speaking at the 27th Congress of the CPSU in February, 1986, emphasised : "The changes in current world developments are so deep-going and significant that they require a reassessment and a comprehensive analysis of all factors. The situation created by the nuclear confrontation calls for new approaches, methods, and forms of relations between the different social systems, states and regions."

It has to be stated, however, that the governig quarters of the imperialist powers, above all the US, still think in terms of outdated stereotypes and presume they can win a nuclear missile war. They provoke and engineer local or "limited" conflicts in an attempt to take social revenge in the struggle against the anti-imperialist and national liberation movements.[1]

There has appeared a doctrine of "neoglobalism" designed to justify the strategy to "rollback" the national liberation movements and to "legitimise" the regional wars of imperialism against the emergent nations of Asia, Africa and Latin America. Coupled with this is the policy of global armed confrontation with the Socialist nations, in the name of fighting the "spread of Communism".

These doctrines are only seemingly new. It is just like turning an old coat. It is an attempt at reviving the spirit of the cold war,

1, See Gennady Kadymov. *Local Conflicts in the Making*. New Delhi, Allied 1986. pp. 1-44.

the Dullesian strategy to "rollback Communism", the policy of armed suppression of the forces of progress, national and social liberation, by all means.

Times have changed, but the philosophy of imperialism and its postulates have not. The British Empire of the 19th century, having secured domination of the seas and arrogated to itself the title of "ruler of the seas", expected to establish its dominance in the world through "gunboat diplomacy". In our days, there is no British domination of the seas, nor anything like the British colonial empire, but its methods have been inherited by other claimants to spheres of influence and colonies and to world supremacy.

There were some "theorists" at the turn of the century, first in Italy, and then in Germany and Japan, who tried to explain the need for those powers to capture new "living space" to redraw the boundaries of colonial empires and, in the long run, secure world domination.

What those claims of the German and Italian fascists and Japanese militarists ended up in is a matter of common knowledge. The countries of the anti-Hitler coalition smashed up the aggressors, the Soviet Union playing a decisive role in their defeat.

History does not stand still. New types of weapons are cropping up and the new aspirants to world supremacy are striving to achieve the old ends with such weapons. US imperialism is not only escalating the nuclear and "conventional" arms race on the land, at sea and in the air, but trying to take this race out into space.

However, no weapons will help Washington keep in check the peoples who are anxious to get rid of foreign domination. Hence the US bid to use local or "limited" conflicts to establish the "American interest" in one country or another in one region or another. Yet it cannot fail to see that a minor war in the present world can lead to a major one, a global conflict with unpredictable consequences for the US itself. That is what makes imperialist strategists think of "double guarantees" of impunity on the world stage. They are hoping to obtain US preponderance over the Soviet Union in strategic arms. For the sake of this unattainable dream, the US has been stubbornly refusing to second the persistent Soviet proposals for a nuclear test ban and has been trampling upon the Soviet-American treaty on the limitation of strategic offensive arms. Washington's reckoning is that it will have, in consequence, a free hand to impose its own will on sovereign peoples and nation and freedom of action in local conflicts.[2]

At the time of the early conquests, a colonial power could well do with one or two frigates and a small landing force to conquer any country. Today imperialists need something far more solid to do so.

The logical and thinking of the days of the conquerors are being extrapolated into the space age. The strategy and tactics of "local" conflicts are being worked out, scenarios and models constructed and rehearsed, conflict situations tried out, vast resources set aside for military programmes, new arms and services are created, and the huge war machine set in motion.

The danger of this kind of thought and action, both for the small nations and for world peace in general, is obvious. It has already plunged nations into conflicts, quite frequent in the post-war years. There have been over 130 armed conflicts since the end of the Second World War, which have claimed 35 million lives. For the most part, these conflicts have taken place in the countries of Asia, Africa and Latin America. During these years, US imperialism has used armed force against other nations and peoples on more than 250 occasions, suffice it to recall the war that US waged in Korea (1950-1953), the US intervention in South Vietnam (1964-1973), in the Dominican Republic (1965), the aggression against Grenada (1983), the aggressive actions of American imperialism in the Middle East against Lebanon, the undeclared wars against Nicaragua. against Afghanistan, and the acts of armed provocation and outright aggression against Libya.

"Local" conflicts are becoming integral to the global foreign policy strategy of American imperialism. It is necessary to expose its tactics with determination, bring the forces of all peoples and nations together in opposition to the aggressor, and nip war preparations in the bud. There is a growing danger, year after

2. *Ibid.*

year, of regional conflicts escalating into a worldwide conflict which can put the lot of entire humanity at stake.

Speaking in Vladivostok on July 28, 1986, Mikhail Gorbachev said : "Whenever independence becomes a tangible international value and there emerges a threat to the exploiter interests of imperialism, it resorts to its favourite methods; economic blackmail, intrigues and plots against the leadership of the country in question, interference in internal problems, and maintenance of separatists with finance for and even direct armament of counter-revolution and terrorists."

The American military bases scattered all over the world provide material support for state terrorism. Aggression against sovereign states is undertaken from US aircraft-carriers and their military bases. They are a means of waging "minor wars."

US imperialism's aggressiveness is growing like a snow-ball, inflicting irreparable damage to small nations. It should be nipped in the bud as soon as the aggressor's intentions become clear, because the consequences of "minor wars" may be unpredictable for the entire world.

The power politics of the US and the other imperialist powers gives priority to the military-strategic imperative. Hence the main postulates of their imperial policy which prescribe having the largest fleet and controlling the straits for ruling the seas, bringing one's troops and weapons as close as possible to the enemy's territory for gaining time superiority for a surprise attack, establishing peripheral "zones of vital interests" for safeguarding one's security, gaining control over the communications and so on.

The military-strategic approach in world affairs became particularly prominent in the US right after the Second World War, when Washington came to view any situation in the world from the position of its potential threat to US interests. Gradually, the military-strategic postulate turned into stereotypes of American thinking. Since after the Second World War the US turned into a global power, Washington started thinking in the imperial categories of *pax Americana*. No regions and countries remained in the world where the US would not have its "vital interests" at stake.

Some of the first US actions associated with the declaration of the Truman Doctrine in 1947 and the start of the "cold war" were the efforts to prevent revolutionary change in the Balkans and in the Mediterranean by force. Using the slogan of "rolling back communism", the US and its allies started landing their troops and setting up military bases in Greece and Turkey.

For this expansionist course the US needed a theoretical foundation, so "doctrines" surfaced very soon which were meant to justify the American policy of "minor" wars against the national liberation movement which spread out in the fifties. Having performed a simple operation involving the falsification of the essence, objective and tasks of the liberation movements in Asian countries and labelled them "communist expansion" supposedly threatening the "vital interests of the US", American imperialism undertook the mission of armed suppression of these movements.

The countries and regions against which the US directs its military might are changing, but its allegiance to military-strategic priority in judging about world affairs remains.

After the end of World War II in the Pacific, American imperialism decided to lay hands on the colonies of its weakened partners in Southeast Asia. However, the accomplishment of those goals came to face a major threat from the wide-spread national liberation movement supported by the socialist community. This movement developed its radical forms in Indochina where it turned into a struggle for social liberation.

The fear of socio-economic and political changes made the US ruling circles interfere in the internal affairs of the countries of Indochina. That was the time of the emergence in the US of the concept of global political and strategic importance of the Indochina peninsula for the US, which became known as the "domino theory" and determined the American strategy in Southeast Asia. Its foundation was laid by President Eisenhower. Regarding Indochina from the viewpoint of military confrontation with the national liberation forces on a global scale, Eisenhower believed that in case of the victory of the national liberation revolutions in Vietnam, Laos and Cambodia (now Kampuchea), not only Thailand but also Burma and Malaysia "will end up in jeopardy" with an added risk for East Pakistan, South Asia and also Indonesia.

The main idea about the American strategists' theory was that the US had to ensure the "defence" of the anti-popular puppet government in South Vietnam and to raise a barrier against "communist penetration" into Sotheast Asia which would otherwise "pose a threat" not only to the countries of the region but also to Australia and New Zealand. It was alleged that the loss of Indochina would directly affect the security of the US. The "domino theory" was made part of the practical US foreign policy. Speaking in the House Foreign Relations Committee, the then US Defence Secretary Robert McNamara insisted that the retention under American control of the bases located on the very periphery of the socialist camp was of "vital importance" for US national security.

Assistant US Secretary of State for Far Eastern Affairs M. Bundy said that if Vietnam "fell" (the term used by the Americans to describe the gaining of national independence by the Vietnamese people), the United States would find it much harder to retain Thailand and Philippines under its control and to help the British in Malaysia in their struggle against the rational liberation movement there. The reason why Vietnam has not fallen, insisted Bundy in 1965, is because the US came to its help at a time when no other power could have performed that mission.

In the mid-60s the US administration decided that Indochina was the place where a blow had to be dealt to the forces of socialism and national liberation. The arguments in favour of US armed intervention there rather than elsewhere in Asia was outlined in a State Department publication which was issued in 1965 under the characteristic title "Why Vietnam?".

These arguments were based on the assessments by President Eisenhower of the global political and military-strategic importanee of that region and also on the "domino theory" transformed later by President Johnson into a concept of preserving the "strategic balance" in Southeast Asia. This concept proceeds from the inadmissibility of the "loss" of Southeast Asia for the US, which would precipitate serious change in the alignment of forces contrary to the interests of the "free world." The then US Secretary of State, Dean Rusk, openly said that the "loss" of South Vietnam would make the defence of the remaining part of Southeast Asia a more expensive and difficult business.

In the mid-60s the US came to view Indochina as a convenient bridgehead in Asia. According to the American strategists, the reliable system of communications via the Hawaii and the Philippines and control over Indochina enabled the Americans in case of a global conflict to open another front on the south-eastern flank of the socialist system, to exert pressure on Burma and to force India into abandoning its policy of non-alignment. Indochina was a crucial link in the chain of American military bases and bridgeheads along the borders of socialist countries. The bases in Japan, South Korea, on Okinawa, in Taiwan, the Philippines, Indochina and Malacca served as a springboard from which the US military intended to strike at the socialist countries.[3]

So how did Washington understand its political interest in Indochina? With its presence there and with the preparedness to supress the national liberation movement in South Vietnam and Laos and to force Cambodia to give up its neutrality, the US wanted to prove to other countries the hopelessness of the attempts to gain national independence and also to display its determination to "defend its allies."

As if that was not enough, articles appeared in the American press which questioned certain aspects of the "domino theory" and especially its supposedly passive, defensive orientation. This led to the emergence of new concepts calling for active action,—notably the doctrines of "flexible response', and "local wars".

These new ideas did not utterly dismiss the old concepts which served as a foundation for the new tactic of carefully doses use of strength with the preservation of the general strategic line and continuity in foreign policy.

In the global strategic sense the US objective in Indochina was not only to retain and broaden the positions of imperialism in Southeast Asia, but also to split the unity of world socialist system, to sour Soviet-Chinese relations and to undermine the alliance of the forces of socialist and national liberation. Another objective was to avoid a direct armed conflict with the Soviet Union. The principal goal, however, was the assertion of American domination in the region and the conversion of Southeast Asia into a zone of exclusive US influence.

---

3. *Ibid.*

President Reagan has inherited the imperial approach and the ideas of Dwight Eisenhower as well as his military-strategic imperative in assessing the complex and controversial socio-economic and political processes in the countries of Asia, Africa and Latin America. The only difference is that the concepts of the previous administrations have been replaced with the "doctrine of neoglobalism" which is said to be a brainchild of the current US President himself.

The change of names, however, does not alter the essence of the matter or the stereotypes of political thinking which have set in the American leadership since the 50s. The "Reagan doctrine" contains verbatim repetitions of the terms and nations used by J.F. Dulles about "rolling back" communism on a global scale, which also implies the "rolling back" of national liberation movements. The "doctrine of neoglobalism" means a policy of neo-colonial invasions and wars and of overthrowing constitutionally elected governments which do not suit the US.

Today, thirty years after the presidency of Eisenhower, Renald Reagan says assessing the situation in Central America and around Nicaragua that the victory of the revolution in that country was a "cancerous tumour" which must be removed and that the disease was threatening other countries in Central America and may spread to El Salvador, Costa Rida, Honduras and other countries. "If we don't want to see the map of Central America covered in a sea of red eventually lapping at our own borders, we must act now," he urged.

Panic-laden shouts "Communists on our doorsteps" are designed to exacerbate the situation in North America to the utmost and to trigger off a wave of chauvinism in order to create conditions for direct intereference in Central American affairs.

US secretary of State George Shultz poured more oil on the flames. Following in the footsteps of Dean Rusk, his recent predecessor, who did much to kindle the war in Vietnam, he demanded that the American people should support the so-called "freedom fighters".

Doctrines of the 50s may be resuscitated and reanimated. But if attempts to translate them into reality failed at that time, it is much harder to implement such doctrines today. If in the 50s the US, relying on the nuclear potential, hoped to get away with impunity, now there is a nuclear missile parity between the US and the Soviet Union. Involvement of the US in local conflicts, which may escalate into global ones, holds out serious and unpredictable consequences for the US itself.

Washington painfully racked the brain how to avoid a conflict becoming global, while retaining freedom of action at the regional level, that is, in Asian, African and Latin American Countries. As a result, the "doctrine of new globalism" was born. Its essence boils down to the substantiation of "low intensity" wars. Caspar Weinberger, the chief of the Pentagon, just as Robert McNamara in his day, came forward with the idea of dosed application of US military strength in regional conflicts and pursing subversive activities in the first place against the developing countries. Indeed, anything new is a thing of well-forgotten past.

In assessing the essence of the "doctrine of neo-globalism" Soviet leader Mikhail Gorbachev emphasised that this had "total diregard for the generally recognised norms of international relations, it is an encroachment on the sovereignty of states, the same old hopeless attempt to deprive the peoples of the right to build their life as they wish."

American politicians themselves believe that the essence of the new doctrine lay in forming a "new structure" for the entire system of international relations, based on the "decisive influence" of the US on the course of world events. In other words, it is again a question of establishing American world or, according to the new terminology, global hegemony.

The brunt of the small wars should be borne by "anti-Communist freedom fighters"—mercenaries like Nicaraguan "contras" and Afghan "dushmans". The US undertake to provide financial and material support for such subversive actions. But the state on mercenaries in unreliable and so the Pentagon is planning not only the developing of new arms, but also the creation of new arms of service intended for waging war on their own on the territories of other states.

US Secretary of State George Shultz elevated "low intensity" wars to the category of major tasks in ensuring US national security, American policy, according to him, is oriented in the long term on most diverse conflicts which hold an intermediate position between a large-scale war an universal peace.

The probability of retribution creates a stiff and unsuitable framework for the US and sets limits to it. Such a situation does not suit Washington. It is trying to wrest free of the binding parity in nuclear-missile arms with the Soviet Union, pinning its hopes on achieving superiority over the USSR in the development of the "ultimate" weapon. The reference is to the development and deployment of space strike weapons.

Of course, the stake on "space retribution" is not more than a chimera, but the Pentagon regards it as a means of blackmailing "unsuitable" states to change the social *status quo*.

Technically, American imperialism has, of course, gone a long way from the times of the beginning of the cold war and the "domino theory". Now not only guns of battle ships threaten the peoples who have embarked upon the path of independent development, also nuclear-tipped missiles and, in the future, nuclear-pumped laser guns and other types of new plane the US still proceeds. But on the conceptual plane the US still proceeds from power politics, military-strategic priorities. Indeed, this is the thinking of a cave man who relied on his club as the decisive argument, transposed into the nuclear ahe.

Modern times inevitably dictate the need for different thinking, for different norms of contacts between peoples and states. In the present-day conditions it is necessary not to refurbish obsolite "doctones', but to restructure the system of international relations, to exclude from practice both "small" and "large-scale" wars. It is high time to understand the illusoriness of achieving "absolute superiority" in the creation of "super-weapons" capable of ensuring world domination.

Any war is relatively easy to start, but more difficult to finish, American imperialism, as any aggressor, pinned hopes on its strength and expected an easy and quick victory, with no particular material and moral losses. A simple arithmetic calculation of the number of the warships, aircraft, artillery and other weapons, compared with the enemy's potential, seemed to point convincingly to US superiority and consequently to the possibility of a rapid and effective triumph.

But war has its own logic. There appear circumstances and factors which fail to lend themselves not only to arithmetic, but also to political algebra and even higher mathematics. They belong to the spiritual spheres to the resolve of a nation to protect its freedom and independence to the last drop of blood, to endure sacrifices and privations to which no hired "gentleman of fortune" would agree. Ho Chi Minh, the late president of Vietnam, issued this call during the US intervention : "Nothing is more valuable than freedom and independence". It became the motto of the entire Vietnamese nation.

The sad experience of US intervention in Korea and Vietnam, in the Middle East and Iran, in Latin American and African countries is a graphic confirmation of the invincible forces of freedom-loving peoples, of the inevitable collapse of aggressors. Imperialist-unleashed wars lead not only to material losses and casualties, but also to grave moral and political loses, cause a crisis of confidence' complicate relations with allies, and place the country concerned into a position of political isolation in the international arena.

The invasion of Grenada was depicted as a big victory for the US. But if we imagine that aggression had been carried out not against a little island country whose population and with its people determined to defend their country, the outcome would have been entirely different. This is demonstrated by the experience of Vietnam and other Indo-china countries, by the abortive attempts to invade Cuba, the disgraceful failure of intervention in Lebanon and Iran, the setbacks suffered by the "dushmans" in the undeclared war being waged against Afghanistan by the USA.

Planning "limited" wars, the US as a rule calculates to wage them by other hands, using predominantly mercenaries. So was the case in Vietnam where the American involvement in the conflict increased by stages. It all began from a small thing, from attempts to stabilise the puppet regime of Ngo Dinh Diem by allocating him aid to build up an army of some 20,000 men and para-military formations of the Self-Defence Corps numbering 32,000.

That soldiery had to be armed and trained to fire. Soon additional sums were required. In 1954-1959 the US brought 424 million dollars' worth of arms into South Vietnam. Washington almost completely maintained the puppet regime, meeting the overwhelming part of Saigon's expenses for military and civilian purposes.

The Military Assistance Advisory Group (MAAG) appeared in Saigon, which was visited by high-placed representatives of the US administration and the Pentagon. In May 1956, in breach of the Geneva accords on Vietnam, the first contingent of US servicemen consisting of 350 men arrived in Saigon, who, as was officially announced, were to "repair French arms."

Subsequently the number of American specialists in various arms grew while military missions multiplied qualitatively and quantitatively, there appeared the temporary Equipment Recovery Mission—TERM, then the Training Reorganisation Inspection Mission—TRIM, and the Combat Arms Training Organisation—CATO.

Early in the 60s, Ngo Dinh Diem addressed urgent appeals to the US to send to his help the cream of American cut-throats. Among the advisers there appeared the first 400 commandos to train "special forces" and take part in punitive operations of the Saigon regime against patriots. The CIA greatly stepped up its activities in Vietnam in those Years. It began forming subversive groups and sending them into neighbouring Laos and Cambodia (Kampuchea).

Good Uncle Sam sent to South Vietnam not only "Green berets" but also new quantities of arms. Americans were drawing up operational plans of combat and also a strategy for herding the local population into "strategic hamlet" (Staily Plan). The USA got more and more involved in South Vietnamese affairs, shouldering not only the material upkeep of the rotten regime, but also the onus of direct militarty operations.

Direct American aggression in Vietnam began in February 1965 with a bombing of DRV territory and landing of 3,500 US Marines in Da Nang. But the resolute resistance put up by the Vietnamese patriots required from Washington additional cannon fodder. After a year the number of US troops topped the 200,000 mark. In 1967, they numbered some 500,000 and at the end of 1968, over 550,000 men. The war in Vietnam was seen bv 4.5 million Americans, which left an idelible mark on the nation's consciousness.

Nothing, however, helped. The rotten regime could not be saved. Instead of a small punitive operation the US found itself involved in a protracted war. It was said in the US at that time that the Americans entered a tunnel with no light seen at the end.

In Vietnam, the US used the latest lethal weapons on a large scale. According to a commission led by Senator Edward Kennedy, the explosive power of the six million tons of bombs dropped by US planes on Vietnam was equivalent to 50 atom bombs of the tupe that was dropped on Hiroshima. It was in those years that the Americans claimed that they were carrying out bombing raids with "surgical precision". But the facts totally refuted such claims. Dwelling houses, schools, hospitals and other civilian buildings were being destroyed. Bombing raids were made not against targets, but open spaces where all buildings were already demolished. The US chemical war in Vietnam, according to an international commission for the investigation of American military activities in Vietnam, upset the ecological balance in that part of the Asian continent. The fields became infertile, the water poisoned, and no animals and vegetation were left on large areas.

Places where people earlier lived can no longer support them. All this had and is having ruinous effects on the life of whole generations.

"Toys" with explosive devices, fountain-pens that blast off one's fingers, beatle-mines and other "gifts" of US imperialism to Afghan children, which counter-revolutionary rebels are bringing into the country, were first used in Vietnam. It was there that this experience was accumulated. Now US advisers share it with the Afghan counter-revolutionaries. These base acts are committed under cover of lies being churned out by the US mass media and statements of high-ranking Washingtom officials in which they try to accuse Soviet troops of using the lethal "toys".

US politicians and scholars are still discussing the "lessons of Vietnam". Some of them say and write that the USA does not observe the "rules" of war conduct. Don't send "our" troops, use mercenaries more, they argue. Others assert that a careful study of force alignment in a state should precede involvement in a conflict, don't link America's prestige with political groups not having support in their own countries, they say. Still others, in particular, the Reagan administration, call for "ceasing to be ashamed of Vietnam."[4]

Unfortunately, sound assessments which would condemn and reject the very idea of interventionism, of using force to solve international issues are rarely heard in the USA. Criticism is limited to the methods only; the man-in-the-street is being asked to believe that individual forms, not the substance, of the US ruling circles' policy are erroneous.

The Reagan adminintration criticizes its predecessors from the right for their insufficient toughness and consistency in pursuing the confrontationist and war line. By sticking to interventionism it wants to reverse the previous failures and setbacks. Actually the White House gets the USA involved in new adventures which, with small variations, reproduce the already known cycles once travelled by other US presidents.

Everything indicates that the Reagan administration intends to play the old game in new conditions, now not in Southeast Asia, but in Central America, the Middle East and Africa.

We have already mentioned the undeclared war the USA has been waging against Nicaragua since 1981. The first steps are now being taken to "North-Americanize" the conflict in Central America. There is no doubt that this will lead to a general destablisation in the region, as was the case in Vietnam where war spread from South to North Vietnam, then to Laos and Kampuchea, in fact to the entire Indochinese Peninsula, subjecting to trial and peace in Southeast Asia.

The USA is already involved in the internal struggle in El Salvador. According to foreign newsmen who have visited that country, US military advisers are directly participating in combat operations. North Americans train over half the men in the Duarte regime's army, carry out night air raids together with its pilots and make flights on their own.

All the necessary preparatory moves towards a "large-scale war" in Central America have already been taken: bases have been

4. *Ibid.*

built in Honduras, and US troops sent there. Bases in Florida and elsewhere in the Caribbean have been equipped for their use by "rapid deployment forces". Planned aggressive actions are being fine-tuned in unceasing war games.

The buildup of US forces in Central America, the aggression in Grenada, the Reagan administration's drive to get through the US Congress allocations for "contras" and the President's bellicose statements have caused the condemnation of the world public. US allies fear that the senior partner's actions may involve them in dangerous adventures.

"Western solidarity" is beginning to crack up. Britain and France, whose policies are closely bound up with the US line, make numerous reservations on some issues. Thus, the perfidious US invasion of Grenada, even without preliminary consultations with the allies, caused shock. A number of countries expressed "regret". British Prime Minister Margaret Thatcher, who can hardly be suspected of non-loyalty to the Reagan administration, declared that Western countries cannot invade other nations only because events that do not suit them occur there. It is to be recalled that Grenada is a member of the Commonwealth. The governor of this island state is appointed by Britain, yet Washington did not consider it necessary to even inform its chief NATO ally of the aggression.

International consequences of "gunboat diplomacy" off the shores of Libya were also negative for the USA. Mediterranean states, including some US allies in NATO, were extremely concerned about the US action and about the possibility of Americans using bases on their territories and drawing them into an explosive conflict.

US allies are beginning to understand that they have to pay a heavy price for their military ties with the USA—the surrender of their own sovereignty. With the unceremoniousness of the "senior partner", they may, against their will, get involved in a conflict that contradicts their interests.

Everywhere, be it Grenada, Lebanon, Libya or Afghanistan, US imperialism resorts to the barbaric methods of warfare. While prattling about "surgical operations" purportedly for "preventive aims" of struggle against terrorism, Washington actually sanctions any bandit actions of its military. Suffice to mention the fact that "surgical operation" by US bombers in Grenada resulted in the destruction of a mental hospital in Saint Geirge's killing dozens of patients. On August 30, 1983, US ships wantonly shelled the residential areas of West Beirut and its southern suburbs. Simultaneously US planes operating from aircraft carriers bombed the mountain areas of Lebanon. As a result of this "surgical operation" there were significant casualties among civilians. The piratic attack on Libya in April 1986 also was presented as a "surgical operation." Journalists who visited the affected sites told the truth to the world public about the aftermath of the US bombings on Libyan cities. Mainly civilians and civil objects had suffered. Women, old men and children were killed in Tripoli and Benghazi. Many people were left without shelter.

Now they say these were results of 'aiming errors" of US pilots. This reminds one of the "error" of Maddox destroyer acoustician who mistook the noise of the engine of his own ship for the sounds of Vietnamese torpedoes.

If the USA unhasitatingly resorts to arms for minor "surgical operations" then were is the guarantee that it will not use more powerful weapons to deal with major political crises and conflicts where a conventional bomb stike will be insufficient? For, the use of nuclear weapons is so alluring There is no barrier for the Americans in this regard.

The United States' strategic allies, such as Israel and South Africa, in a critical situation won't stop at extreme means, Israel has already carried out an air raid on the nuclear reactor in Iraq, without thinking about possible heavy consequences for all Middle Eastern countries.

With great ease, US imperialism resorts to a military force in solving issues. This is criminal and extremely dangerous. Now that any conflict can turn into a nuclear one, the brandishing of a nuclear missile truncheon, state terrorism or global demonstration of force testify to the absence of political wisdom. Restraint and weighed actions on the international scene are political wisdom.

The consequences of the US interventionist policy are only too obvious. It entails direct US intervention into conflicts with ever growing participation of US armed forces. The US again assumes the role of a "world policeman." After another short-lived wave of chauvinistic sentiment, the US involvement in a conflict depresses the US public. Prolonged conflict a split US society and give rise to a political crisis. Internationally, the US testing of it allies' loyalty increases the isolation of the United States. But the intensification and widening of the struggle waged by the peace loving forces against the policies of diktat and violence is a major result of US interference in the internal affairs of other states. Paradoxically, US aggressive actions produce results unexpected for the United States. The policy of violence and war is doomed and has no future. And the sooner the White House sees that, the better for the US and its prestige as a world power.[5]

The Soviet Union and other peace loving forces offset the logic of war with peace logic. They offset the stepping up of regional conflicts with the policy of peaceful settlement of issues. In a nuclear missile age this is the only way of thinking acceptable for mankind. The USSR and other socialist countries reject wars as a means for solving political and economic contradictions among states and settling ideological differences.

The 27th Congress of the CPSU (February-March 1986) formulated the concept of excluding wars, big and small, from the life of mankind. It is based on a new approach to the evaluation of world processes. The Congress called on the statesment of countries, big and small, to master the science and the art of behaving with restraint, acting with discretion, and living as civilised people should, maintaining proper international contacts and co-operation. There must be no violence, *diktat* or domination in relations among states.

"The times persistenly demand a new understanding of the present stage in the development of civilisation, of international relations, and of the world," said Mikhail Gorbachev in Vladivostok on July 28, 1986. "This is a controversial and complex world, but it is objectively united by the bonds of interdependence.

5. *Ibid.*

International relations have evolved, under which, for all the differences and clashes of interests, one can no longer live by the millennia-old traditions of "the law of the first".

Life has advanced the following alternatives for the international community : Co-operation in searching for a lasting peacenot confrontation. Peaceful co-existence of states with different social and economic systems—not encouragement and creation of crisis situations and conflicts. And the search for political solutions to the arguments cropping up-not "gun-boat diplomacy" or sabre-rattling. To make the ideals of peace and co-operation a reality, the material force used in warfare must be eliminated. The military arsenals, and above all the stockpiles of the most dangerous weapons of mass destruction—nuclear and chemical arms—must be reduced and in the long run eliminated.

This lofty task of removing before the end of the current century the terrible threat of total extinction in a nuclear missile war is advanced in the January 15, 1986 statement by Mikhail Gorbachev. It contains a concrete programme for the elimination before the year 2000 of all nuclear weapons and other means of mass destruction. The unilateral Soviet moratorium on all nuclear explosions has been in force since August 6, 1985 - the 40th anniversary of the American nuclear bombing of Hiroshima. It has been extended until August 6, 1986 and then extended again till January 1, 1987. Meanwhile the US, regretfully, has been continuing nuclear tests.

The Soviet Union's peace initiatives have called forth favourable response all over the world. The non-aligned countries have likewise called for nuclear-free zones and sones of peace in many parts of the globe. Twenty-five countries have joined the Treaty on Latin America as a nuclear-free zone (the Treaty of Tlatelolco). The member countries of the South Pacific forum declared that vast region a nuclear-free zone (the Avarua Treaty). The Treaty has been signed not only by the newly-freed nations, but also by Australia and New Zealand - the advanced capitalist states of the region. There have been initiatives to establish nuclear-free zones in Africa, the Middle East, and the South and South East Asia.

Gorbachev said that the Soviet Union "approached with understanding the striving of many states to create nuclear-free zones in various regions of the globe. We are for such zones, say, in Northern Europe, in the Blanks, in South East Asia, and in Africa. The efforts of the South Pacific states to establish a nuclear-free zone in that region are also worthy of approval."

The search for ways of settling conflict situations through the collective efforts of states is the most fruitful form of strengthening peace in the regions, and stabilizing the situation. The Afro-Asian and Latin American states co-opperate regionally and advance alternative political solutions to acute conflict situations.

The striving to develop neighbourly relations among states persists. The policies of confrontation and war are being condemned more and more strongly. They contribute to the isolation of the initiators and upholders of such policies on the world scene. The conclusion that the forces of war and reaction are not omnipotent, and that they can and must be curbed is supported by the practice of international relations.

CHAPTER TWELVE

NUCLEAR WEAPONS AND STAR WARS

ONE OF THE RESULTS of the arms race started by the imperialists is that the 20th century is approaching its end under the question mark whether mankind will manage to get rid of the nuclear menace or the policy of nuclear confrontation exacerbating the risk of a nuclear conflict will get the upper hand.

The latter variant would threaten the very survival of human civilization. According to the data of the USSR Academy of Medical Sciences, the immediate effects alone of the combat use of nuclear weapons would kill at least 2.5 billion people or about half the global population. A simultaneous surface explosion of several tens of thousands of nuclear bombs would contaminate hundreds of millions of square kilometres with radioactive fallout. Scientists have established that nuclear war would inevitably precipitate climatic cataclysms such as the onset of a global "nuclear winter".

This means that never before has mankind been faced with such an urgent task of normalising the international situation and of creating effective safeguards against the slide towards nuclear-missile war as today. Nevertheless, the world keeps spending up to a trilion dollars on weapons every year, while 800 million people are starving and 900 million remain illiterate. The arms build-up continues, although the existing nuclear arsenals are sufficient for annihilating 58 billion people or twelve times more than the present population of our planet. Moreover, today the world is on the brink of the arrival of fundamentally new types of weapons and of the extension of the arms race to space.

The war danger is a threat of global magnitude. The Atlantic has polluted not only itself, but also the Pacific and Indian Oceans". These words by the late Indian Prime Minister Smt. Indira Gandhi very accurately reflect the danger to universal peace posed by the militarist thinking of the US administration which sees our planet only as a combination of war theatres, where the Asian-Pacific region, according to Washington's designs is second in importance after Europe.

Throughout the whole postwar period Asia practically has not known a single more or less lengthy spell of peace and stability. Seats of tension and fierce conflicts have sprung up on the territory of the continent where nearly two-third of the world population are living, causing innumerable troubles and suffering to the local peoples and distracting them from the settlement of their pressing problems.

Among the primary causes of the complicated relations among various Asian and Pacific states one should certainly mention the specific character of their historical development. There is probably no other region on the Planet with neighbouring states having such disparity in the levels of economic development and such great difference in socio-economic systems, culture, religion and traditions.

And yet the main cause of unabating tension in Asia is the continuing interference in the affairs of the Asian states by the imperialists seeking to turn the Asian-Pacific region into an arena of confrontation with socialism and with national liberation forces.

The United States has repeatedly tried to rope various Asian countries into its military adventures. Today, Washington is placing a major stake on the involvement of Asian and Pacific states in the so-called Strategic Defense Initiative (SDI) which is commonly known as the Star Wars programme. In its political and propaganda campaign aimed at selling SDI to Asia, the United States actively employs both old and new arguments. These include the assurances that the weapons systems which may appear as a result of the work under the SDI programme will be exclusively defensive and non-nuclear and will eliminate missiles instead of people. There is also a popular argument that the economics of Asian states can supposedly drive great benefit from the technological spin-off resulting from the research and development for the needs of the Star Wars programme. Very indicating in this respect is the report "Strategic Defence Initiative Prospects for Asia" which was released in the beginning of March this year by the Asian Studies Centre of the ultra-conservative American outfit called the Heritage Foundation which has the dubious honour of being one of political "midwives" of the Star Wars programme. The report alleges, among other things, that SDI will considerably bolster up the US deterrence forces deployed in the Pacific region, will reduce the threat of Soviet nuclear blackmail of the American allies in Asia and will become a noticeable contribution to the consolidation of security in the region as a whole.[1]

The Asia-Pacific region witnessed the first use of atomic weapons when, in 1945, the US dropped the bomb on the Japanese cities of Hiroshima and Nagasaki. In Asia, in the '60s, the US waged large-scale chemical warfare against the patriots of Vietnam.

US hydrogen bombs were first tested in Pacific islands in the '50s, as were weapons for future space wars. In October 1959 a missile launched from a B-47 bomber intercepted *Explorer*-6, an artificial satellite. In the '60s, in Pacific islands, the US was the first to set up two ground anti-satellite system; in 1963 on Kwajalein Atoll using Nike-Zeus anti-missiles, and in 1964 on Johnston Island employing modified Thor-Agenas. Numerous missiles were launched to intercept target satellites.

According to statements by the US Chief of Joint Staff, Admiral William J. Crows, the Asia-Pacific region now has the role of a "frontline" in SDI plans.

Since 1971 the "zone of responsibility" of the United States Pacific Command (PACOM) has embraced the Pacific and Indian Ocean basins-100 million square miles or half the Earth's surface. A huge military machine has been set up there by the US and associated countries. The second largest group of US general-purpose forces (after-Europe) is deployed in the Pacific. It Includes 4,74,000

1. *See* Gleb Ivashentsev. *Asia and the "Star Wars"* Plans. New Delhi, Allied, 1986, pp. 1-28.

men, 200 warships and over 1,100 combat planes. A special role is given to naval, forces, especially the US Seventh Fleet, 340 carrier-based aircraft.

The Far East is the location of over 300 military bases and facilities, including 32 in Japan, 40 in South Korea and 11 in the Philippines. Up to 1,50,000 US servicemen are billeted there.

As William Arkin, director of the Washington Institute for Policy Studies, has noted, the US Pacific nuclear buildup is seen by the Reagan administration as a top priority. *Tomahawak* cruise missiles, largely to be nuclear-tipped, have begun to be deployed, in addition to the 400 Seventh-Fleet nuclear ammunition. According to foreign press data, nuclear delivery vehicles loom at US bases in Japan, South Korea, and the Philippines. The US administration's focus no inter-mediate range weapons attests to a wager on local nuclear war-limited, for example, to the Far Eastern theatre of operations. Tinian, one of the Mariana islands, has been made a nuclear warhead depot. Kwajalein Atoll is a large military base; its lagoon is being used for ICBM tests. An atomic submarine base is to be set up in the Palau islands.

A big US force exists in the Indian Ocean : about 30 military bases, including the major one on Diego Garcia in the ocean's centre. UP to 180 combat planes (80 nuclear-capable) operate from US carriers there. The number of US warships exceeds 60, including 2 carriers, 5 cruisers and 3 atomic submarines. Everything bespeaks of US plans to establish control over the Strait of Malacca, the gateway from the Pacific to the Indian Ocean.

There are contingency plans for ship transfers from the Mediterranean Sea and the Pacific, to quickly add to US Indian Ocean naval power, both in amount and qualitatively. Washington continues to take practical steps to create a 50-warship-strong Fifth Fleet (including carriers) there. Combined with the Mediterranean's Sixth and Pacific's Seventh, this fleet will threaten the whole of Eurasia from the south.

Washington wants to enlist its allies, especially NATO members, in its Indian Ocean military buildup. One can already speak of 2-3 British destroyers, frigates and auxiliary ships permanently stationed there, plus regular calls of a British task force, including a carrier and escort ships. A permanent French naval group of 8-9 combat ships is also there. There have been periodic visits by FRG warships since 1980.

The new US-led "multilateral Asia-Pacific military-political structure" will have a particular role for Japan, which is becoming increasingly involved in the global aggressive strategy of Washington. US and Japanese top leaders miss no opportunity to stress the "special partnership" of the two countries and their shared foreign-policy aims and military objectives. In January 1983 Nakasone's government officially sanctioned Japanese war technology transfers to the US, and in November of the same year an inter-governmental agreement fixed a transfer procedure and provided for a bilateral *ad hoc* commission to this end. By identifying themselves more and more with the US life, Japan's ruling circles hope through political and military concessions to alleviate the trade and economic contradictions: Japan's 1985 record 45-billion-dollar surplus in trade with the US has greatly antagonised the Americans.

Tokyo has been among the first to endorse the stationing of US intermediate-range nuclear missiles in Europe, to back Washington's plans to extend the arms face to outer space and declare readiness to co-operate in their implementation. The newspaper *Asahi*, commenting on the government's attitude to the Star Wars programme, wrote that Premier Nakasone had of late been increasingly shifting from "understanding" to open support of the US stand. "We are concerned", it said editorially, "that the Premier is demonstrating readiness by practical steps to back and Star Wars programme, including the provision of Japanese technology to the US for these purposes".

This involves the US administration's intensions to gain access to the Japanese work in optical electronics and milimetre-band large-scale information transmission, which must lay the foundation for the "nerve centre" of a future network of US military spacecraft in orbit. The Japanese press suggests that Tokyo is also likely to accept a part of the financial cost of the expensive space armaments. By drawing Tokyo into military-technological co-operation under SDI, the US would like to significantly weaken Japan's competitiveness in civilian branches (the area of world rivalry between the two countries' monopolies) and correct unfavourable mutual-trade balance.

Although Japan under Article 9 of its Constitution renounces the use of war as a means of settling disputes, as well as threats to use force, and, in accordance with the "three non-nuclear principles", has committed itself not to possess or manufacture or import nuclear weapons, the world's fifth largest "nuclear support" system is located on its territory. This system ensures control, communication and the gathering of intelligence for US air-and sea-based nuclear forces.

In line with the US "forward-base strategy", Japan's zone of responsibility covers a triangle limited by the sea routes from Tokyo to Guam Island and from Osaka to the Philippines. Japanese and US forces will jointly block the international Tsugaru, Korea and La Perouse Straits in an "emergency", and the aim is not concealed : to lock Soviet naval ships in the Sea of Japan.

Co-operation between the Japanese "self-defence forces" and their US partners is regulated by the "guiding principles" adopted in 1978 by the Japanese cabinet without a public or parliamentary discussion. It includes the holding of joint reconnaissance operations, logistics and the provision by Japan of various facilities to the US armed forces "in the case of a situation in the Far East outside Japan which will have an important influence on Japan's security".

The first step towards integrating communications, as well as data collection and processing between the US and Japan has been to reinforce joint operations among the three Japanese fighting arms, each of which earlier acted autonomously. There has to be an improvement in the communication systems. The new drive for mutual standardisation between the US and Japanese services will secure communication between F-15 fighters, destroyers and anti-submarine patrol places. In 1984 Japan's National Defence Agency launched its new underground Command Computing Centre in Tokyo, the nerve centre of the naval, air and land forces. Though the national legislation of the Japan and a special parliamentary resolution of 1969 evisages the development and use of Japanese artificial Earth satellites exclusively for peaceful purposes, these principles are being constantly violated. For example, when Japanese warships intercommunicate through US ship-to-ship communication satellites, the Defence Agency of Japan asserts that these principles are not applicable here since the satellites are the property of the United States, not of Japan.

In the opinion of the Stockholm International Peace Research Institute (SIPRI), the updating of Japan's reconnaissance and communication system aims to "provide wartime survivability and endurance to fight and control a nuclear conflict and to facilitate the successful use of nuclear weapons."

The line of militarising Japan and getting it into Washington's SDI scheme meets with growing public protest at home. A 1985 national opinion poll has shown only 14.2 per cent support for increased arms spending, as against 54.1 per cent in favour of the previous relatively low level. Highly influential political forces of Japan oppose SDI. Millions of Japanese are peace supporters. Nuclear-free zones have been declared in 900 Japanese cities, towns and villages, which total over half the country's population. All this reflects a desire truly to denuclearise Japan, thus contributing to the full removal of nuclear weapons from the face of the Earth.

The entire US military-strategic set up in Asia and the Pacific and Indian Oceans is being enlisted in SDI realisation. At the end of 1984, the Press Trust of India reported a US military buildup in the Indian Ocean driven by the development and sophistication of anti-satellite and space wars technology. US Defence Secretary Weinberger also mentioned Indian Ocean anti-satellite installations in a congressional debate on the arms budget for 1985. The nuclear-missile base on Diego Garcia is being expanded and updated. A space tracking station is being built there, one of SDI's big five. Hence also new functions for the US Air Force satellite tracking station at Mahe in the Seychelles.

US base in the Far East and the Pacific also accommodate weapons, equipment and communication systems for Star Wars in increasing quantities. This involves the tracking stations in South

Korea – at Chagsan, Pohang and Osan ; communications centres, including the satellite ones in Japan—at Yokota, Kadena, Kami Seya and Camp Zama ; and the Subic Bay naval and Clark Field air bases in the Philippines, the largest outside the US. All these centres are part of the US Pacific Command's integrated satellite communication system "Commando Lion". In Australia, where a whole complex of US naval and air bases and communication centres is located, special mentions is made of the station at Nurrugar which processes the date from spy satellite, including the *Big Bird* and KH-11. US expert James Bamford suggests that this satellite communication centre also receives signals from infrared warning devices for detecting ballistic missiles exhausts.

"These facilities are very important", explains Dr. Robert Harkevy, US specialist on military bases from Pennsylvania State University. "They are the guts of the nuclear system".

Essentially, SDI gives a new impetus to shoring up this US "nuclear system" in the Asia-Pacific region. But only a person who is not versed in world affairs may seriously believe that the aim is purely defensive. Washington is creating a machine of aggression there, directed against the socialist countries, the non-aligned states and the forces of national liberation.

"The realisation of the Star Wars scheme poses a direct threat to the Asian and Pacific countries. First, there is greater danger that these countries may be drawn into a US-Soviet nuclear conflict against their will as a large part of SDI military capability is located on their territory or near their borders. Besides, there is the higher risk of various tragic accidents which will become more likely with more computerised decision-making and larger amounts of lethal equipment on the Earth and in outer space.

Second, is there a guarantee that the United States will resist the temptation to use SDI military capability against a country of the region if Washington suddenly decides, as it frequently did in the past, that some elements in the policy of that country "contradict US vital interests" ?

Third, the exceptional contagiousness of a "virus of aggression" should be remembered. If Uncle Sam continues to assert his world interests by the first-law method, minor predators inevitably will suit. Consequently, implementing SDI will badly aggravate the problem of regional conflicts.

Fourth, the overall rise in political and military tension in the area will destabilise and disrupt international economic ties.

Each of these questions merits separate discussion.

The concept of Asian security is designed to take full account of the realities of the present nuclear-missile era. These realities, as noted above, have not bypassed the Asian continent.

"In this nuclear age", Prime Minister Rajiv Gandhi has emphasized, "peace is the basic yearning of all peoples of the world. Yet at no time in history has the danger to peace been greater. This danger comes from the very weapons that have been developed in the name of security. The stockpiles are growing. It is a good sign that there is repeated public expression of a desire to reduce and eliminate nuclear weapons. The onus of disarmament is that of the nuclear-weapon powers. But can any other nations remain unconcerned ? There can be no greater leveller and decimator than a nuclear war. Nuclear death will not inspect people's passports. It will not care for nationality as it will not care for life."

Emanating from imperialism's militarist policy, the growing nuclear threat in Asia requires that the concept of Asian security includes a complex of such commitments and measures as a pledge by all the nuclear powers not to be the first to use nuclear weapons in Asia or elsewhere in the world or to use nuclear weapons against non-nuclear countries and regions in Asia ; adoption by non-nuclear weapon states of the three non-nuclear principles— not to possess, not to produce, and not to allow nuclear weapons on their territory ; signing of the Treaty on the Non-Proliferation of Nuclear Weapons by those Asian states which have not yet done so ; and a complete halt to all nuclear-weapon tests in Asia and in the Indian and Pacific Oceans.

As for the Soviet Union, it consistently abides by these obligations in its policy in Asia as well as on other continents. Its efforts are directed, despite imperialist intrigues, at averting a nuclear arms race in Asia, at preventing the continent from becoming an arena of nuclear rivalry.

The Asian nations are highly appreciative of the fact that at the Second Special Session of the UN General Assemby on Disarmament in June 1982, the Soviet Union declared its commitment not to be the first to use nuclear weapons. Significantly China has also undertaken such a commitment. If the tantamount to a total ban on the use of nuclear weapons.

As early as 1978 the Soviet Union declared that it would never use nuclear weapons against those states which had renounced the production and acquisition of nuclear weapons and had no such weapons on their territory. The Soviet Union also expressed its willingness to conclude a special agreement on this issue with any such non-nuclear state.

It is relevant to mention that a number of Asian nations voiced anxiety about the deployment of SS-20 missiles in the Asian part of the Soiet Union. In taking that step the Soviet Union was guided solely by defence considerations. Speaking on French television in October 1985, the Soviet leader Mikhail Gorbachev emphasized: "We have as many missiles in Asia as we need to balance the corresponding potential of the Union States in that region—neither more, nor less. If the Union States does not increase the number, we shall not do so either. If the situation changes for the better, we shall react accordingly."

Asian security is not impaired by the USSR's retaliatory measures in response to the network of military bases speardheaded against the Soviet Union and other socialist countries built by the United States. As was pointed out at the 27th Congress of the CPSU, the practical solution of questions pertaining to the military balance in Asia is envisaged by the Soviet disarmament programme at the relevant stage.

Of significant importance to Asia is the commitment of the nuclear powers to prevent the proliferation of nuclear weapons in any form. Thanks to the USSR's efforts, the 1968 Treaty on the Non-Proliferation of Nuclear Weapons, which has more than 130 signatories, including the majority of Asian nations, has come into force.

But there are some 30 states which have not signed the treaty, including two nuclear powers - China and France. The Zionist state of Israel reportedly has a nuclear arsenal of its own; Pakistan is trying to manufacture the first "Islamic", atomic bomb. All this must be a source of serious concern among the neighbours of these countries.

The revelation that the Israelis by dint of their nuclear stockpile rank sixth among nuclear weapons nations will not shock as much as it will cause dismay. Those who carefully followed the Israeli modus operandi in nuclear matters were aware a long time ago that Tel Aviv was bent on becoming a nuclear weapons power with the intension of dominating West Asia. Tell-tale reports of Israeli involvement in hijacking of nuclear fuel shipments; of clondestine "losses" of nuclear fuel from US facilities; the blatant attack on the Iraqi Osirak reactor outside Baghdad some years ago, were all pointers to things to come. It has now been revealed by a person who, it is claimed, had worked in an underground nuclear factory in Dimona which had been built by France and monitored for some time by the US time by the US before surveillance was withdrawn with the obvious intention of facilitating an ally's passage to the nuclear club, that Israel now has at least 100 nuclear weapons. It is significant that neither France nor the US had tried to prevent it from happening. If anything Washington, Britain and France have contributed to Israeli capability to deliver a nuclear bomload by air and with missiles through aircraft production programmes like the Mirage (from which Israel has built the Kfir and other derivatives), the supply of aircraft like the F-16 and of Lance missiles which cover all of West Asia. It has thus been an international conspiracy. For West Asia, its implications are obvious the US would like to impose stategic arrangements in the region which will ensure Israeli dominance. To that end it has subverted Arab sovereignty and is now engaged in trying to destroy the Palestine Liberation Organisation led by Yasser Arafat without whom, it has generally been agreed, there can be no peace in West Asia. US complicity in the proliferation of nuclear weapons (and attempts to sabotage the programmes for peaceful uses of nuclear energy by such developing countries as India) are underscored by its refusal to prevent the racist regime of South Africa from going nuclear (with Israeli collaboration) even after it was warned of a possible nuclear test in South Africa detected by a Soviet satellite. It explains the US administration's extreme reluctance to join international efforts to end racism there.[2]

Under the circumstances, US certificates of nuclear ractitude (which are mandatory under the Symington complacency. The US strategy for Asia is to boost Pakistan's conventional military capability under the guise of bolstering it against a Soviet invasion through Afghanistan and winking at Pakistan's attempts to join the club of nuclear weapons states of which, it is to belatedly acknowledged by the west, Israel is already a member. Whether it is bulding an "Islamic bomb" is also now a moot point, given the manner in which it allowed the Pan Am Karachi episode to appear as if Abu Nidal's group Palestinians, and therefore Libya, was responsible for the massacre. It would have been a useful excuse for the US Sixth Fleet to teach Libyan leader Muammer Gaddafi a second lesson. It is going to be Pakistan's bomb and it will, first of all, serve Pakistan's interests on the subcontinent.

J.R. Airemath, Indian ambassador and permanent representative to the International Atomic Energy Agency (IAEA), has observed that Israel's growing nuclear capability posed a serious threat to peace and security.[3]

In his address to IAEA's 30 the general conference at Vienna, Austria, which considered, among other things, Israel's nuclear threat and South Africa's capabilities, Hiremath said India was sympathetic towards the demand of Arab countries to impose a certain measure of international discipline on Israel with regard to its nuclear prowess.

He said strenuous efforts to compel Pretoria to bring its nuclear programme under scrutiny had led only to frustration because of the non-co-operative attitude adopted by that government.

2. Nuclear conspiracy, *Patriot* 8 October, 1986,4.
3. *The Times of India* (New Delhi) 7 October, 1986.

Hiremath cautioned that Israel's policies had led to the escalation of tension and it continued to occupy territories belonging to its neighbhours. Israel, he pointed out, had launched long-range attacks on sovereign Arab countries far from its borders such as Iraq and Tunisia.

This added an ominous and new dimension to its capability to destabilise or dominate the region, he said.

Hiremath said India acknowledged the existence of Israel as a state. However, Israel must withdraw from all Arab and Palestinian territories occupied by it, including Jerusalem.

Hiremath said Israel must also restore the inalienable rights of Palestinians including their right to a national state of their own and recognise the Palestine Liberation Organisation as the representative of the Palestinian people.

Unless these conditions were met it would be difficult to envisaged peace in West Asia, he said.

The Indian representative expressed satisfaction that even countries, willing to make allowances, had decided to increase sanctions against South Africa, which had raised unacceptable issues with regard to its semi-commercial enrichment plant.

Signing the Non-Proliferation Treaty (NPT) by states which have not yet done so would serve to strengthen stability on the Asian continent.

The Soviet Union has consistenly called for a quantitative freezing of nuclear weapons as an effective step towards reducing such weapons. The Asian states have been highly responsive to the initiative on this issue taken by the leaders of six countries—India, Argentina, Greece, Mexico, Tanzania and Sweden. Their initiative was set forth in a Declaration of 1984 and confirmed in the 1985 Delhi Declaration. It was highly commended in the Soviet Union. Unfortunately the United States and other western powers greeted it with hostility.

The USSR's unilateral cession of all nuclear explosions from August 6, 1985 to January 1987 found a broad response among the peace-loving forces of Asia. According to many press organs of the Asian countries, this important initiative was fresh testimony to the peaceful nature of Soviet foreign policy.

The Soviet leadership attached great importance to the joint message sent in October 1985 by the "Delhi Six" leaders to those of the USSR and the United States. In his reply to the leaders of these states Mikhail Gorbachev emphasized : "*It* (the message) *confirms that we have common goals, that your proposals as to the cessation of the arms race, particularly the nuclear arms race, and the prevention of the militarization of space are consonant with our approach.*" The Soviet Union indicated that it was prepared even then to sign a treaty banning all nuclear-weapon tests provided, of course, the United States and the other nuclear powers manifested the political will to take this important step.

Despite the fact that the United Sates did not join the Soviet moratorium on nuclear-weapon tests, in the beginning of 1986 the Soviet Union announced its prolongation for another three months, until March 1986. In reply to this goodwill gesture Washington carried out a nuclear explosion on March 22. As the *Daily* (Bombay) noted, the nuclear explosion carried out in Nevada in opposition to world public opinion was a shock to the international community. This move demonstrated beyond all doubt that US strategic course was directed at perfecting weapons of mass destruction. To counter that course the USSR and the non-aligned countries came out for a ban on nuclear weapons.

In March 1986 the Soviet Union said it would abide by its moratorium even after March 31 until the first American nuclear explosion. And although the United States did not stop their nuclear tests, on May 14, 1986 the Soviet Union decided to extend its moratorium on nuclear tests till August 6, 1986, the date on which more than forty years ago the first atomic bomb was dropped on the Japanese city of Hiroshima by the United States resulting in the death of hundreds of thousands of people. Thereby the Soviet Union again urged the United States to consider most responsibly the measure of danger looming over mankind, and to heed the opinion of the world community.

Peace-loving forces in Asia and the rest of the world express full support for the USSR's constructive approach to the Soviet-American talks on nuclear and space weapons held in Geneva, and especially for the Soviet proposal for agreeing on a total ban on space-based strike weapons and for a drastic cut in armaments capable of reaching each other's territory. The Asian nations are aware that progress at these talks will to a large extent determine the issue of Asian security.

The concept of Asian security necessarily presupposes refrainment by the Asian and Pacific states from participation in the plans to militarize outer space. There is growing awareness in the Asian countries that the creation of "Star wars" weapons, which is the aim of the US administration's Strategic Defense Initiative increases the danger of nuclear war and leads to destabilization of the situation in the world in general and in Asia in particular. Prime Minister Rajiv Gandhi sharply rebuked the Americans for claiming that the anti-missile weapon system being built in the United states was of a "peaceful" nature and promoted "greater security". "*We've heard such assertions before,*" he said, "*when submarines were being equipped with nuclear weapons, when cruise missiles and MIRVed intercontinental missiles weapons, were being deployed. The escalation of armaments leads to increased danger of war.*" The US Administration's programme came under criticism in China too.

The Asian nations welcome the Soviet leadership's assurances that Moscow will not be the first to deploy weapons in outer space, and that as an alternative to the US Administration's sinister "Star Wars" plans the Soviet Union is putting its "Star Peace" concept before the world community.

The programme for the complete elimination of nuclear and other types of weapons of mass destruction by the end of the present century, put forward on January 15, 1986 by Mikhail Gorbachev, is regarded in Asia as a valuable contribution to the joint search for a comprehensive approach to the formation of a system of security and lasting peace in that region.

The programme is consonant with the sentiments of the Asian nations, who have experienced the inhuman destructiveness of such weapons. It was precisely the peoples of Asian countries (Japan and Vietnam) who were once the targets of nuclear and chemical weapons.

Here are several authoritative opinions testifying to the massive response caused by the momentous Soviet initiative.

"*That Statement*," said Kim Il Sung, General Secretary of the Central Committee of the Workers' Party of Korea and President of the Democratic Republic, "*reflected the most cherished aspirations of the peoples of the whole world.*"

"*The realizations of the Soviet programme*," the Vietnamese leader Le Duan told the 27th Congress of the CPSU, "*will enable mankind to enter the 21st century with the hope of living in a world where war will stop being a means of resolving controversial issues in relations between countries.*"

"*Mikhail Gorbachev's Statement signifies an alternative to the nuclear arming of outer space : it is a search for realistic ways of liberating Earth from nuclear weapons*," Prime Minister Rajiv Gandhi noted.

"*Never before has a schedule for disarmament been drawn up as is now done in the proposals of Mikhail Gorbachev*"—commented the Chinese journal *Liao Wang* in its February 1986 issue.

During talks in January 1986 in Ulan Bator between Soviet Foreign Minister Eduard Shevardnadze and Mongolian leaders, the Mongolian side declared its unceasing support for the Soviet concept of a comprehensive approach towards ensuring peace and security in Asia, and observed that a most valuable contribution to its materialization were the all-embracing Soviet proposals for disarmament, promulgated on January 15, 1986. Their implementation would drastically change the Asian continent and raise security in that vast region of the world to a qualitatively new level.

The intensifying actions of the peace forces in the Asian nations against the imperialist policy of escalating the arms race, especially in nuclear weapons, and against the "Star Wars" plans of the United States, show that this region has been more and more actively joining the world wide movement to avert a thermonuclear catastrophe and prevent the threat of war from outer space.

Mikhail Gorbachev's August 18, 1986 statement on Soviet television extending the unilateral Soviet moratorium on nuclear tests till January 1, 1987 has evoked an enthusiastic response from all who cherish the cause of world peace. The Soviet moratorium was not only an invitation to the other side to follow suit but also an action indicating the seriousness of the Soviet programme for nuclear disarmament and the sincerity of the Soviet calls for a new policy based on realism, peace and co-operation.

One finds it hard to imagine what the United States is counting on, with respect to a summit it expects in November or December, if America is still planning, as its government has declared to tear up the SALT-Treaty. This means that the meeting is to take place a couple of weeks after or before this blow to the entire fibre or treaty-based relations between the two countries.

The impression is that the White House is keen, not to abide by the understandings reached in Geneva, but to demolish as much as possible before 1988 so that this administration's successors will find it difficult to restore anything.

This is undercutting SALT and sapping the ABM Treaty. This is varitable bulldozer syndrome.

The United States is eager to break out of all the treaty-based constraints, with both international law and international organisations also being increasingly regarded by it as a nuisance. An offensive is under way on the entire range of even the modest limitations on the arms race that have been set by the earlier treaties and efforts are being to scuttle even the very possibility of further talks.

Can the United States continue its current policy indefinitely without risking to blow up both itself and the rest of the planet ? And will the world community and the Americans themselves allow this policy to be maintained indefinitely ?

Stepping up the arms race by Washington and the entire NATO bloc towards a nuclear abyss permits no delay in taking major practical steps capable of sharply reversing the course of developments for the better. The Soviet leadership has repeatedly stated and proved this not only with proposals, but with deeds. One of the most vivid examples is the Soviet unilateral moratorium on nuclear tests, which Moscow has strictly adhered to in the course of a year and now has extended it to the first day of next year. "Our striving to transfer the course of international development to the tracks of detente," said Mikhail Gorbachev, "meets our philosophy, our socialist morality."

The Soviet Union, following a thorough and all-round analysis of the world situation, has come to the only possible conclusion for human reach : pre-nuclear thinking lost its significance at the moment when the poisonous mushroom of an atomic explosion rose above Hiroshima. Today, it is impossible to ensure one's own security without taking into account the security of other states.

The Soviet policy aimed at ending nuclear tests makes it possible to erect a strong barrier in the way of nuclear arms race. In brief, the Soviet Union proposes, without detriment to anybody's security, prohibition of nuclear explosions, putting an end of the perfection of nuclear weapons and to the development of its new destructive varieties, and thus beginning to move towards the abolition of all nuclear arsenals on earth. The question of reliable control over the verification of an agreement on ending explosions has ceased to be an obstacle. The Soviet Union has repeatedly declared that it does not object to international control either. The consent to the installation of American monitoring equipment in the USSR is a clear proof. But, unfortunately, Washington is stubbornly exploiting this problem, trying to conceal its unwillingness to disarm.

In deciding to extend the moratorium, the Soviet Union was well aware that during the period of moratorium the US continued underground nuclear explosions. And in the course of forty years the US had conducted far more nuclear tests than the USSR. So the Soviet Union had sufficient reasons for resuming its nuclear testing. And still it extended the moratorium. The logic here is simple : if there are no tests, the nuclear weapons which both sides have stockpiled in abundance will not be upgraded.

The moratorium the USSR introduced in August 1985 was welcomed by men of good will from all continents. World public opinion rightly saw in this step an example of the correct approach to modern problems, the way to avoiding a nuclear disaster.

When the moratorium expired on August 6, a considerable and authoritative section of the world community called upon the USSR to extend it and upon the US to join it. This call was made in the Mexican Declaration by leaders of six countries of four continents and also by the majority of the countries participating in the non-aligned movement. Politicians and public figures, individuals and organisations in many countries, including the United States and other NATO states asked Moscow not to resume nuclear testing and to give those who insist on underground nuclear explosions one more chance to see reason.

But forces are active in the US, which bank on a continuation of the arms race, see in it a bonanza and cherish the hope of weaning the Soviet Union down and provoking it into slamming the door.

"At the same time", said Mikhail Gorbachev, "we know with whom we are dealing. Therefore, the security of our country is sacred to us. This must be clear to all. This is a matter of principle."

So, after scrupulously weighing all pros and cons, the USSR extended the moratorium. The Soviet Union believes that the peoples of all countries and world public will correctly evaluate the prolonged silence on Soviet nuclear testing ranges.

"On behalf of the Soviet people, I an appealing to the wisdom and dignity of the Americans not to miss another historic chance on the way towards ending the arms race," "I am asking," continued Gorbachev, "US President Ronald Reagan to evaluate once again without bias the situation which has taken shape, to discard everything extraneous, cost off delusions about the Soviet Union and its foreign policy."

The Soviet Union is confident that agreements on ending nuclear tests can be reached speadily and signed this very year at the Soviet-American summit meeting. That even would, undoubtedly, become the main real outcome of the meeting, a considerably step towards ending the arms race. It would be a kind of prologue, said Mikhail Gorbachev, to further pregress at the talks on nuclear weapons and on their elimination, to a radical improvement of the whole situation in the world.

The United States appears to be unmoved by repeated Soviet gesture in extending its unilateral moratorium on nuclear tests. For the third time, Moscow has extended its moratorium this time upto January, 1987. This was not only in response to the apeal of the six-nation meeting at Mexico, but also to world public opinion which is increasingly concerned over the slide towards the point of no return.

Indeed, by carrying out a series of nuclear tests during the period of the moratorium, no doubt designed to develop space weapons under the SDI programme, Washington has shown scant regard for the growing world public opinion against the SDI and the nuclear arms race.

The US argument, apparently rejected even by US experts, is that the tests are needed to counter what Reagan calls "massive Soviet buildup." In any case, the State Department made it clear recently that test ban is a "long-term goal" as far the US in concerned. Are we then to presume that Washington has no plans to follow up the logic of the US-Soviet summit agreement to avoid a nuclear war ?

The summit clearly recognised that a nuclear war could not be won and must not be fought. "Recognising that any conflict between the USSR and the USA," the summit communique said, "could have catastrophic consequence, they emphasised the importance of preventing any war between them, whether nuclear or conventional". Surely, the world expected concrete steps from Washington. But there have been none. If there are any, they are negative and directed to "disarm" the Soviet Union in some way or other in vital areas of strategic defence.

It was because of this, that the six nations—India, Mexico, Greece, Argentina, Tanzania and Sweden—took up the initiative and appealed to both the major nuclear powers that the moratorium should be made mutual.

Earlier, the US objected to the cessation of nuclear tests on the ground of verification problems, though the USA and the USSR had perfect technical means for verification. It was then that the Soviet Union agreed to setting up onsite verification facilities. And now the six-nation group at their Mexico m eeting has offered to establish temporary monitoring stations at existing test sites and to operate them for an initial period of one year. What is the US response ? Washington now says that verification is not the main thing :

Indeed, the problems of verification has never been the main issue. The real cause for the US objection was mentioned in an official letter by the US Arms Control and Disarmament Agency to the US Congress on September 7, 1983. Claiming that a halt to nuclear weapons tests would not be "in the best interest of the USA" the letter admitted that "the nuclear tests are specially required for the development, modernisation, and certification of warheads." In other words, to develop space weapons.

The tragic accidents at the Chernobyl nuclear power plant at the launching of the U.S. Challenger space shuttle had shown once again how fragile is any security based on complex technology alone. That is why the Six declared at their Mexico meeting that if a repetition of Hiroshima on a global scale was to be prevented it was not merely more knowledge or new technologies which were needed, but more wisdom. They went on to point out that they could not accept that a few countries should decide the nuclear fate of the world.

The Soviet Union has put forward after the Second World War more than one hundred specific proposals in the UN and clesewhere to strengthen peace, prevent the arms race and for the reduction of arms. Most of these proposals are still relevant, including the fundamental one or complete disarmament. But the US response has always been negative.

The logic of the summit agreement should have led Washington to accept the Soviet proposal that each side undertake not to be the first to use nuclear weapons. But Washington has reserved the right to use force in certain circumstances. What is one to infer from this ? It means that the US has not given up the use of force in the pursuit of its foreign policy goals.

That is why Mikhail Gorbachev, while speaking on the extension of the moratorium till January 1987, gave a clear warning that the security of the USSR was dear to the Soviet people. "It would be wrong to hope to intimidate us," he said. And to those who are hoping to turn the strategic balance in their favour through the SDI programme, Gorbachev had an answer. He said that the USSR would not remain indifferent, but would take counter-measures, and added: "it will not be what the US expects, but will be the answer that will devalue the Star Wars programme."

Dr. N.P. Singh, a public personality of Nepal, Member of the Presidium of the World Peace Council, said: "The main goal of the Soviet initiative is removing the danger of being burned in a nuclear conflagration, which is hanging over mankind, and ensuring stable peace all over the world. That the Soviet Union has unilaterally extended its moratorium on nuclear tests is an indication of its goodwill and is a good example to other nuclear powers."

Vo Nguyen Yiap, Deputy Chairman of Vietnam Council of Ministers, referred to the Soviet Programme as a great Document of Peace. "The USSR," he said, "has again showed its readiness to start putting into practice the aspirations of all nations."

Commenting on the Soviet leader's Statement, Bangla Desh's Prof. Kabir Choudhry, eminent public figure and scientist, said: "As a representative of a developing country. I find it very important that the implementation of Soviet initiatives is likely to release astronomical sums, presently spent on military needs, to be used in aid to the developing countries for the benefit of entire mankind."

National newspapers of Asian countries, their radio and TV networks, and news agencies concentrate on those points of the statement which link the programme of nuclear disarmament with the issues of peace and security in various regions, including the Asian-Pacific region. The Soviet Peace Programme, a commentery of the UNI of India says, corresponds to the interests of all world nations, including Asian. It puts in the hands of the world community a universal instrument that can be used in the struggle not only for a peaceful future, but also for a future based on all achievements of progress.

Soviet peace initiatives are not confined to Soviet-American relations. They are meant to mark diarmament and detente available to every part of the world, every country and nation. They immediately concern Europe, where the positive process ushered in by the European Conference on Security and Co-operation (Helsinki, 1975) shall be consolidated and developed. They concern Asia was well. The Soviet Union sees its Peace Programme as its contribution to the all-round approach to Asian and Pacific security being elaborated.

Soviet peace initiatives deserve special examination as pertaining to Asia and the Pacific. Those initiatives do not counterpose one country or group of countries to another, and are not meant to isolate or boycott any. Their goal is to prevent a thermonuclear conflict in that part of the world, and incorporate it into the global process to eliminate nuclear danger and promote detente.

Not only the United States threatens, Asia and the Pacific with nuclear conflict. France is testing its nuclear weapons in the South Pacific. Isreal and South Africa have nuclear arsenals ;

Pakistan is about to acquire one. Not only Australia, Canada and Japan, but Indonesia, Iran, the Philippines, Thailand, South Korea and Taiwan will be able to manufacture or purchase nuclear weapons in the next decade, SIPRI experts hold.

The Soviet Union wants all Asian and Pacific countries not to contend for military superiority but to engage in peaceful co-operation based on mutually balanced interests. Highly indicative of that are the Soviet proposal to have the confidence-building measures active in Europe extended to the Far East, and the emphasis our country lays on non-use of nuclear weapons, nuclear test ban and non-participation of Asian and Pacific countries in the Star Wars project.

It is essential today to display mutual reserve and not to commit any action that would deteriorate the political situation in Asia and the Pacific. The policies of the US and its allies, however, may only increase tensions. To all appearances, certain political forces in the United States and Japan see inter-state contention as the only possible prospect for the region. To encourage that contention, they are trying to knock together the so-called Pacific Community, which might be eventually transformed into a closed regional grouping or one more military bloc.

"There is deep conviction in the Soviet Union that the establishment of large-scale co-operation on a basis of equality and mutual benefit of all countries of the Asian-Pacific region irrespective of difference in their social systems meet the basic interests of the countries of that part of the world and will promote a restructuring of international relations on an equitable, democratic basis. The USSR is ready to participate actively in such regional peaceful co-operation and to use for such purposes all the economic, scientific and technical potential at its disposal," says the Soviet Government Statement of April 23, 1985.

The nuclear disarmament programme suggested by the Soviet Union has another crucial aspect. The arms race eats up mammoth sums and material resources. To overcome the present confrontation trend and turn the world towards detente and disarmament means not only to give peace and security to humankind but to save tremendous extra resources for creation and development. This "Disarmament for Development" principle shall replace the reverse, Armament Instead of Development", imposed by militarism.

According to UN estimates, even a 10 per cent reduction of global war expenditures would save about 80 billion US dollars. If allocated to newly-free countries' development, the money would raise their fixed capital by about 30 per cent, and give a mighty impetus to the fight against famine, epidemics, child mortality, and other social evils. It takes only two billion dollars a years to implement all UN programmes in health care, environment protection, education, food and technical aid. Finance and material aid to developing countries' agriculture, which will eventually bring them to self-sufficiency in food supply, costs three billion. To provide enough drinking water for their entire populations would cost a billion a year, and to eliminate children's infectious diseases, about the same sum.

The United Nations has declared 1986 the Year of Peace, an important and responsible step, greeted by the world public.

Different countries, however, support it differently. Like most countries, the Soviet Union thinks that the Year of Peace must usher in new practical steps to stop the arms race, and turn the world from confrontation to detente.

The year 1985 was one of great hope—a hope that peace will be consolidated, an international relations improved. The spirit of Geneva is the name of that hope.

During the Geneva summit meeting between Mikhail Gorbachev and Ronald Reagan, the sides came to an understanding that nuclear and any other warfare has to be roled out in Soviet-American relations, and that there can be no victors in a nuclear conflict; that neither side will strive for military superiority. The Soviet and US leaders confirmed the understanding of January 8, 1985, according to which the Geneva talks were to be concerned about non-militarisation of space and reduction of nuclear arsenals on Earth.[4]

4. Gleb Ivashentsev. *op. cit.*

The Joint Soviet-American statement made in Geneva is not a treaty, of course. But Moscow sees it as an important principle-setting document making it obligatory for both the leaders to act accordingly. That was confirmed once again in the report of Mikhail Gorbachev, the Soviet leader, to the June 1986 Plenary Meeting of the CPSU Central Committee, where he put forward new large-scale Soviet initiatives to bridle the arms race. This viewpoint is not to the liking of some influential circles. The US monopoly capitalist Right-wingers see growing international tension as justification for military allocations, global ambitions, interference into other countries' affairs, and attacks on the rights and interests of the American working people. The recently adopted US military budget beats all records and envisages more expenditures on space military programmes. Target satellites were being launched for anti-missile weapon tests. Ever more underground nuclear tests are made. Characteristically, the US tried to vindicate SDI by saying that it would render nuclear weapons superfluous, while now it claims that nuclear devices were necessary to implement SDI. Will the year of Peace allow nuclear death into space ?

Chapter Thirteen

A WORLD OF UNITY

TO ENSURE PEACE and security in Asia through the joint efforts of the states concerned is a political concept which the Asian nations themselves devised, proceeding from their own historical experience. The very logic of the struggle to consolidate national independence and defend it against provocations and pressure on the part of imperialism and regional reaction suggested to them the necessity to co-ordinate and pool their efforts in the interests of peace in Asia.

Already in the second half of the 1940s, immediately after the Second World War, the developing states made an attempt to build the foundations for security in Asia. For instance, in the autumn of 1945 the Chairman of the Provisional Government of Vietnam, Ho Chi Minh, addressed a proposal to the Government of Indonesia pool the efforts of the two countries to combat colonialist intrigues and promote neighbourly co-operation in South-East Asia. The idea of forming an Asian Community designed to defend the political and economic independence of the devoloping states was put forward in 1947 by the leader of independent Burma, Aung San. The First Asian Relations Conference, held in the spring of 1947 in New Delhi and attend by enjoys from 27 states, marked a major even in the life of Asia. In his speech at the Conference Jawaharlal Nehru called for the creation of a "world of unity" in Asia.

In the early 1950s the peace forces in Asia managed to achieve significant results in their struggle against imperialism's armed intervention, to ensure on the continent—the flashpoints of military danger in Korea and Indo-China were extinguished. The documents of the 1954 Geneva Conference on Indo-China reflected the principles of peaceful settlement of differences and neighbourly co-operation between the countries of Asia.

India and the People's Republic of China (PRC) devised the Five Principles of Peaceful Co-existence (*Panch Sheel*) :

(1) Mutual respect for each other's sovereignty and territorial integrity;

(2) Non-aggression ;

(3) Non-interference in each other's internal affairs ;

(4) Equality and mutual benefit ;

(5) Peaceful co-existence. These principles, which were first formulated in 1954 in the preamble to the Indo-Chinese Agreement on Trade and Relations Between the Tibetan Region of China and India, became a reliable basis for restructuring international relations in Asia on a qualitatively new foundation in the interests of peace and security for all the Asian nations.

The historic Bandung Conferenee, held in April 1955, played a significant role in consolidating newly-independent countries of Asia. The convocation of the conference and the decisions it took were the logical results of the struggle waged by the newly-independent states against traditional colonialism and neo-colonialism.

Seeking to regain lost positions, the imperialist powers were set on launching a large-scale counter-offensive on the newly-independent countries and harboured various plans to suppress the national liberation movements.

Although the war in Indochina had ended by that time with the signing of the Geneva agreement of 1954 and a peace settlement had been achieved in Korea, the imperialist powers began to create, under the pretext of organizing a "collective security" system against communism, military alliances and blocs. They sought to make the yet-weak sovereign states join them, engaged in sabre-rattling on the borders of the socialist countries, sent troops to newly-independent countries, escalated international tension and provoked new armed conflicts.

The deterioration of the situation in Asia and Africa at that crucial time brought to the fore the task of relying all anti-imperialist and peace forces in the struggle against imperialism, colonialism and rascism and in difference of the sovereignty and the political and economic independence of the newly-liberated countries.

The Bandung Conference was to give answers to these and other crucial problems facing the peoples of Asia and Africa and provide them with guidelines in the struggle against the policy of Cold War and imperialist blocs and for peace and peaceful co-existence.

The convocation of the first Afro-Asian conference attracted public attention all over the world. The Soviet Union considered that conference not namely as a forum for discussion of problems of concern for Afro-Asian countries but also a potent weapon in the struggle against imperialism and colonialism and for peace and international security.

The majority of the participants rejected the imperialist thesis that countries could co-exist only on the basis of the "policy from strength" and that the principle of co-existence was "not clear" and even "dangerous". In spite of the desperate efforts of a number of pro-imperialist states to bury the principle of peaceful co-existence, the overwhelming majority of delegates supported that fundamental principle, consistently defended the cause of peace and rejected war and armed conflicts as a means of settling disputes. The participants demanded a ban on atomic and thermonuclear weapons and an end to the arms race.

The Bandung Conference was of historic importance. It showed that all Asian and African countries, regardless of their social system, could unite on the common platform of struggle for peace and international security. It also showed that different countries could waive their differences in the interest of co-operation, peace and international security.

The Bandung Conference not only recognized the five principles of peaceful co-existence but further elaborated them and united them in a coherent system which provided a political and legal basis for relations between states with different social systems. It adopted the Declaration on the Promotion of World Peace and Co-operation, which said that all nations should practise tolerance and live together in peace with one another as good neighbours and develop friendly co-operation on the basis of the following principles ;

1. Respect for fundamental human rights and for the purposes and principles of the Charter of the United Nations.
2. Respect for the sovereignty and territorial integrity of all nations.
3. Recognition of the equality of all races and of the equality of all nations-large and small.
4. Abstention from intervention or interference in the internal affair of another country.
5. Respect for the right of each nation to defend itself singly or collectively, in conformity with the Charter of the United Nations.
6. (a) Abstention fiom the use of arrangements of collective defence to serve the particular interests of any of the big powers.

   (b) Abstention by any country from exerting pressures on other countries.
7. Refraining from acts or threats of aggression or the use of force against the territorial integrity or political independence of any country.
8. Settlement of all international disputes by peaceful means, such as negotiation, conciliation, arbitration, or judicial settlement as well as other peaceful means of the parties' own choice, in conformity with the Charter of the United Nations,

9. Promotion of mutual interests and co-operation.

10. Respect for justice and international obligations.

The 10-point programme adopted by the Bandung Conference on the basis of the *Panchsheel* principles consolidated the legal foundations of the people's struggle for freedom and independence and provided guidelines for the struggle to make international relations more equitable. The 10-principles of the Bandung Conference were a major contribution to the cause of strengthening peace and security in Asia.

The non-aligned movement (NAM) which emerged in the early 1960s became an important form of unifying the developing nations. The ideas of Bandung were carried forward in the movement's multifaceted activities aimed at improving international relations and combating the aggressive, expansionist policy of imperialism and neo-colonialism.

The organization of *regional economic co-operation* in the mid-1960s was a new phenomenon in the international life of the Asian countries. In that period two regional organizations came into being in Asia : in 1964—the Organization for Economic Co-operation (OEC), comprising Turkey, Iran and Pakistan ; and in 1967—ASEAN (Association of South-East Asian Nations), which today has six members ; namely, Indonesia, Malaysia, Singapore, Thailand, the Philippines and Brunei.

The 1970s were marked by the outstanding victories of the forces of peace and national and social progress in Asia, such as the successful completion of the anti-imperialist struggle of the peoples of Inda-China and the formation in that region of independent states—the Social Republic of Vietnam, the Laotian People's Democratic Republic and the People's Republic of Kampuchea ; the triumph of the April Revolution of 1978 in Afghanistan and the anti-monarchy revolution of 1979 in Iran. The process of detente opened up the possibilities for positive advances in the system of international relations in the Asia-Pacific region as well.

The course of events in Asia in the 1980s demonstrated with fresh vigour that its nations will not put up with imperialist encroachment on their freedom and sovereignty, that their resolve to achieve peace is invincible.

An important factor in today's international relation is the non-aligned movement, which currently involves 101 states, about two-thirds of them in Asia. For nearly a quarter of a century now NAM has been fighting against imperialism and colonialism, for peace and freedom of the peoples.

The participants in the non-aligned movement denounce all imperialist doctrines aimed at justifying the build-up and deployment of armaments, especially nuclear weapons in various parts of the world. Being aware that catastrophic consequences to world civilization would ensue from a nuclear war, they are vitally interested in having the funds now wasted on armaments used for peaceful development.

Adherence to the fundamental principles of the non-aligned movement was demonstrated at the Seventh Conference of Heads of State or Government of Non-Aligned Countries (New Delhi, March 1983). The Conference brought out the unity of the movements members in their demand for a lasting and just peace, in their repulsion of imperialist intrigues against developing states and national liberation movements, including those in Asia.

The Delhi Conference frustrated the attempts by imperialism and international reaction to exploit the heterogeneity of the NAM to hamper the non-aligned countries' co-operation with the socialist states. In their speeches, many delegates to the Conference, including those from Asian states, exposed the false thesis imposed on the non-aligned countries that argues that the movement should oppose the "policy of the two superpowers" and not the aggressive policy of imperialism.

Both the developing and socialist countries need peace to tackle their constructive tasks. And this is quite a strong reason for continuing to pool their efforts in the struggle for international security. As is increasingly made evident by international experience, the solidarity of the socialist and non-aligned countries in the struggle for peace, and for the establishment of genuinely equitable and mutually beneficial co-operation between nations, is an effective resistance to imperialism's militarist course in Asia and other parts of our planet.

In response to the increased aggressiveness of imperialism and regional reaction in the eighties, many Asian nations came forward with a complex of substantive initiatives. They apply to practically all regions of the continent—South and South-East Asia, the Middle and Far East, and also to the adjoining areas of the Indian and Pacific Oceans. The essence of these proposals (they were advanced on a national, regional and on a broader international scale) is the desire of the Asian nations to turn the principle of renunciation of the use of force in interstate relations in Asia into a law of international life, in order to solve Asia's most acute problem—the elimination of the hotbeds of tensions—and work for a political settlement of the protracted international conflicts.

Certainly to erase the tensions and current differences is possible only if the legitimate interests of all concerned parties are fully and justly considered, and, of course, it is necessary to have a political basis for settlement which does not infringe on these interests. There must also be a negotiating mechanism suitable for each specific conflict. It is highly significant that thanks to the joint efforts of the socialist and non-aligned states, the appropriate political platforms for achieving a just settlement of nearly all the present regional and bilateral conflicts in Asia already exist or are being elaborated. The appropriate negotiating mechanisms either exist or can be set up. This emphasizes the constructive and realistic nature of the initiatives which were advanced by the Asian states who stand for the consolidation of peace on the continent.

An important place in the complex of these initiatives rightly belongs to the proposal, *put forward by the Mongolian people's Republic* in 1981, *to elaborate and conclude a convention on mutual non-aggression and non-use of force in relations between states in Asia and the Pacific.* To discuss and co-ordinate the specific clauses of the convention it is proposed that a conference of Asian and Pacific states be convened with the participation of the permanent members of the

UN Security Council (the USSR, the United States, Britain, France and China). The convention could carry forward and endorse, with reference to the concrete situation in the region, the relevant clauses of the UN Charter and UN resolutions on renunciation of the use of force. It should highlight the clauses from among those that stipulate effective steps to be taken by the participating states to lower the level of military confrontation, curb armaments and promote disarmament. The realization of this initiative of Mongolia, which has evoked great interest in many Asian countries, would undoubtedly constitute a major move toward ensuring peace and security on the Asian continent.

The constructive foreign policy of the Korean People's Democratic Republic makes a valuable contribution to the improvement of the situation on the Korean Peninsula, in the Far East as a whole and to the creation of favourable conditions for effecting the peaceful and democratic reunification of Korea. The peace-loving countries of Asia are giving increasing support to the important initiatives of the Korean People' Democratic Republic aimed at achieving a political settlement of the Korean problem, as well as to its proposal on signing a peace treaty to replace the existing ceasefire agreement, on adopting a Declaration Non-Aggression between North and South, on a mutual reduction of armed forces, and on turning the Korean Peninsula into a nuclear free zone.

An International Conference for Denuclearisation and Peace on the Korea Peninsula was held in Pyongyang in the first week of September 1986. Comrade Kim Il Sung delivered at a banquet given on September 6, 1986 in honour of 'participants to the Conference.

"In the south of the Military Demarcation Line, there are more than 40,000 US troops equipped with nuclear weapons and nearly one million South Korean soldiers. The tension and the danger of nuclear war on the Korean Peninsula are the direct products of the United States Korea policy and Asia strategy. The United States has brought into the small land of South Korea a great amount of nuclear weapons, an amount which is four times as large as it has in the NATO area in terms of the density of nuclear deployment. Not satisfied with this, the United States is going to ship more or new types of nuclear and chemical weapons into South Korea in the future and build scores of special nuclear armouries there.

"Our fair and reasonable peace proposals, including the proposal for tripartite talks to replace the Korean Armistice Agreement with a peace agreement and adopt a non-aggression declaration between the north and the south, have already been widely known to the people of the world.

As long as the United States Korea policy and Asia strategy remain unchanged and as long as the US keeps its troops in South Korea, resorting to manoeuvres for aggression, it is impossible to guarantee durable peace on the Korean Peninsula and settle the question of the reunification of our country. If we are to ease the tension and guarantee peace on the Korean Peninsula and settle Korea's reunification question in a peaceful way, we must get all the nuclear arms and the US troops withdrawn from South Korea. If the US troops are complelled to withdraw from South Korea and a nuclear-free, peace zone is established on the Korean Peninsula by the joint struggle of our people and the progressive people throughout the world, one of the most dangerous sources of nuclear war in the world will be removed and great progress will be made in preserving peace in Asia and the world. If the people throughout the world who love peace and justice are closely united, they can be invincible and, by their united efforts, frustrate the imperialists' moves for a nuclear war and defend-peace. By forming a broad united front and vigorously conducting the anti-war, anti-nuclear, peace movement, all the peace-loving people of the world must check the imperialists' reckless manoeuvres to build up nuclear arms and militarise outer space, and must realise complete nuclear disarmament and frustrate their scheme of aggression and war, which is becoming more blatant with every passing day. Working for peace is a consistent foreign policy of the workers' Party of Korea and the Government of the Republic. Our party and Government will, in the future too, resolutely fight to prevent nuclear war and preserve peace in firm unity with the peoples of socialist countries, non-aligned nations and all the peace-loving people throughout the world, under the unfurled banner of independence, friendship and peace."

The constructive efforts of the South-East Asia countries to promote a political settlement of the region's controversial issues and to establish there lasting peace and stability are finding growing support in Asia and beyond. Special mention should be made of the fact that three states of Indo-China Vietnam-Kampuchea—greatly contribute to the creation of an atmosphere of good-neighbourliness, trust and co-operation in South-East Asia. At the biannual conferences of their Foreign Ministers held since 1980, these countries always advance constructive proposals aimed at turning South-East Asia into a zone of peace and co-operation.

The countries of Indo-China declare their readiness to participate in an international conference on peace and security in South-East Asia support the ASEAN countries proposal to turn that region into a nuclear-free zone, with to improve relations with China on the principles of peaceful coexistence. Vietnam, Loas and Kampuchea, in order to implement the accords possible between them and the ASEAN countries, call on the permanent members of the UN Security Council to participate in guaranteeing these accords. Desiring to promote the normalisation of the situation in South-East Asia and to create there a zone of peace, good-neighbourliness and co-operation, the Soviet Union has announced its willingness to participate jointly with the other permanent members of the UN Security Council in guaranteeing such accords.

In response to the ASEAN countries' proposal that talks be held on normalizinng the situation around Kampuchea, the states of Indo-China have emphasized that the question of who exactly will attend the talks is especially important. Kampuchea is willing to enter into negotiations with the various Khmer groupings based abroad with the exception of the criminal Pot pot clique that exterminated a third of the country's population.

In 1985, Vietnam and Kampuchea announced their intention to complete the stage-by-stage withdrawal of the Vietnamese volunteer units from Kampuchea by 1990 (From 1982 to 1986 units of Vietnamese volunteers, having returned home).

At least 12th Conference of Foreign Ministers of Vietnam, Laos and Kampuchea, confirming their previous proposals, these states declared that the solution of the problem around Kampuchea would both help to ensure lasting peace in South East Asia and to reach an agreement on setting up a zone of peace and stability there. The Conference's communique commended the 1985 meeting between the Foreign Ministers of Vietnam and Indonesia, and expressed the readiness of the three countries of Indo-China to negotiate with Thailand, on the basis of the principles of peaceful coexistence, solutions to the problems in their relations.

The proposals of Vietnam, Laos and Kampuchea map out a clear-out political framework for promoting neighbourly relations between the ASEAN countries and the states of Indo-China. A basis for such relations has been gradually taking shape, and certainly they themselves can set up the mechanism for the relevant talks. But what is important is that they not be prevented from reaching agreement.

"*The world needs peace ; peace is essential to every continent and in every ocean*," Le Duan, General Secretary of the Vietnamese Communist Party's Central Committee, told the 27th Congress of the Commnnist Party of the Soviet Union (CPSU), "*It's time to get a dialogue started between the states of Indo-China and the member countries of ASEAN so as to solve the problems existing between them. South-East Asia should be turned into a zone of peace, stability, friendship and co-operation.*"

The proposal, put forward by the non-aligned coastal states of the Indian Ocean, that that region be declared a zone of peace free of foreign military bases and threats to the security, independence and sovereignty of those countries, still remains on the agenda of world politics. Supported by the United Nations, this proposal was adopted as the Declaration of the Indian Ocean as a Zone of Peace in 1973.

Today the efforts to create such a zone in the Indian Ocean rest on the convening of an international conference sometime before 1988 in order to discuss this issue as per the decision of the 40th Session of the UN General Assembly (1985).

The Soviet Union's constructive stand on the Indian Ocean area is well known to Afro-Asian nations, particularly its support for the efforts of the non-aligned countries to set up a peace zone there. The Soviet Union expressed its willingness many times to resume the 1977-78 talks on limiting military activities in the Indian Ocean. which were broken off by the United States. But Washington pursued different aims. At the same time that US representatives were involved in negotiations, the Pentagon completed a plan for the strategic development of the Indian Ocean, and for the five-year period from 1981 to 1985 allocated 30,000 million dollars for this purpose.

The Soviet Union's 1980 proposal regarding the Gulf area received worldwide attention. Its provisions guaranteed that the non-aligned status chosen by the states in the area would be respected, that the nuclear powers would refrain from drawing these states into military groupings with their participation and also refrain from building military bases or deploying nuclear weapons there.

The Soviet Union strives for military methods of solving interstate problems to be also excluded from Asia and for the complex development of the continent not to be further complicated by threats and the use of force on the part of imperialism and hegemonistic tendencies. The Soviet policy in Asia is a policy of strengthening peace, of resolute resistance to the enemies of peace, solidarity with all forces of social progress. It is a line of peaceful co-existence, co-operation and good neighbourly relations with all states interested.

With the aim of spreading the process of detente to the Asian continent, the Soviet Union proposed in the late 1960s the idea of ensuring security by collective efforts of the states of the continent. At the same time, the Soviet Union stresses its readiness to take a very attentive approach to all proposals proceeding from the endeavour to safeguard lasting peace and security in Asia and from the viewpoint that this peace and security have to be ensured by collective efforts.

The Soviet initiative put forward during the Indo-Soviet summit meeting in 1982 also remains valid. The Soviet Union proposed then that while waiting for an international conference on the issue of declaring the Indian Ocean a zone of peace, all states whose ships sail in that ocean should refrain from taking any steps capable of complicating the situation. This proposal was reconfirmed by the Soviet side at the Indo-Soviet summit talks in May 1985. The joint statement on the results of Prime Minister Rajiv Gandhi's visit to Moscow expressed from Soviet support for the speediest possible implementation of the UN Declaration of the Indian Ocean as a Zone of Peace, as desired by India and other non-aligned states.

The first conference of the leaders of seven South Asian countries (India, Bangladesh, Bhutan, the Republic of Maldives. Nepal, Pakistan and Sri Lanka) held in December 1985 in Dacca. Bangladesh, marked a major event in the life of the South Asian states. It founded a new regional organization in Asia, namely, the South Asian Association for Regional Co-operation (SAARC). Its Charter emphasizes that co-operation among the countries of South Asia must be founded on the principles of sovereign equality, territorial integrity, political independence, non-interference in the internal affairs of other countries, and mutual benefit. It was noted that the purpose of the Association is to promote peace, stability, friendship and progress in South Asia through the strict observance of the principles of the UN Charter and of the non-aligned movement.

It is hoped that SAARC's formation will open up the way to good-neighbourliness and co-operation among the South Asian nations, and that it will help to improve the situation in the Indian Ocean zone, in Asia, in the Pacific and the world in general.

A sovereign, non-aligned state against which a large-scale co-ordinated armed intervention, primarily from the territory of Pakistan, is being perpetrated—would definitely enhance Asian security. This could be achieved through the realization of the constructive proposals put forward by the Government of the Democratic Republic of Afghanistan, which provide for a complete and unconditional cessation of armed and any other kind of interference in the internal affairs of the country with guarantees that this not be resumed.

The Soviet Union backs Afghanistan's efforts to protect its sovereignty, and would like to withdraw its limited contingent of troops stationed there at the request of the Afghan Government. The time-limit for a stage-by-stage withdrawal has already been agreed upon with Afghanistan, and it was effected from October 15, 1986.

CHAPTER FOURTEEN

THE COMMON SEARCH

THE ENTIRE HISTORY of the Soviet Union's foreign policy, including in Asia, convincingly show the USSR's solidarity with all the forces of national and social progress and its determination to strengthen peace and give a firm rebuff to those who are against the security and sovereign rights of nations.

Way back in 1920 the great Lenin wrote that the tasks of Soviet foreign policy in Asia "are the same as in Europe: peaceful coexistence with all peoples, with the workers and peasants of all nations awakening to a new life—a life without exploiters".

The principles of friendship and equality formed the basis of the first treaties which the Land of the Soviets signed with its neighbours in 1921—Iran, Afghanistan, Turkey and Mongolia. The first foundations of peace and stability in a substantial part of the Asian continent were thereby laid in those early days.

In the early 1930s, when the clouds of military threat began to gather thickly over Asia, the USSR proposed to Japan and China the signing of non-aggression pacts, and called for a Pacific pact to be signed by the Soviet Union, the United States, China and Japan. At the international conference convened in Brussels in 1937 by decision of the League of Nations, the Soviet delegation demanded the application of collective sanctions against Japan for its acts of aggression towards China. Regretfully, all these Soviet initiatives came up against a wall of silence opposed by those to whom they were addressed. Had they been realized, a solid barrier would have stood in the way of the aggressor.

In the postwar period the Soviet Union, jointly with the developing states, stepped up its efforts to consolidate peace in Asia. The world knows the constructive role of the USSR as the initiator and active participant in a number of major international conferences and agreements aimed at ensuring peace in various parts of the Asian continent. Among them are the Geneva Conferences of 1954 (on a settlement in Korea and Indo-China) and of 1962 (on Laos), the Tashkent Meeting of 1966, the International Conference of 1973 on Vietnam, the Geneva Peace Conference of 1973 on the Middle East, etc.

In the late 1960s and early 1970s the Soviet Union advanced the idea of safeguarding security in Asia by its countries and peoples having relations based on the principles of peaceful coexistence. Important initiatives directly affecting various parts of Asia were set forth in the Peace Programme for the 1980s approved by the 26th Congress of the Communist Party of the Soviet Union (1981).

The present programme of the Soviet foreign-policy activities is comprised of the guidelines for the struggle for peace and security in Asia and the rest of the world formulated by the 27th Congress of the CPSU (1986).

The political opponents of Moscow often assert that the Soviet Union's attention to questions of peace and security in Asia is due to transient considerations. This is not true. The Soviet Union's interest in the peaceful development of political processes on the Asian continent, with which the Soviet country is closely linked geographically, economically and historically, is logical and natural. A substantial part of the USSR's territory, and socialist and non-aligned countries friendly to the USSR are situated in Asia. The security of the Soviet Union and its friends, as well as world peace depend largely on the trend of developments in Asia.

The demagogic assertions that a "Soviet threat" hangs over Asia are entirely unfounded and meant to misinform people. Such insinuations, to which Washington has recently been increasingly resorting, have one single aims to conceal irrefutable evidence testifying to the US military preparations in Asia and in the Indian Ocean and Pacific areas.

The Soviet Union does not threaten anybody in Asia, Pacific, Europe or other coutinents and never has. As far as strengthening its defences is concerned, the Soviet Union does only what is necessary to maintain its security.

Whatever contradictions there may be between the Asian states and however different their approaches to existing problems may be, the Soviet people are convinced that there is one overriding factor : the Asian nations are linked by common historical destinies and vital interests, and they are coping with tasks in many ways similar. The Soviet leadership believes it is precisely this "which dictates the necessity of co-operation and good-neighbourly relations built on a broad-based agreement on security that couforms to the interests of each and every country in the region". By its multifarious activities toward establishing sound principles in international relations in Asia, toward strengthening security there, the Soviet Union makes a valuable contribution to the formation of such an agreement and to its implementation in political life.

The rich experience of the Asian nations in the fight for peace and stability on the continent suggested the fundamental principles underlying the Soviet concept of Asian security and determined its broad-based, comprehensive character. The Five Principles of Peaceful Coexistence and the Ten Principles of Bandung are the starting point of that concept, in which the constructive initiatives put forward in recent years by the socialist and the non-aligned countries of Asia play a prominent role.

The Soviet concept of security also includes the Soviet initiatives of the first half of the 1980s. Let us name some of them. Formulated by the Soviet Union in 1981, the proposal to hold talks on confidence-building measures in the Far East is aimed at easing tensions in that region. These talks could be attended by the USSR, China, Mongolia, North Korea, Japan (all of whom are Far Eastern neighbours), and also the United States, which has military bases in Japan, South Korea and other countries in the area, and conducts intensive military activities there. However, as the specific details point out, it by no means ruled out that movement in this direction could not be started on a bilateral basis as well, e.g., with a meeting between the USSR and Japan. Readiness was also expressed to discuss possible measures to enhance mutual trust along the Soviet-Chinese border area.

The proposal on confidence-building measures in the Far East still stands, and the USSR urges all states concerned to take a serious approach to the holding of talks relevant to this.

The proposals on a Middle East settlement, put forward by the Soviet Union in July 1984 as an instrument for solving the Middle East problem, suggest that an international conference be held attended by Syria, Jordan, Egypt, Lebanon, the Palestine Liberation Organization (the sole legitimate and genuine representative of the Palestinian people), and Israel. Since under the prevailing circumstances the Soviet Union and the United States have been playing an Important role in Middle Eastern affairs, they too should attend the proposed conference.

The Soviet Union proposes that such a conference be held simply because this is virtually the only rational and effective way to end the long-standing state of war in West Asia and establish a lasting peace there. And these aims should be attained without further bloodshed, without intrigues and backstage deals, and with due consideration for the interests of all parties concerned without exception.

In the main coinciding with the joint Arab platform worked out at the Fez (Morocco) summit in 1982, the Soviet initiative is accepted in the Arab world. At the Soviet-Syrian summit talks held in June 1985, for example, the two sides stressed the need to step up the efforts of the Soviet Union, Syria and other Arab countries toward convening an international conference as a practical way of achieving a lasting and just settlement in West Asia. At the Soviet-Algerian summit meeting in March 1986 those two countries expressed their conviction that lasting peace in the Middle East could not be ensured by means of separate agreements, and condemned all attempts to seek pseudo-solutions on that basis.

During the visit of friendship paid by Prime Minister Rajiv Gandhi to the Soviet Union in May 1985, the Soviet leaders announced an important initiative for elaborating a general comprehensive approach to the problem of Asian security. It involves working out a common policy, through the joint efforts of the Asian states, regarding the problem of security in Asia—a policy which takes into account the constructive initiatives put forward by the Asian nations in recent years, and, to certain extent, the experience of the all-European process. In working toward this various methods are possible—bilateral talks as well as multilateral consultations, up to and including an all-Asia forum to be held some time in the future for the exchange of opinions and a joint search for constructive solution.

The numerous positive responses to the USSR's initiative testify that many Asian states do wish to sit down at the negotiation table and work out together ways of solving the problems of security. Some, unfortunately, think diffrerently. In an attempt to belittle the importance of the Soviet initiative some resort to hackneyed arguments, among other things which claim that as a consequence of the geographical and other types of "isolation" of the Asian countries, the formula of security for Europe is inapplicaple to Asia, and so forth.

To be sure, one cannot fail to see the specific situation in the Asian countries, the distinctive way of life there, the political, social and economic realities which often differ significantly from those of Europe. But by proposing that the experience of the all-European conference be used, the Soviet Union had no intention whatsoever of recommending a mechanical transfer of the Helsinki accords to Asian soil. The Soviet Union believes, however, that the basic principles can be applied to Asia. After all, the adoption of these principles, including respect for sovereignty, non-interference in each other's internal affairs, non-use of force, peaceful settlement of disputes, the right of nations to self-determination, and development of equitable and mutually beneficial co-operation resulted in West European detente. Their application in Asia is especially possible given that the same principles formed the basis more than thirty years ago, of the Five principles of Peaceful Co-existence and the Ten Principles of Bandung, whose significance for present-day Asia is generally recognized.

Yet the essence of the problem lies in something else : peace is indivisible, and in the present nuclear-missile age this axiom of political life stands out in bold relief. For in yofsy's complex international situation any local conflict is fraught with the danger of becoming a large-scale clash, or even a global catastrophe. That is why the peoples of Asia are vitally interested in the security of the whole continent, of the whole world; security is as necessary to them as it is to the peoples of Europe, or for that matter anywhere. If a nuclear war breaks out its incinerating flames will devastate all the continents of our planet and threaten the very existence of human civilization.

Under these circumstances, it becomes increasingly obvious that the problems of the contemporary world, including those of Asia, are so complicated and intertwined that they can only be solved through the joint efforts of all states and peoples. Indeed, the adoption of joint measures to strengthen security in Asia, which the Soviet Union had been calling for so persistently, takes on a greater urgency due to the sharply intensified military activities on the part of the United States and its western allies in that vast region.

These feverish militarist preparations dictate the necessity to take more effective measures to protect Asia against foreign intervention. This is precisely why the Soviet Union advanced the concept of a comprehensive approach to the problem of Asian security and simultaneously proposed that every permanent member of the UN Security Council should undertake not to interfere in the affairs of the countries of Asia, Africa and Latin America, not to threaten them with force, and not to draw them into military blocs. For its part, the USSR expressed readiness to take upon itself such a commitment.

In the opinion of the Soviet Union, it would be advisable to incorporate in the concept of Asian security such measures as the creation of peace and nuclear-free zones in various parts of the Asia-Pacific region ; the freezing of the level of military activeness in Asia and in the Indian Ocean and Pacific areas, prevention of the establishment of new military blocs in the region or the expansion of existing ones ; ıhe dismantling of foreign military bases on the territories of the Asian nations, and in the Indian Ocean and Pacific areas ; refraining from giving outside support to subversive anti-government and terrorist armed groupings.

Since imperialism has sharply aggravated the international situation, ever greater importance is attached to the measures proposed by various countries of Asia with the aim of improving the situation in certain areas, of creating peace and nuclear-free zones there. In addition to the idea of a zone of peace in South-East Asia (with which we have already dealt), the possibilities are now being examined for setting up such zones in other parts of Asia, e.g., in the Middle East and on the Korean Peninsula. These zones, the Asian countries feel, could be build on such principles as elimination of all foreign military bases in the zones of peace, non-deployment of nuclear weapons, non-interference in the internal affairs of other states, and peaceful settlement of disputes without foreign interference.

The Soviet Union and other socialist countries welcome the proposals for setting up zones of peace and non-nuclear zones in various parts of the world. The United States looks at this issue differently. The very concept of creating such zones contradicts the course, proclaimed by the US Administration, toward turning vast expanses of the globe, including in Asia, into spheres of its "vital interests".

The Soviet Union is a consistent champion for freezing the level of military activities in Asia and in the Indian and Pacific Oceans. As early as March 1982 the Soviet Union announced its willingness to reaeh agreement on mutual limitation of actions by the navies of the opposing blacs. The Soviet Union proposed discussing the question of extending confidence-building measures to the seas and oceans, especially in those areas where the busiest maritime routes life. The Soviet proposals are aimed at turning as much as possible of the World Ocean into a zone of peace in the nearest future.

In April 1986 the Soviet Union suggested that a conference of Pacific countries be appropriately prepared for and held to consider questions of security, including economic security, Needless to say, all Pacific countries which wish to participate in examining security matters and in elaborating decisions must be allowed to do so. A number of states have already eome up with various proposals for strengthening security in that region. These proposals deserve serious attention.

The Soviet Union proposes starting negotiations between an interested Pacific countries on the promotion of equitable, mutually beneficial and stable commercial-economic, technological, scientific and cultural co-operation. It is prepared to take a most active part in such regional peaceful co-operation, to use for this purpose its tremendous economic and scientific-technical potential.

The consolidation of neighbourly relations and friendship among all Asia-Pacific countries, and the pooling of their efforts in the common search for constructive solutions to problems of security in Asia and in the Pacific area would not only improve the situation in this vital region, but also contribute to global peace.

CHAPTER FIFTEEN

ECONOMIC SECURITY AND DEBT

THE UNEVEN growth of the foreign debt has been typical of the developing countries' economic evolution in the recent decades. Since the mid-1950s the external debt of the Third World has grown 100 times, to a trillion dollars in early 1986. Of course it is necessary to consider the high rates of inflation characteristic of the capitalist economy, especially in the 1970s and 1980s. However, even after giving allowance for inflation, the foreign debt grew at least 20 times in this interval, out-pacing the overall economic growth of the developing nations.[1]

The geography of the overseas debt is very broad. Among the debtors are the more backward countries such as Burma, Sri Lanka, Niger, Senegal, Sudan, Togo, the Dominican Republic and Bolivia, and the recognised economic leaders of the Third World, including Brazil (102 billion dollars at the end of 1985), Mexico (98 billion dollars), Argentina (50 billion dollars), the Philippines (27 billion dollars), Egypt (19 billion dollars), and Nigeria (19 billion dollars). (*Notar sobre lu ecocomia y el desserollo*, 424/425, December 1985, p. 17.). In South and South East Asia, virtually all countries groan under the burden of debt. At the end of the 1984 the foreign debt of some countries of the region was as follows (billion dollars) : Indonesia, 29; India, 20; Thailand, 12; Pakistan, Malaysia, 9; Sri Lanka. 8; and Burma, 2.

For the Third World, the foreign debt averages a third of the Gross National Product (GNP). For dozens of countries the

1. See Lev Kloch Kovsky. *Debt Burden of Developing Countries*. New Delhi, 1986, pp. 3-6.

external debt varies from 60 to 80 per cent of the GNP or more.

The debtors have greatly exceeded the generally accepted 20 per cent share of a country's export receipts allocated for debt servicing. According to UNCTAD, debt servicing absorbs from 30 to 50 per cent of foreign exchange receipts in Pakistan, Burma, Tanzania, Zimbabwe; Madagascar, Morocco, Ecuador and Peru. Some debtors channel over half of their currency receipts into debt servicing. For instance, in 1985, the Philippines spent 66 per cent of the export revenues for the purpose.

On the whole, the Third World spends 120 to 140 billion dollars a year to repay its foreign debt. This is unbearable burden for the economies of the developing nations, depriving Asia, Africa and Latin America of the funds they desperately need for economic growth and to handle pressing issues such as poverty, diseases, hunger, illiteracy and unemployment. As UN statistics show, in the developing world 570 million people are threatened by death from starvation, 800 million adults are illiterate, 250 million children do not go to school, and 15,000 million people do not have medical assistance.

In the early 1980s, the recession in the centres of capitalism profoundly afflicted most of the developing nations as well. As is usual with it, international capital wanted to settle its problems at the expense of its less developed partners. In these circumstances, more and more debtors were providing unable to discharge their commitments under the external debt. In 1982, 35 countries were overdue with debt servicing, amounting to 140 billion dollars, an all-time record. (International Credit Policy and the Foreign Policy of States : the Mexican Debt and Payment Crisis, Geneva, 1983, p. 28. Exchange Arrangements and Exchange Restrictions. Annual Report, 1983, IMF, W, 1983, p. 39). In 1982-83 the Western banks rescheduled 24 developing countries' aggregate debt of 67 billion dollars and supplied them with 30 billion dollars in new loans to keep them afloat. (B. Belassa. The Problem of the Debt in Developing Countries, paper prepared for the conference on the International Monetary System and Economic Recovery, Turin, 30-31 March, 1984, p. 1). In the previous quarter century there were only 60 cases of rescheduling, less than 3 a year for 21 countries, with delayed repayments totalling 32 billion dollars.

The monetary problems of the developing countries have overgrown into a dramatic crisis of the external debt, constituting a grave threat to the economies of Asia, Africa and Latin America and the overall capitalist international credit and financial system. This greatly wories the capitalist world. If the huge pyramid of bebts looming over the capitalist economy collapses in the long last, the magazine Foreign Policy said, the capitalist world would plunge into an economic crisis for decades or more.[2]

The West is trying to shift the blame for the debt crisis onto the debtors, accusing them of irresponsibility, extravagance and mismanagement. Lamberto Dini, the Director General of Banca d'Italia, said that worsening financial problems in developing countries result from their inadequate domestic policies, the consequences of which have been aggravated by the concurrence of extremely adverse external factors. (International Debt, Financial Stability and Growth, Paris, 1983, p. 13.) He is seconded by Wilfried Guth, Chairman of the Board of Directors of Die Deutsche Bank, West Germay. Admitting that the debt crisis reflects the cumulative effect of a long slump, excessive interest rates (nominal and real) and growing protectionism in the industrial world, Wilfried Guth alleges at the same time that the debtors have not exerted adequate efforts to adapt to the worsening economic situation in the world. (The Banker, London, 1983, N689, p. 25). Managing Director of the International Monetary Fund, Jacques de Larosiere, speaking of the reasons for the crisis, gave first place to what he termed as the superexpansionist fiscal and currency policies of the debtors. (American Express Bank Review London, 190.06. 1984). A similar opinion was voiced by the Council of Economic Advisers to the US President, pointing in its annual report to an alleged erroneous economic policy of the developing countries which resulted in an excessive demand and an inflated rate of national currencies. The idea behind all these statements reflecting the calculated policy of the West is to shift the blame for the debt crisis to the developing countries and force them to assume the burden of its consequences.

2. *Ibid.*

This profoundly selfish stand of the imperialist countries meets with growing anger in the developing countries meets with growing anger in the developing countries and is wrathfully denounced by all pragressive and democratic forces, "Our countries should not be blamed either for being underdeveloped or being in debt. Our countries should not be blamed for having been colonies, neocolonies, banana, ore, or oil republics compelled to produce raw materials, exotic commodities and fuel at low prices and with cheap labour", said the Cuban leader Fidel Castro, when he was the Chairman of the non-aligned movement.

In the last quarter of a century the foreign debt of the Latin American countries has grown 65 times and reached 380 billion dollars.

Under the existing order, the debtors annually pay the interest and part of the basic debt. Between 1982 and 1985 the sum equalled 106 billion dollars. As calculated by experts, this money would be enough to build 25,000 schools for 40 million children on the continent who have no chance now to go to school.

In many Latin American countries the debts devour nearly half of the receipts from their exports. This sharply deteriorates their already alarming economic situation : every six seconds a child dies of hunger or disease; nearly every second Venezuelan lives in extreme poverty; poverty is the lot of 8 million Argentinians and 60 per cent of Brazilians. Cuts in allocations for social needs threaten nearly all Latin American countries.

The majority of the Latin American leaders agree that the responsibility for the present deep financial crisis in the region rests with the United States which is artificially lowering the prices of minerals and agricultural produce, the main sources of currency receipts for the Latin Americans. It is the United States which bans the sale of many Latin American goods in its markets. And, finally, it is the US banks which, lending money to the neighbours, predatorily raise the rates of interest.

As a result of the US plundering policy, the economies have been practically "working" in the past few years only to cover foreign debts. In 1978-84 these countries paid to the Western usurers the sum equalling their debt by the end of that period, while the debt itself had doubled. What economics development can one talk about in this situation.

Instead of sitting down at the negotiation table with its southern neighbours and finding a reasonable solution to the debt problem, Washington offers them new loans in exchange for a free hand for its corporation and banks operating in Latin America. Taking advantage of the difficult economic situation of these countries, the United States is trying to make more dependent financially and then to use this for impudent interference in their, internal affairs.

The debt problem continues to haunt the bankers. They had in the years when there was a surfeit of petrodollars given loans to all and sundry without examining too closely the credit worthiness of the borrowers or the purposes to which these funds were to be utilised.

In these days the bankers were only enthusiastic to land and the borrowers were able to indulge in their most extravagant fancies without a thought about how the loans were to be paid back. Even when the funds were invested in productive projects the gestation period was too long and borrowers could only service their debts with further borrowings.

Thus, some day or the other the chickens had to come home to roost and with economic recession and falling oil prices the bankers and the leading institutions had an attack of nerves. If a major debtor like Mexico or Brazil defaulted the consequence for financial system could be too horrible to envisage; it could indeed be the Crash.

Peru's President Garcia has not only said that his country will only devote 10 per cent of its export income to debt servicing but this in no case will exceed the new credits it receives from abroad. The Government had found the past agreements with the IMF to be totally unacceptable but there was no way Garcia could avoid a confrontation with the IMF.

On 15 August, 1986 Peru failed to honour the deadline for the payment of US $ 190m of debt and two days later the IMF declared Peru ineligible for new loans. The battle has been joined. Peru had prepared the ground. It has accumulated sufficient reserves and brought them. Its current financial situation is not too gloomy and it might succeed in holding out for some time. But if others do not follow Peru will be forced to yield and the bankers will insist on punishing a defaulter.

The banks and the international lending institutions, were only two anxious to render assistance to the major debtor countries and arrange for new financing to pay off old debts and servicing charges but even these measures were not sufficient. The real problem was that the debtor countries, which had borrowed to expand or modernise their productive resources, could only earn sufficient foreign exchange to service their debts if their exports could find a market in the developed countries.

Most of those countries export primary materials and the potential for increasing exports remained extremely limited. Thus, with the collapse of the tin market Boliva hardly and anything to export and it was forced to default. For a poor country defaulting actually offers no solution. It continues to need new loans to strengthen its productive base. Countries remain poor and underdeveloped because investment in productive facilities has been low and they have not been able to raise sufficient funds internally. Without the support of the international financial system it will be impossible for a small and poor country belonging to the capitalist system to function effectively and therefore, the vast majority of the indebted countries are in no position to defy the bankers.

The debt look is simultaneously tightening around the African countries. Africa's foreign debt has grown from 12 billion dollars in 1972 to 170 billion in 1985. By the end of this year the sum may top 180 billion. According to Western economists, the African countries annually spend about 17 billion dollars on repaying the debt. As was reported by West Africa magazine, the sum will soon exceed 20 billion dollars, that is more than half of the African States aggregate annual income.

However, the problem of the debt to the West is not confined to the financial robbing of Africa. The debt loop is used at the same time as an instrument of imperialist pressure on the countries that have found themselves in it "with the aim of imposing on the debtors the "reforms" that would suit the West.

Today word capital is intimidating the developing countries with the spectre of their financial bankruptcy, demanding that they give up practically all the gains of their independence.

The same egoistic approach was manifested at the recent Special Session of the U.N. General Assembly on the Critical Economic Situation in Africa at which imperialist powers obstructed the adoption of a resolution that would help ease the crisis.

Not long ago Nigeria, one of the largest African countries, refused to meet the terms imposed on it and stated it would not pay to the creditors more than 30 per cent of its foregin currency receipts. The Washington Institute for International Financing. which reflected the bank's point of view, immediately sent a letter to the International Monetary Fund recommending it to take the strictest measures against that country.

It would be logical if the developing countries problem of foreign debt servicing (it now stands at nearly 1,000,000 million dollars) is readdressed to their creditors—advanced Western countries. The unprecedented foreign debt is rooted in the colonial times when Africa, Asia and Latin America were robbed of the riches compared to which their foreign debt is no more than a drop in the ocean. That shameless looting greatly interfered with the development process in the African, Asian and Latin American countries. Hence a paradoxical situation when the creditors are eventually in debts to the debtors.

The foreign debt burden aggravated by the general backwardness gives rise to a wide range of social and economic problems in the developing countries, such as growing inflation, steadily declining real incomes, and limited possibilities for schooling. The latter is particularly dangerous as it objectively leads to still greater technological backwardness and, eventually, to greater dependence on Western technology.

The foreign debt problems has a political facet, too. As a result of the continuing economic crisis, the peoples which have won their democracy at the cost of many hardships could find themselves thrown back to military dictatorship. This applies to some South American countries whose foreign debt is particularly high.

The fair solution of the foreign debt problem is even more difficult to attain in view of the Third World's failure to work out a common platform for negotiations with the advanced capitalist powers which act in unison. The imperialists' old "divide and rule" principle is still working.

A radical solution to the problem could be the termination of debt servicing and the write-off of all debts. This is actually the only varient based on objective reality. The inability of the debtor countries to meet the schedule of debt service payments confirms the above. Very remarkable in this respect is the decision by President Alan Garcia Perez of Peru to earmark not more than 10 percent of export earnings for the needs of foreign debt servicing.

The most important task faced by the developing countries in the field of world economy is to pool their efforts. A need has long been pressing for a special agency with a task of drawing out a common platform for the entire Third World. Certain constructive moves in this direction have already been made. An international conference held in Kuala Lumpur, the capital city of Malaysia, last May passed a decision on forming a special working group with the task of working out the structure and principles of a so-called "South-South Commission" which would co-ordinate the efforts of the developing countries in their dialogue with their creditors which so far has been the dialogue of the "deaf".

The foreign debt problem will doubtlessly be a key issue on the agenda of the forthcoming Non-aligned Summit in Harare.

The foreign debt crisis dovetails with the most important problems of world politics. It is contingent upon the most pressing problems of our time—the termination of the arms race and the transition to disarmament.

The arms race in the developing countries wastes their funds and makes them poorer, while enriching the transnational corporations of the United States and Western Europe, which are vitally interested in keeping the existing conflicts in Asia, Africa and Latin America going.

Even a tiny portion of the funds spent by advanced countries on the arms race would be enough to finance aid programmes, the implementation of which could considerably improve the well-being standards in the developing countries. This is what makes so acute and important a proposal by Mikhail Gorbachev on using part of the funds released through disarmament consistently advocated by the Soviet Union to finance economic progress in developing countries.

The imperialist-instigated arms race is a serious factor behind the growing economic difficulties of the developing world. Imperialist powers, while whipping up brink-of-war jitters, are seeking not only to get the developing nations more and more involved in their rackless militaristic plans but, by all means, to make up for their vast military expenditure at the expense of the economic interests of the countries of Asia, Africa and Latin America, and through their intensified exploitation. The arms build-up in the US has reached unprecedented proportions. Indeed, there has never been so terrible a waste of resources for military ends in time of peace. Marx's statement that preparations for war "are just the same, in the direct economic sense, as dumping some of a nation's capital into the water" is relevant when applied to the US today.[3]

US military spending is leaping ahead, which is directly related to the Reagan Administration's militaristic course. The outlay for the Pentagon more than doubled from $ 141,000 million in 1980 to $ 302,503 million in 1985. In other words, about one-third of the US budget is for war preparations. According to the Congressional Budget Office, one trillion and ninteen thousand million dollars were earmarked for "defence needs" from 1982 to

3. See Lev Klochkovsky. *op. cit.*, pp. 13-46.

1985, i.e., almost 80 per cent more than in the preceding four years.

In the next five years, the Pentagon is planning to spend a further two trillion dollars, which is over three times the present total annual income of the population of the world's fifty economically least developed countries. Incidentally, actual US military spending exceeds the official figures, because sizable expenses relating to militarist purposes come under the civilian heads of the budget notably those of the National Aeronautics and Space Aeronautics and Space Administration, Departments of Power Transport, Commerce to mention just a few.

Imperialism is forcing the developing world into the arms race as well. This begets dangerous conflicts and hampers the social and economic progress of emergent nations. The Moloch of militarism is devouring more and more of the scanty material resources of those nations. Their military spending is growing at a fast rate. It jumped from $ 17,000 million in 1965 to 39,000 million in the early 70s, and topped $ 100,000 million in the mid-80s ($ 118,300 million in 1984—World Armaments and Disarmament SIRI Yearbook, 1985, London, p. 27). In other words, the military appropriations of developing nations increased 7-fold in the two decades. They were rising faster than did the military expenses of the imperialist States. The share of the imperialist States. The share of the developing world in the global military expenses is 1960 was 4.5 per cent, while at the present time it is as high as 19 per cent. Military appropriations swallow up more of the GNP in developing countries than they do in advanced capitalist countries. Militarisation in the developing world is outpacing economic growth.

Militarisation is bearing hard on developing economies, causing a tremendous waste of economic resources and hampering social and economic progress. A serviceman's unkeep in the developing countries is estimated at 10 times the average per capita income of the population. In many developing countries, military expenses surpass appropriations for agricultural development. Militarisation draws off six times the expenses for health-care and three times the outlay for education. Experts figure out that the

$ 100,000 million which the countries of Asia, Africa and Latin America spend on military purposes could be used to build 300 oil refineries, 1000 chemical fertilizers factories, 1,600 sugar refiners, 10,000 hospitals or 20 million flats. That is the enormous economic and social price that the developiug world has to pay for international tensions today. With military spending rising as it does, the lot of large sections of population in the developing countries is bound to grow from bad to worse in the near future.

Militarisation is doing tremendous damage to Asian countries. Some Asian countries closely connected with the US spend a substantial proportion of their means for military ends. For example, the army and police appropriations eat up over half the national budget of Pakistan. Thailand's military spending comes second in size after appropriations for national debt repayment. No wonder that the economies of those countries are increasingly beset by a wide range of difficulties.

Pakistan has to grapple with most dramatic financial problems. Its asset build-up rate is the lowest by any standards (it is one-third of India's and half of Burma's and Sri Lanka's). Because of the shortage of finance, the government has had to cancel the sixth Five-Year Economic Development Plan, replacing it by a three-year "sliding plan for Pakistan's economic recovery" for 1985/86—1987/88.

But there is no recovery in sight. In recent years, there has been a trend for Pakistani exports to decline, while the country's annual foreign trade deficit has grown to three thousand million dollars. Interest payment alone for credits and loans from the US, used mostly for arms purchases, constituted 22 per cent of the overall export earnings in 1984-85. In the near future, expenses for military purposes will rise still further on account of the latest military-economic deal between Washington and Islamabad for a term of six years. The scale of the new deal is estimated to double the present $ 3,200 million accord.[4]

Quite a few negative economic developments are in evidence in Thailand. It has galloping inflation, drastically reduced economic

---

4. *Ibid.*

growth rates, and an abortive five-year plan (for 1982-1986) in many respects (above all, in industry). Many industrial enterprises operate below capacity. There are more bankruptcies and mounting unemployment. Those are the consequences of the fateful arms race.

One cannot fail to note that militarisation has an adverse effect on the development of many political and social processes. It contributes to rampant reaction, violation of democratic freedoms, and increased repression of working people, of progressive and democratic forces. A UN document rightly described the arms race as a waste of resources, diversion of the economy from its humane pursuits, an obstacle to national development and a threat to democratic freedoms.

The aggressive policy of imperialist powers, above all, the US, is a major factor behind increased international tensions and a faster arms build-up in the developing world, including Asian countries. Washington is seeking greater military presence in Asia, making full use of its military bases (notably in the Philippines) and trying to enlarge the existing military bases and other military installations and create new ones. There are over 300 US military bases and other installations in Asian countries. The US has established close on a hundred air force bases and airfields, 30 naval and parts equipped to accommodate warships, set up 50 arms depots, including nuclear arms depots, 100 troop control centres, monitoring, intelligence, communications and other stations in areas adjacent to the Southern borders of the USSR.

The Pentagon never stops producing its closest Asian allies into the arms build-up. That is the purpose behind the intense propaganda efforts of American diplomacy to sell the idea of the Pacific Community. Asian observers in exposing Western schemes have been pointing out that although, technically, the Pacific Community is supposed to mean an economic alliance, it is actually being planned as a military alliance.

All these acts are generating a climate of military and political tension in Asia, which compels the peace-loving Asian nations to

in the first place, is to perpetuate the financial difficulties of the Third World. They want these problems to continue so that the emergent nations could be effectively tied to imperialism.[6]

International capital can no longer employ the methods it used to resort in the past. In 1902 Venezuela, confronted with dramatic financial problems, announced a moratorium on its foreign debt. Following this, its creditors, i.e. Britain, Germany and Italy, dispatched a joint naval squadron to Venezuela which seized the country's export stocks.

Neo-colonialism is using more refined yet equally brazen methods. In a bid to exploit the developing countries' financial dependence to promote its own interests, the United States is increasing pressure on the developing countries to ensure major economic changes to suit US interests and get new concessions for private foreign investors.

The International Monetary Fund (IMF) is to play a particularly important role in this respect. Since the Second World War the IMF has vigorously promoted the aggressive financial policy of the imperialist nations.

In the current complicated situation, the IMF co-ordinates the efforts of imperialist states and their multinational banks with regard to the developing countries. The IMF acts as middlemen in reviewing the terms of the return of the external debt by Asia, Africa and Latin America. The IMF elaborates agreements to refinance developing coutntries' foreign debt and controls their implementation. IMF officials often proclaim their readiness to assist the developing countries in their economic rehabilitation, solvency recovery and in boosting economic progress. However, the agreements concluded show that the IMF upholds the interests of imperialist countries and their financial corporations. It pursues the following objectives : to force the developing countries to return the loans and pay exorbitant rates: not to allow the formation of a "club of debtors" by exposing each of them to the common

6. *Ibid.*

front of the imperialist creditors; and to enforce upon the developing countries extremely tough refinancing schemes.

In the course of the debt crisis, the IMF has come to play a more important role in the economic activity of many developing countries and its possibilities to interfere in the debtors' internal affairs have grown significantly. Commenting on IMF activities, A. Ferer, a well known Argentine economist, said that the debt burden posed a grave threat to the national sovereignty of the peoples and their right to self-determination. (EL Pais, Madrid 27-05-1985).

The "Stabilisation programmes" the IMF is imposing upon debtor nations aim to curb the public sector, reduce social spending, devaluate their currency, extend privileges to foreign investors, freeze wages and increase private investors' incomes in other ways. Giving in to IMF pressure and accepting its terms, many developing states find their problems augmented.

A case at hand is the Philippines which in 1985 signed an agreement with the IMF on partial refinancing of its external debt. In exchange for postponed repayments the Philippines had to assume a number of fettering commitments. As a result the liquidation of government-run enterprises has started. In particular, the company United Conconut Oil Mills, which enjoyed government support, has been disbanded. The government has cancelled its monopoly on sugar sales and exports. The largest government-run company, National Sugar Corporation, has been privatised. Foreign capital, which is becoming increasingly active, his intensified pressure on national entrepreneurs. In the first three months of 1985 a total of 800 national companies went bankrupt. The economic situation of the Philippines is worsening. Unemployment has reached 3 million. As Arthur Aguilar, President of Management Consultants, aptly put it, "all of us are going deeper into the pit."

Not content with this, the IMF exposes the Philippines to growing pressure. Late in September 1985 the IMF accused the Philippines government of having failed to comply with the agree-

average of 6.5 per cent a year, as in 1984-85 the GNP went down by 10 per cent.

The growing influence of transnational banks (INB) has been causing particular concern in the countries of Asia, Africa, and Latin America. In the last decade, they have been carrying through a large-scale credit expansion in the developing world. In the 70s. the private bank crediting of developing nations was expanding at twice the rate of public financing. Eurocurrency credits, granted by transnational banks, have become the most dynamic element of private bank crediting. While as late as the mid-60s, the developing nations were still virtually barred from this source of finance, in the latter half of the 70s' they absorbed over half the Eurocurrency credits (52 per cent for 1976-79 when this kind of borrowing was at its peak). In consequence, the developing nations' debt to private Western banks sky-rocketed from $ 39,000 million 1973 to $ 325,000 million by the end of 1982, with the debt of the countries outside the OPEC soaring from $ 32,000 million to $ 247,000 million (bank for International Settlements. Fifty-Third Annual Report, p. 120).

It is important to stress that the profit-hunting banking corporations have imposed high-interest credits on developing nations in many cases, quite often using bribery, personal connections with the oligarchy and other methods. As a Mexican economist M. Vienche has rightly noted, the initiative in bringing the developing nations into the loan capital market has been taken by creditors.

The vast proportions of credit expansion have enabled the leading TNBs to appreciably extend their foothold in the developing countries. Although several thousand Western banks have been involved in crediting those countries, just about half the loans have been granted by 30 major banks with headquarters in the US, Britain, Japan, and West Germany, North American banks have been particularly prominent. Nine leading US banks (including Citicorp. Bank of America, Chase Mahattan, Manufactures Hanover Trust, and J.P. Morgan) have lent to the developing countries three times the equivalent, of their own capital. The countries of Latin

America, for instance, received 40,000 million dollars worth of loans from the said American banks. Rather sizeable loans have been granted also to some Asian countries (for instance, the Philippines and Indonesia). TNB credit operations involve many enterprises of the public sector and leading groups of national private capital. Considering the long-term character of the debt problem, the said credit connections have become avenues of strong and most effective influence by international banks on various aspects of the economic life of developing nations.

Leading international banks have been using credit operations in developing countries for their vast enrichment. The American Citicorp and Chase Manhattan banks received 20 per cent and 13 per cent of all of their incomes respectively, in Brazil alone in the late 70s, and the early 80s. They have been deriving tremendous benefits from financial operations in Asian countries which make billions of dollars' worth of interests payments to them every year. On the whole, the TNB financial operations for crediting the developing countries have enabled extensive and most profitable recycling of petrodollars, which has helped maintain economic activity in capitalist centres and permitted banks to get fat profits. They received $ 173,000 million as interest payments alone in the space of 8 years – from 1976 to 1983. The foreign debt crisis has been compelling the countries of Asia, Africa and Latin America to make every effort for mitigating their financial difficulties. They have been reducing their imports and cutting other hard currency expenses to the bone. The total imports of the developing countries dropped by about $ 30,000 million in 1982-84. Some Latin American countries had their almost halved. The Philippines trimmed its imports by 28 per cent. There was a notable import fall off in some other Asian countries. However, these cuts are of little consequence as more finance go to Western creditors.

The TNBs are extremely tough on the issue of debt service payments by the developing nations. Their approach, basically, is to hold the debtors themselves entirely responsible for their foreign debt crisis. Expressing this point of view, the Managing Director of the International Monetary Fund, Jacques de Larosiers has declared that the debtor nations must overcome the debt crisis by their own efforts through a restrictive economic policy. The debtor countries must, he claims, demonstrate that they are taking effective steps to regain their financial viability.

In actual fact, the refinancing of the foreign debts of the developing nations is causing their debt burden to grow and widens TNB opportunities for their intensified exploitation. An analysis of the accords concluded between the creditor banks and developing nations in 1982-1985 prompts the following conclusion : first, refinancing operations make debt service much more expensive all the accords envisage a spread and an additional bankers' commission. Those are not trifles ; the minimum spread is 1.95 per cent of the Libor rate that of commission—1.05 per cent ; second, accords on debt rescheduling are stopgap solutions because they are signed for no more than three years, as a rule (except the new credits with repayment deadlines of between 6 and 8.5 years). The banks appear to be holding the debtors on a "short leash", as it were, monitoring the regularitate rescheduling over and over again, and ; third, the negotiations cover, for the most part, the basic debt, but not the interest (only in recent times have the TNBs begun to grant limited credits to this and) fourth, considering the large debts of the private sector of developing countries, the creditor banks demand a government guarantee.

There has been a mounting propaganda rumpus in the West for some time over the "difficulties" the TNBs are supposedly experiencing because of the debt crisis, a high measure of risk and great responsibility of Western bankers. What is passed over, however, is a vast discrepancy of crisis consequences for creditors and debtors. As far as the TNBs are concerned, they more than offset their "difficulties" with superprofits they gain from their loan operations in the developing world. As the Latin American economist R. Devlin has noted, in 1983 creditor banks got between 70 and 130 million dollars' worth of profit in Latin America alone through "spreads", commission payments, increased interest rates and other indirect payments as compensation for "the risk" of crediting Latin American debtors has no justification at all, in Devlin's opinion, because that "risk" has been fully taken into account in the original accords.

Furthermore, international banks do not stop short of blackmail and outright repression in dealing with the developing countries which cannot meet the hard terms imposed on them. At the very first sign of any irregularity, the imperialist creditors "cut off the oxygen" to the debtor nation by suspending crediting. In 1983, for instance, the IMF suspended the granting of loan, as provided for by the accord, to Brazil because the Brazilian government had failed to meet all of the Fund's requirements. That served as a signal to the world's commercial banks which also suspended the crediting to Brazil. The same device was applied to Argentina ; in 1985, the IMF stopped granting credits to her, seizing upon Argentina's failure to comply with a 1984 accord. International banks acted similarly. The US Government broke off the negotiations about a US Treasury loan to Argentina. Similar pressure and blackmail tactics have been widely used against a number of Asian countries.

So international banking capital is using the machinery of "settlement" of the foreign debt crisis to bring the emergent nations more into the debt bondage and step up their economic-bleeding.

The dictatorial practices of transnational banks and of the international organisations which express their interests (above all, the IMB) are incurring growing indignation in the developing world. Austerity measures, wage freeze and price increased imposed by international capital have been raising social tension in many developing countries, affecting the vital interests not only of the large masses of working people but of middle classes as well, and inducing all sections of society to rise in protest. In some countries (as the Dominican Republic) spontaneous action against the financial rule of imperialism has come to be suppressed by force of arms. In this context, the West has resorted to new tactics aimed at heading off the mounting discontent in Asia, Africa and Latin America.

In the middle of 1985, the former US Secretary of State Henry Kissinger broached the idea of a new "Marshal Plan" for Latin

America as the region most affected by the debt crisis. He proposed the setting up of a new financial body to provide loans for the development projects of Latin American countries and establishing a fixed interest rate (inflation rate +3 per cent). The Vice-President of the US Federal Reserve System, P. Martin, has urged setting a "ceiling" lending rate for old and new debts as well as an exchange of debts for the bonds of the International Bank for Reconstruction and Development and conversion of debts into the shares of public enterprises in developing countries.

In October 1985, the US Secretary of the Treasury, James Baker, set forth a so-called "safe growth programme" at the 40th annual IBRD and IMF session in Seoul. The "Baker Plan" involves, above all, 15 major debtors, including countries in Latin America, Africa and Asia. The aggregate debt of these countries amounts to $437,000 million, with $275,000 million coming from TNBs (Fortune 12,23,1985, Financial Times 10,28,1985). The US Secretary of the Treasury called for the crediting of developing nations with money from international financial organisations (IMF, IBRD, and the Asian Development Bank) to be increased by $9,000 million in the space of three years and for guarantees to Western private banks for a further 20,000 million dollars of commercial credits to the said countries. That offer was properly interpreted by the developing nations as yet another ploy. It is worth recalling that the countries listed in the "Baker Plan" alone will have to pay about $150,000 million as interest rates on previous loans to the West in the next three years. So can the miserable extension of the credit operations by international financial organisations (by around $3,000 million a year) and the vague promise to stimulate more credits from private banks substantially alleviate the financial condition of the said countries ? Of course not. That has been admitted even by the Western press. The British *Financial Times* noted, for instance that the US initiative would hardly be practicable for resolving the increasingly dramatic foreign debt problem. The US device has been designed to reassure the developing nations and to generate more illusions about Western readiness to aid them.

At the same time, the "Baker Plan" has far-reaching hidden aims. It fits into the strategic line of the international capital for a fundamental review of the major options of the domestic economic policies in the developing nations. In exchange for fresh credits, the debtor nations have to make essential changes in their legislation and in their industrial, financial and foreign trade policies, which boils down to the continued dismantling of their public sector, liberalising economic relations with the West, and creating most favourable conditions for foreign capital operations.

A no less important hidden objective behind the American enterprise is to blow up the emergent united front of debtor nations. The "Baker Plan" has been brought forward, as a matter of fact, to counter the programme of a "group of 24" (developing nations) which colled for reshaping international economic relations and the world capitalist monetary system on terms of equality, conducting a constructive global dialogue to secure a long-term solution to the foreign debt problem, and easing debt service payments, above all, by fixing reasonable deductions from export earnings. As official American spokesmen have emphasised, fresh loans will be granted on a bilateral basis only. There has been a noteworthy remark by James Baker regarding the new loans to Peru which stands, by the principle of deducting 10 per cent of export earnings for debt service payments. If she held on to that stand, Baker declared, she would, naturally, get no more money at all.

At the present juncture, the Reagan Administration is making considerable efforts to induce its NATO partners and Japan to give the utmost support for the implementation of the "Baker Plan". At the same time, Washington is seeking support from developing nations. However, none of them, except Ecuador, has so far consented to join the "Baker Plan". Moreover, the Cartagena Group, which is the main Latin American foreign debt agency, turned down the "Banker Plan", as a matter of fact, at its conference on December 16-17, 1985.

The foreign debt crisis is a serious threat to the developing states' international economic security. As it is noted in the resolution "International Economic Security", adopted by the 40th session of the UN General Assembly, solving the problem of the developing countries' foreign debt is of immense importance for normalising the world economic situation and for creating conditions favourable for economic and social progress of the newly-free nations. It is impossible to achieve a real solution to the foreign-debt problem without restructuring international economic relations to make them just, equal and democratic. The loan and credit interests rates need to be reduced, the currency exchange rates stabilised, protectionism renounced, the international currency-financial system restructured to take account of the interests of all states, and the financial institutions operating within its framework democratised. An end must be put to the practice of making advantage of the currency-financial difficulties of individual countries for pressuring them politically and for interfering in the home affairs of sovereign states.

As it was stressed in the special memorandum of the USSR Government on international economic security, "stabilisation of the general economic and currency financial situation and implementation of the UN resolution on restructuring international economic relations on a just, democratic basis, first of all the Charter of Economic Rights and Duties of States and the Programme of Action for the Establishment of new International Economic Order, are major pre-requisites improving international economic relations."

But the imperialist power and international financial capital clearly show their unwillingness to even slightly waive their advantages and privileges. They strive to preserve inequality in international economic relations and try to use the foreign debt lever for gaining new advantages.

There are some specific trends in the West's approach to the problem of the developing countries' indebtedness. First of all, the Western propaganda, machine, taking into consideration the heightening of economic and social tension in developing countries, manoeuvres to reassure public opinion by drawing a radiant picture of the possibility of self-regulation of the capitalist currency-financial system. For instance, the French newspaper *Le Monde* has declared the foreign debt problem a "fiction" and said that international inflation will sooner or later devalue the Third World's debts. Some representatives of the Western banking community and government circles portray the current crisis as a temporary shortage of currency resources. In the view of the majority of experts, the debt crisis can be settled : the indebted countries are in a stage of more or less acute non-liquidity but are not insolvent, J. Westphalen (Deutsch-Sudamerikanischen Bank of the FRG) writes : It is possible to overcome the crisis, above all, if there is a long invigorations in the world and if energetic joint efforts are made both by the debtors and the creditors.

As for the transnational banks, they prefer moves which guarantee, above all, their economic interests. The idea of "buying out" from the private banks the debts of the developing countries which are on the brink of bankruptcy is widely spread in the West. The idea is that the banks sell (at a 10 to 15 per cent or even greater discount, depending on the equality of the debt of some specific indebted country), or in other words, rediscount the short and medium term liabilities of the debtors either at their central banks, the IMF or the IBRD, or at an international financial institution set up specially for this purpose. In turn, these organisations convert the aforesaid liabilities into long-term ones with a fixed interest rate. The authors of this idea intend in this way to rid the private banks of the "hopeless" or "dubious" debts, which encumber their financial position, by shifting the burden on the tax-payers.

At the same time, the proposal to pay off the liabilities of developing countries with shares of public-owned enterprises and other developed capitalist states.

Fulfilment of such recommendations would certainly enable the West to widen the sphere of its control over the economy of developing countries and also to considerably undermine the positions of the public sector which is today the principal force countering the expansion of monopoly capital.

As for the numerous intiatives of the developing countries which could help resolve the foreign debt problem and strengthen their economic security, they are, as a rule, rejected point blank by the West. The latter emphatically turns down all attempts at holding multilateral talks on the debt problem. Fearing a united front of the debtors, the transnational banks insist on an "individual approach" Demanding strict compliance with the liabilities, the West does not stop at resorting to open threats the blackmail. The punishment for a refusal to pay will be served, American periodical *Business Week* writes, seeking to scare the developing countries. The economy of the debtor country will be placed, in effect, on to a barter footing, while its ships and aircraft will be confiscated by the creditor banks, the weekly says.

In the present-day situation, the developing states and the progressive and democratic forces of the whole world make over more resolute efforts to strengthen international economic security. To achieve this, the Soviet Union has advanced a viable proposal, the basic principles of which are :

First, exclusion of all forms of discrimination from international practice; renunciation of the policy of economic blockades and sanctions if this is not directly envisaged in the recommendations of the world community;

Second, joint quest for ways for a just settlement of the problem of debts;

Third, establishment of a new world economic order guaranteeing equal economic security to all countries;

Fourth, elaboration of principles for utilising part of the funds released as a result of cuts in military budgets for the good of the world community, above all, of the developing countries;

Fifth, the pooling of efforts in exploring and making peaceful use of outer space and in resolving global problems on which the destiny of civilisation depends.

As Mikhail Gorbachev stated in the Report at the 27th Congress of the CPSU "in the future it would be important to convene a World Congress on Problems of Economic Security at which it would be possible to discuss as a package everything that encumbers world economic relations."

CHAPTER SIXTEEN

BILATERAL AND MULTILATERAL RELATIONS

AT THE BEGINNING of the year 1986 the Soviet Union submitted an ingenious peace programme, the implementation of which by the end of this century would rid mankind of nuclear weapons. It was contained in a statement made by the Soviet leader Mikhail Gorbachev.

People of common sense, whether living in Europe or Asia, in Africa or Australia, in Micronesia or America, support the new Soviet initiatives. It is quite natural. The existing nuclear potential would be able to destroy one million such cities as Hiroshima. The halting of the arms race and the liquidation of nuclear arsenals have become the fundamental, inevitable condition for the survival of mankind. And it is absolutely necessary that the endeavour to avert nuclear catastrophe bring its first concrete results as soon as possible for the trauma of nuclear threat not to be transferred from our generation to our children, grandchildren and great-grandchildren.

Mikhail Gorbachev's statement is a continuation of the highly principled policy of the Soviet Union, of its endeavour to rid the world of the danger of nuclear death. Since the end of World War II, the Soviet Union has submitted some 200 peace proposals on various international forums. They were mainly aimed at averting the danger of nuclear war. Of their large number let us recall at least those submitted in the past five years. The 26th Congress of the Soviet Communist Party in 1981 formulated concrete initiative steps directed against the stockpiling of nuclear weapons and the deployment of new missiles and proposed to set up an international committee for averting nuclear disaster.

In 1982, at the 2nd special session of the U.N. General Assembly, the Soviet Union declared its pledge not to be the first to use nuclear weapons.

The session of the Political Consultative Committee of the Warsaw Treaty member states in January 1983 adopted a political declaration stressing that war is an inacceptable means of solving international problems and disputes and that it must cease threatening human civilization once for all. The same forum proposed to conclude a treaty on the non-use of force and the preservation of peaceful relations between the Warsaw Treaty and NATO states.

At the 38th U.N. General Assembly session in October 1983; the Soviet Union submitted draft resolutions for denouncing nuclear war and freezing nuclear armaments. The fact that the majority of the member states of this important international organization voted for these draft resolutions proves that they gained great support.

In January 1985, the Politburo of the Soviet Communist Party Central Committee discussed a report on Soviet-US relations and on the basis of the results of talks between the Soviet and US Foreign Ministers, it gave significant impulses for a Soviet-US dialogue on space and nuclear weapons. It emphasized in particular that a real progress must be made on the road towards halting the arms race and averting the threat of nuclear war, and resolute measures adpoted to liquidate nuclear arsenals.

The Soviet leader Mikhail Gorbachev said in April 1985 : "We are convinced that it is possible to avert a world war. Experience shows, however, that the struggle for the preservation of peace and the safeguarding of world security is not easy and requires more and more efforts."

With this resolve the Soviet Union attended the significant international dialogue held in Geneva in November 1985. However, the far reaching importance of everything positive that has been agreed upon in Geneva can be manifested only through concrete deeds. This principle is consistently observed in the Soviet foreign policy. This is also the basic motive for which the Soviet Union submitted at the present time in particular such important initiative proposals as are contained in Mikhail Gorbachev's statement. The significance of this statement rests mainly in that it organically combines mobilizing prospects with the action plan of their achievement. The statement constitutes a concrete, specified program of nuclear disarmament. It solves this immensely complex task in three subsequent stages, each covering a limited period and embracing realistic gradual objectives.

It is logical that the first stage encompasses above all a reduction in the nuclear potentials of the two main nuclear powers—the Soviet Union and the United States. Their arsenals of strategic nuclear weapons are to be reduced to 50 per cent in five to eight-years. These questions are to be discussed on the already existing platform constituted by the Geneva talks on nuclear and space weapons. The Soviet Union also proposes to make progress in the first stage in the solving of another grave question, namely medium-range nuclear missiles and tactical nuclear missiles. In this field, too the Soviet initiative is quite concrete: the Soviet Union proposes the liquidation of Soviet and American medium-range missiles in Europe, both ballistic and Cruise missiles.

The main goal of the second stage is the involvement into the process of nuclear disarmament also of other countries having nuclear weapons, that is Britain, France and the People's Republic of China. This would open up the way for all countries having nuclear weapons to star the liquidation of these dangerous means of mass annihilation following the 50 per cent reduction in the Soviet and US nucleas potentials. The second stage should also see the achievement of another gradual target, i.e. the conclusion of a Soviet-US agreement banning offensive space weapons. It would gradually change from a bilateral into a multilateral agreement joined by the leading industrial states. This would reliably bar the way for the militarization of outer space.

The third and final stage, which should not begin later than 1995, would consummate ths reduction of nuclear arsenals by their complete liquidation. Mankind would thus be able to start a new century, the first century of the third millenium, rid of the greatest threat in its existence.

A typical feature of the new Soviet peace proposals is a close connection between the near and prospecive goals. Of great importance in this respective is the Soviet call for putting an end to all experimental nuclear explosions. The Soviet Union has pledged to extent its one-sided moratorium of 1985 by three months.

What is very important about Mikhail Gorbachev's proposals is that they take into account the developing countries' interests. One part of his statement concerns Asian security. It says that the programme of liquidation of nuclear and chemical weapons is in harmony with the outlook of the nations on the Asian continent for which the problems of peace and security are as urgent as for the European nations. "How could we omit to recall that Japan, its cities of Hiroshima and Nagasaki, fell victim to nuclear bombing and that chemical weapons were used in Vietnam," Mikhail Gorbachev emphasized. He appreciated the constructive initiative proposals submitted by Asian socialist countries, India and other member countries of the Non-Aligned Movement. "We regard it to be of great importance that the two nuclear powers on the Asian continent—the Soviet Union and the People's Republic of China—undertake not to be the first to use nuclear weapons."

Undoubtedly, the implementation of the Soviet peace programme would basically change the situation in Asia, ridding nations also in this part of the world of their fear of nuclear and chemical disaster and raising security in this region to a qualitatively new level. Mikhail Garbachev pointed out that this programme is to help find - along with all Asian countries—a general comprehensive attitude to the creation of a system of a secure and lasting peace on this continent.

This programme, however, concerns not only Asia but also other developing continents. As Mikhail Gorbachev emphasized "the transition to active steps in the sphere of halting the arms race and reducing military arsenals is also an inevitable prerequisite for solving constantly deteriorating global problems such as the destruction of the environment, the need to seek new energy resources, eliminate economic backwardness and combat diseases. The 'armaments instead of development' principle, imposed on the world by militarism, must be replaced by the opposite—disarmament for development. The yoke of debts coming to billion which strangles dozens of countries and even whole continents, is a direct consequence of favourish armaments. The sum of over 250,000 million dollars wrung from the developing countries every year practically equals the U.S. military expenditure. This coincidence is far from accidental in its nature. It is the objective of the Soviet Union that every measure concerning reduction in armaments, every step on the road towards the liquidation of nuclear weapons bring greater security to nations and moreover, make it possible to earmark larger funds to improve the living conditions of people. It is not accidental that nations striving to eliminate their backwardness and achieve the standard of highly advanced industrial countries link their prospects of emancipation with their indebtedness to imperialism which exploits their economies, with the reduction and liquidation of armaments, with cuts in military expenditures and the transfer of resources to social and economic development."

Mikhail Gorbachev pointed out that "the Soviet Union disapproves of attempts to make the implementation of measures in the sphere of disarmament dependent on so-called regional conflicts. They are to conceal unwillingness to embark upon the road of disarmament and the endeavour to impose on sovereign nations alien will and such orders which would make it possible to preserve extremely unjust living conditions in certain countries for the benefit of others, exploit their natural, human and cultural resources for egotistic imperial purposes of individual states or aggressive groups. The Soviet Union has always been and will be opposed to this. It has been and will be a consistent advote of the freedom of nations, peace, security and the strengthening of the international legal order. Its aim is not the fomenting of regional conflicts but their liquidation by collective effort, on the basis of equitable principles and the sooner the better."

The noble gesture of the Soviet Union, its important initiative proposals contained in Mikhail Gorbachev's statement express the aspirations of peace-loving people all over the world. They express the hope that the 20th century, which has given mankind an immense resource of energy obtained by atomic fission will definitively and once for all put an end to the danger posed by the misuse of this revolutionary scientific discovery against the interests of mankind. In these proposals the world public sees a concrete and realistic way of ridding this generation and generations to come of the threat posed by nuclear weapons and making the external longing of mankind for a life in peace come true.

To ensure reliable security in Asia it is absolutely necessary that all states of the continent should actively co-operate in the commercial-economic and other fields on a bilateral and multilateral basis. Such good neighbour co-operation is an effective way of improving the international climate in Asia.

Not only does the Soviet Union call on the Asian nations to promote such co-operation, but for its part does its utmost to develop and deepen mutually advantageous ties with all countries of the continent.

And it is perfecting its relations with countries which have chosen the path of socialist construction—Mongolia, Democratic Korea, Vietnam and Laos. The Soviet leaders' talks in 1985-86 with Jambyn Batmunh, Kim Il Sung, Le Dung and Kaysone Phomvihane gave a powerful impulse to the improvement of the multifaceted ties with these countries.

The socialist countries of Asia are unanimous that it is necessary to invigorate the search for constructive and mutually acceptable ways of solving the problems of safeguarding peace and security on that continent. They attach vital importance to holding an all-Asia debate in the future to consider the whole complex of issues relating to Asian security.

The efforts of a number of Asian countries, including the Soviet Union, to normalize their relations with China contribute to peace on the continent. In his Political Report to the 27th Congress of the Communist Party of the Soviet Union Mikhail Gorbachev remarked : "One can say with gratification that there has been a measure of improvement of the Soviet Union's relations with its great neighbour—Socialist China. The distinctions in attitudes, in particular to a number of international problems remain. But we also note something else—that in many cases we can work jointly, co-operate on an equal and principled basis, without prejudice to third countries. In thinking of the future, it may be said that the potentialities for cooperation between the USSR and China are enormous. They are great because such co-operation is in accordance with the interests of both countries ; because what is dearest to our peoples—socialism and peace—is indivisible."

A vivid example of peaceful co-existence of states with different social systems are the teaditionally friendly Indo-Soviet relations, which are marked by a diversity of forms and spheres of co-operation. In August 1986 the peoples of the two countries will celebrate the 15th anniversary of the Treaty of Peace, Friendship and Co-operation between the USSR and the Republic of India. These past years have strikingly confirmed that the Treaty justifies its lofty purpose to the full. It has been and remains an effective instrument in the fight for peace and stability in Asia and the rest of the world.

"A special place," the Soviet leader Mikhail Gorbachev noted in May 1985 during Rajiv Gandhi's visit to Moscow, "is held by the Soviet Union's and India's efforts to remove the threat of war and end the arms race. No one can ignore the fact that friendship and co-operation between our two countries is playing a more and more important and beneficial role in the entire system of international relations."

The process of promoting mutually beneficial co-operation between the Soviet and the ASEAN countries goes on. The USSR's relations are developing successfully with its southern neighbours in West Asia. The Soviet Union is rendering the people of Afghanistan enormous assistance in building a new life. Soviet-Turkish economic co-operation is stable. There has been increasing trade between the Soviet Union and Iran. The USSR's ties with the Arab countries are greatly strengthened by the high prestige of the peaceable Soviet foreign policy in West Asia and the Gulf, by the USSR's tireless efforts to achieve a just and all-embracing settlement in that region.

In improving the international situation in the Far East and in Asia as a whole, Soviet-Japanese relations play an important role. The Soviet Union invariably wants its relations with Japan to be friendly, deep and diversified. The Soviet proposal to conclude a Soviet-Japanese treaty on good-neighbour relations and mutually beneficial co-operation remains valid ; such a treaty would help create a favourable atmosphere for continuing the talks on signing a peace treaty. The Soviet Union has also put forward other proposals, including those concerning economic co-operation and cultural ties.

The visit of Soviet Foreign Minister to Japan in January 1986 marked a major event in Soviet-Japanese relations. During the talks it was noted that a political dialogue between the leaders of the two countries would be of major importance. The two sides confirmed their agreement to continue holding regular consultations at the Foreign Minister level. An agreement on trade and payments between the two countries covering the period from 1986 to 1990, as well as other agreements on matters of bilateral relations, came out of those talks. They both expressed satisfaction with the accord reached between the USSR, Japan and the United States on a number of measures and their means of implementation of increase the safety of fights in the northern part of the Pacific Ocean.

"The resumption in January 1986 of political consultations between the USSR and Japan," *Nihon Keizoi Shimbon* (Tokyo ; April 2, 1986) wrote, "around deep satisfaction in Japanese business circles . . . These circles pin great hopes on the possibility of furthering commercial and economic ties between the two countries."

The Soviet Union is convinced that the establishment of good-neighbour relations and co-operation between all Asian states, represents a real prerequisite that will enable them to pool their efforts, provided they have the goodwill, in working out a common complex approach to the problem of security in all of Asia and in adjoining Indian Ocean and Pacific areas, and to find the ways and means of solving this extremely important problem in the nearest possible future.

CHAPTER SEVENTEEN

THE PARTY, PEACE AND PROGRESS

IT IS WITH unflagging interest that the world public discusses the Soviet Union's new comprehensive programme for the elimination before the year 2000 of the nuclear and chemical weapons on the earth and the prevention of the militarisation of outer space.

Political parties of diverse orientations, voluntary organisations, government and parliament members, scientists and people prominent in the world of culture are voicing support for the new large-scale Soviet peace initiatives advanced in the January 15, 1986 statement by Mikhail Gorbachev, and nothing their timeliness and realism.

The new peace proposals of the Soviet Union are universal because they cover a whole package of problems underlying the global and regional security. The Soviet programme of elimination of the nuclear and chemical weapons involves guarantees of peace and security on the Asian Continent. These problems are no less but possibly more acute for the Asian nations than for Europe. After all, the Asian state of Japan is the only in the world to have suffered from atomic weapons. Vietnam, another Asian State has been a victim of the horrible chemical weapons, used on a large scale by the US brass-hats during the aggression in Indochina.

As to the Asian aspect of the new Soviet peace proposals, they fully take into account the huge peace potential which has been accumulated over the decades by the Asian states in their socio-political activities, and the standards and principles of relations they have elaborated. Suffice it to recall that as far back as the 1950s the Asian countries worked out the "Pancha Sheela" principles which were further developed in the known ten principles of peaceful co-existence, proclaimed during a conference of the independent Afro-Asian countries (Bandung, April 1985).

India and other Asian countries have an important role to play in the development of the concept of the Non-aligned movement as an influential factor of the anti-imperialist and anti-war movements of the emergent nations.

In recent years the Asian states have advanced a number of important initiatives aimed at a political settlement of the regional conflicts and at creating an atmosphere of neighbourliness and mutual co-operation on the continent. In this context in would be proper to mention the proposals of the Democratic People's Republic of Korea to free South Korea from the presence of the US occupational troops and US nuclear weapons and to work for a peaceful democratic unification of that country's north and south.

The initiatives of Vietnam and other countries of Indochina supplement the ASEAN countries' proposals to set up a nuclear-free zone of peace in South-East Asia. The Asian countries are making efforts to develop their relations with the closest neighbour in the region. This is promoted by the important constructive peace initiatives of India aimed at the normalisation of her relations with Pakistan.

The large-scale initiative of Sri Lanka, India and several other Asian states to turn the Indian Ocean into a zone of peace has not been realised as yet. The realisation of this initiative could substantially contribute to the improvement of the political climate in Asia and all over the world.

The constructive proposals of Afghanistan and Mongolia are aimed at a radical improvement of the situation in those areas. Of great international significance far exceeding the limits of the Asian continent is the obligation not to be the first to use nuclear weapons, assumed by Asia's two great powers—the USSR and China.

For the legitimate aspirations of the Asian people for peace and security to come true, the whole of the powerful peace potential and will of the Asian countries must merge into a single whole. Close contacts as well as dialogues and co-operation among all Asian nations are needed for this.

It is this lofty goal which is served by the 1985 Soviet call for a comprehensive approach to the problems facing Asia, and for all of its states to pool efforts in a bid to establish a system of reliable security and lasting peace on that continent. The proposal has been approved by many countries in Asia, because it meets the interests of all Asian states without exception and suggests the only correct way of solving the complex and urgent problems faced by the continent. The democratic public and the peace-loving forces on that continent are only too well aware of the fact that realisation of the Soviet Union's Asian initiative in close interrelation with the other radical steps proposed by Mikhail Gorbachev in his statement would thoroughly change the situation in Asia, rid her peoples and the whole of mankind from fear of the nuclear and chemical threat and elevate Asian security to a qualitatively new level.

Addressing the 27th CPSU Congress in Moscow Mikhail Gorbachev pointed to the growing importance of the Asian and Pacific region in promoting peace and international security. In that vast region, he said, there are many tangled knots of contradictions, the flashpoints of military danger are not dying down and the political situation in some places is unstable. Here, the Soviet Union holds, it is necessary, without postponement, to find the relevant solutions and paths. Evidently, this has to begin with the co-ordination and then the pooling of efforts in the interests of a political settlement of painful problems so as, in parallel, on that basis to at least take the edge off the military confrontation in various parts of Asia and stabilise the situation there.

"We," the Soviet leader Gorbachev said, "are in favour of vitalising collective quests for ways of defusing conflict situations in the Middle East and in all of the planet's turbulent points."

He noted in this connection that counter-revolution and imperialism had turned Afghanistan into a bleeding wound. The Soviet

Union helps the Afghan defend their sovereignty. It would like, in the nearest future, to withdraw the Soviet troops stationed in Afghanistan at the request of the Afghan Government. Mikhail Gorbachev said the USSR has agreed with the Afghan side on the schedule for their phased withdrawal as soon as a political settlement is reached that ensures an actual cessation and dependably guarantees the non-resumption of foreign armed interference in the internal affairs of that country.

Gorbachev called a just political settlement of international crises and regional conflicts, including those in Asia, as one of the fundamental principles of an all-embracing system of international security which the Soviet Union is urging the world community to build.

The Political Report of the CPSU Central Committe lists other fundamental principles of this system, which either are fully in keeping with demands and proposals by the non-aligned and developing countries or move with them in the same direction.

These are, to name just a few, respect for the right of each people to choose the ways and forms of its development indepedently; Prevention of an arms race in outer space; Destruction of nuclear and chemical weapons and renunciation of the development of other means of mass annihilation; A lowering of the levels of military capabilities of countries to limits of reasonable adequacy and balanced and commensurate reduction of their military budgets; Extirpation of genocide and apartheid, etc.

Gorbachev paid a particular attention to the problem of guaranteeing international economic security and establishing a new world economic order. He called for convening in the future a world forum which would make it possible to discuss in package everything that encumbers world economic relations.

The Soviet leader said the USSR, was prepared to discuss with other countries any proposals aimed at improving the world situation. It will be recalled that the Soviet Union has always assessed highly the well-known five principles of *Pancha Shila* and ten principles of Bandung, as well as the initiatives by the Non-Aligned

Movement, regional groups and individual Asian countries—everything that conforms to the idea of turning Asia into a zone of peace and co-operation.

The international policy of the CPSU is based on the humane nature of socialist society, which is free from exploitation and oppression and has no classes or social groups interested in unleashing war. It is inseparably linked with the basic, strategic tasks of the Party in the USSR and expresses the common aspiration of the Soviet people to engage in constructive work and to live in peace with all nations.[1]

The main goals and directions of the international policy of the CPSU are :

—provision of international conditions favourable to the perfection of socialist society and the advance to communism in the USSR; removal of the threat of world war and achievement of universal security and disarmament;

—constant strengthening and expansion of co-operation between the USSR and the fraternal socialist countries and the utmost contribution to the consolidation and progress of the world socialist system;

—development of relations of equality and friendship with newly free countries;

—maintenance and development of relations between the USSR and capitalist states on a basis of peaceful co-existence and business-like, mutually beneficial co-operation;

—internationalist solidarity with Communist and revolutionary-democratic parties, the international working class movement and the national liberation struggle of the peoples.

The CPSU's approach to foreign-policy matters consists in firm protection of the interests of the Soviet people and resolute

1. See *XXVII CPSU Congress : Documents and Resolution*, New Delhi, Allied, 1986.

opposition to the aggressive policy of imperialism combined with a readiness for dialogue and constructive settlement of international problems through negotiations.

The foreign-policy course for peace elaborated by the Party and consistently pursued by the Soviet state in combination with the strengthening of the defence capability of the country has ensured for the Soviet people and for most of the world's population the longest period of peace in the 20th century. The CPSU will continue to do everything it can to secure peaceful conditions for the constructive work of the Soviet people, to improve international relations, and to stop the arms race that has engulfed the world, in order to avert the danger of nuclear war, which looms over all peoples.

There is no loftier or more responsible mission than that of safeguarding and strengthening peace and curbing the forces of aggression and militarism for the sake of the life of present and future generations. A world without wars and without weapons is the ideal of socialism.

The CPSU attaches primary importance to the further development and strengthening of relations of friendship between the Soviet Union and other socialist countries.

The Party is seeking long-lasting relations and many-sided co-operation between the USSR and the other states of the world socialist system. The CPSU proceeds from the belief that the cohesion of the countries of socialism meets the interests of each of them and their common interests, and promotes the cause of peace and the triumph of socialist ideals.

All-round strengthening of relations of friendship and the development and perfection of ties between the Soviet Union and the other countries of the socialist community are a matter of special concern to the Party.

The ruling Communist and Workers' parties are the motive force of these countries' all-round co-operation. To strengthen the cohesion of the Communists of the fraternal countries and to ensure the mutual enrichment of the practice guiding society, the CPSU will continue to help broaden the inter-Party links that embrace Party organisations at all levels, from Central Committees to primary Party organisations; it will promote exchanges of opinions and experience both on a bilateral and multilateral basis.

The CPSU will continue its policy of strengthening interestate relations between the Soviet Union and other socialist countries of affirming them in treaties and agreements, of developing contacts between the legislative bodies and between the public organisations of these countries, and of further stepping up their political cooperation in all forms.

The Soviet people stand for the increasingly efficient interaction of the fraternal countries on the international scene with due regard for the situation and interests of each of them and for the common interests of the community.

As long as the imperialist NATO military bloc exists, the Party considers it necesary to contribute in every way possible to improving the work of the Warsaw Treaty Organisation as an instrument of collective defence against the aggressive ambitions of impearilism and of joint struggle for a lasting peace and broader international co-operation.

In economic relations, the CPSU stands for a further deepening of socialist economic integration as the material foundation for drawing the socialist countries closer together. It attaches special importance to a consistent uniting of efforts by the fraternal countries in key areas of intensification of production and acceleration of scientific and technological progress in order to accomplish jointly a task of historical significance, namely, that of advancing to the forefront of science and technology with the aim of further improving the well-being of their peoples and strengthening their security.

The CPSU proceeds from the belief that integration is designed to contribute to an every increasing extent to progress in the sphere of social production and socialist way of life in the countries of the socialist community, to a speedier evening out of their levels of economic development and to a strengthening of the positions of socialism in the world.

The CPSU will actively participate in the collective work of fraternal parties to coordinate their economic policies, to improve the mechanism of their economic co-operation and evolve new forms of co-operation, to deepen specialisation and co-operation in production, to co-ordinate plans, to exchange advanced experience and to develop direct links between associations and enterprises. It will help enhance the role of the Council for Mutual Economic Assistance and broaden economic, scientific and technical co-operation on the basis of bilateral and multilateral programmes.

While considering equal and mutually beneficial economic co-operation between socialist and capitalist states to be natural and useful, the CPSU at the same time believes that the development of socialist integration should enahance the technical and economic invulnerability of the community with regard to hostile actions by imperialism and to the influence of economic crises and other negative phenomena that are intrinsic to capitalism.

In the sphere of ideology; the CPSU stands for pooling the efforts of the fraternal parties aimed at studying and using the experience in building socialism and in the communist education of working people, at developing the theory of Marxism-Leninism while deepening its creative nature and upholding its revolutionary essence. Invigoration of collective thought, a constant widening of exchanges of cultural and intellectual values, and co-operation in science and culture serve further to strengthen friendship between socialist countries.

The CPSU will continue to enhance awareness of the unity and common historical destinies of the fraternal peoples. Propagation of the truth about socialism, exposure of imperialist policy and propaganda, rebuffing of anti-communism and anti-Sovietism, and struggle against dogmatic and revisionist views—these tasks are more easily accomplished when Communists act in a single front.

The CPSU regards it as its internationalist duty, together with the other fraternal parties, to consolidate the unity and increase the strength and influence of the socialist community. The outcome of the competition between socialism and capitalism and the future of world civilisation depends largely on the strength of the community, on the success of each country in its constructive endeavours, and on the purposefulness and co-ordination of their actions.

The experience of the development of the world socialist system shows that socialism provides every opportunity both for the society's confident advance and for the maintenance of harmonious mutual relations between countries. But neither comes of its own accord.

The levels of countries' economic and political development, their historical and cultural traditions, and the actual conditions in which they exist are different. The social development of socialist countries does not always proceed in a straight-forward manner. Every major stage of this development sets new complex tasks, whose accomplishment involves struggle, search and the overcoming of contradictions and difficulties.

All this, the CPSU is convinced, call for utmost attention, a constructive comparison of viewpoints and effective solidarity so as to rule out any possibility for the rise of differences that could arm common interests. Of special importance are the co-ordination of actions in matters of principle, comradely interest in each other's success, strict implementation of commitments, and a profound understanding of both national interests and common, international interests in their organic interconnection.

The formation and development of a new society are taking place in a situation of sharp confrontation between the two world systems. Seeking to weaken the positions of socialism and disrupt the mutual ties of socialist states, and primarily ties with the Soviet Union, imperialism is employing a whole range of differentiated measures—political, economic and ideological. It tries to exploit problems that arise and makes use of nationalistic sentiments for subversive purposes. The CPSU proceeds from the belief that strong unity and class solidarity among socialist countries are especially important in these conditions.

The experience of the Soviet Union, of world socialism shows that the most factors in its successful advance are the loyalty of the ruling Communist and Workers' parties to the teaching of Marxism-Laninism and a creative application of that teaching; firm links between the parties and the broad mass of working people an enhancing of their authority and guiding role in society, strict observance of the Leninist norms of Party and state life, and development of government by the people under socialism; a sober consideration of the actual situation, timely and scientifically substantiated solution of problems that arise; and the building of relations with other fraternal countries on principles of socialist internationalism.

Whatever the characteristic features of each of the socialist countries, its level of economic development, size, and historical and national traditions, all of them have the same class interests. What unites the socialist countries and makes them cohesive is of paramount importance, and is immeasurable greater than what may divide them.

The Party is convinced that the socialist countries, fully observing equality and displaying mutual respect for their national interests, will continue to follow the road of ever greater mutual understanding and will draw closer together. The Party will contribute to this historically progressive process.

Formulating its policy towards former colonial and semi-colonial countries, the CPSU proceeds from the belief that the embarking of the formerly enslaved peoples on the road of independence, the emergence of dozens of new states and their increasing role in world politics and in the world economy are one of the distinctive features of the present epoch.

The newly free peoples, as Lenin foresaw, are to play a great role in the destinies of mankind as a whole. The CPSU believes that these peoples' increasing influence should promote to an ever greater extent the cause of peace and social progress.

The Party is consistently pursuing a policy of expanding contacts between the Soviet Union and the developing countries, and regards with profound sympathy the aspirations of the peoples who had experienced the heavy and humiliating yoke of colonial slavery. The Soviet Union is building its relations with those countries on the basis of strict respect for their independence and equality, and supports the struggle of those countries against the neo-colonialist policy of imperialism, against the survivals of colonialism, and for peace and universal security.

The Party attaches great importance to solidarity and political and economic co-operation with socialist-oriented countries. Every people creates, mostly by its own efforts, the material and technical base necessary for the building of a new society, and seeks to improve the well-being and cultural standards of the masses. The Soviet Union has been doing and will continue to do all it can to render the peoples following that road assistance in economic and cultural development, in training national personnel, in strengthening their defences and in other fields.

The CPSU is developing closer relations with the revolutionary-democractic parties of developing countries. Especially close co-operation has been established with those of them that seek to base their activities on scientific socialism. The CPSU stands for the development of contacts with all national progressive parties holding anti-imperialist and patriotic positions.

Relations between the Soviet Union and the developing countries have demonstrated that there also exists a realistic basis for co-operation with those young states that are following the capitalist road of development. That means a common interest in safeguarding peace, strengthening international security and ending the arms race. That means a sharpening contradiction between the interests of the peoples and the imperialist policy of imposing diktat and expansion. That means an understanding by young states of the fact that political and economic ties with the Soviet Union help to strengthen their independence.

However different the developing countries may be from one another and whatever road they follow, their peoples share a common desire to develop independently, and to run their affairs without foreign interference. The Soviet Union is fully in solidarity with them. The CPSU does not doubt that it is the sacred right of the newly free countries to decide their own destinies and to choose their own type of social system.

The CPSU support the just struggle waged by the countries of Asia, Africa, and Latin America against imperialism and the oppression of transnational monopolies, for the assertion of the sovereign right to be master of one's own resources, for a restructuring of international relations on an equal and democractic basis, for the establishment of a new international economic order, and for the deliverance from the burden of debt imposed by the imperialists.

The Soviet Union is on the side of the states and peoples repulsing the attacks of the aggressive forces of imperialism and upholding their freedom, independence and national dignity. Solidarity with them in our time is also an important aspect of the general struggle for peace and international security. The Party regards it as its internationalist duty to support the struggle of the peoples who are still under the yoke of racism and who are victims of the system of apartheid.

The CPSU regards with understanding the goals and activities of the non-aligned movement and stands for an enhancement of its role in world politics. The USSR will continue to be on the side of the non-aligned states in their struggle against the forces of aggression and hegemonism and for settling disputes and conflicts that arise through negotiations, and will be opposed to the involvement of those states in military and political groupings.

The CPSU stands for the equal participation of developing countries in international affairs and for an increase of their contribution to the solution of the most important problems of our time. The interaction of those countries with socialist states is vastly important for strengthening the independence of the peoples, improving international relations and preserving peace.

The alliance of the forces of social progress and national liberation is a guarantee of a better future for mankind.

The CPSU proceeds from the belief that the historical dispute between the two opposing social systems, into which the world is divided today, can and must be settled by peaceful means. Socialism proves its superiority not by force of arms but, by force of example in every area of the life of society—by the dynamic development of the economy, science and culture, by an improvement in the living standards of working people, and by a deepening of socialist democracy.

The Soviet people are convinced that the future belongs to socialism. Every people deserves to live in a society that is free from social and national oppression, in a society of genuine equality and genuine democracy. It is the sovereign right of an oppressed and exploited people to free itself from exploitation and injustice. Revolutions are a natural result of social development, of class struggle in every given country. The CPSU has believed and continues to believe that the "export" of revolution, the imposition of revolution on anyone from the outside, is unacceptable in principle. But the "export" of counter revolution in any form, too, is a gross encroachment on the free expression of will by the peoples, on their right independently to choose their way of development. The Soviet Union is strongly opposed to attempts forcibly to check and reverse the march of history.

The Communist Party of the Soviet Union firmly and consistently upholds the Leninist principle of peaceful coexistence of states with different social systems. The policy of peaceful co-existence as understood by the CPSU presupposes: renunciation of war and the use or threat to use force as a means of settling disputes issues, and the settlement of such issues through negotiations; non-interference in internal affairs and respect for the legitimate interests of each other, the right of the peoples independently to decide their destinies; strict respect for the sovereignty and territorial integrity of states and the inviolability of their borders; co-operation on the basis of complete equality and mutual benefit; fulfilment in good faith of commitments arising from generally recognised principles and norms of internationational law and from international treaties concluded.

These are the basic principles on which the Soviet Union builds its relations with capitalist states. They have been affirmed in the Soviet Constitution.

The CPSU will purposefully help to bring about a universal affirmation in international relations of the principle of peaceful co-existence as a generally recognised norm of inter-state relations that will be observed by everyone. It believes that the extension of ideological differences between the two systems to the sphere of these relations is inadmissible.

The Party will work for the development of the process of international detente, regarding it as a natural and essential stage on the road to the establishment of a comprehensive and reliable security system. The experience of co-operation shows that there is a real prospect for this. The CPSU stands for the creation and use of international mechanisms and institutions, which would make it possible to find optimal correlations between national, state interests and the common interests of mankind. It stands for enhancing the role of the United Nations in strengthening peace and developing international co-operation.

The nuclear power bear a special responsibility for the situation in the world. The states possessing nuclear weapons and other weapons of mass destruction must renounce the use of or threat to use such weapons and refrain from steps that would lead to an aggravation of the international situation.

The CPSU stands for normal and stable relations between the Soviet Union and the United States of America, which presupposes non-interference in internal affairs, respect for each other's legitimate interests, recognition and practical implementation of the principle of equality and equal security, and the building of the greatest possible mutual trust on this basis. Differences between social systems and ideologies should not lead to strained relations. There are objective prerequisites for the development of fruitful and mutually beneficial Soviet-US co-operation in various fields. It is the conviction of the CPSU that the policies of both powers should be oriented to mutual understanding rather than hostility which is fraught with the threat of catastrophic for the Soviet and American people, as well as for other nations.

The Party is convinced that all states, big and small, regardless of their potentials, geographic location, and social systems, can and must participate in the search for solutions to acute problems, in the normalisation of conflict situations, and in carrying out measures to ease tensions and curb the arms race.

The CPSU attaches great importance to the further development of peaceful, good-neighbourly relations and co-operation between European states. An indispensable conditions for the stability of positive processes in this region, as in other regions, is respect for the territorial and political relations which emerged as a result of the Second World War. The CPSU is strongly opposed to attempts to revise them under any pretext whatsoever and will combat any manifestation of revanchism.

The Party will make consistent efforts to ensure that the process of strengthening security, trust and peaceful co-operation in Europe, which was launched on the initiative and with the active participation of the Soviet Union, develops and deepens, and comes to embrace the whole world. The CPSU stands for the pooling of efforts by all interested states for the purpose of ensuring security in Asia and for carrying out a joint search by them for a constructive solution to the problem. Asia, Africa, Latin American, the Pacific and the Indian Ocean can must become zones of peace and good-neighbourliness.

The CPSU stands for the development of extensive long-term and stable contacts between states in the sphere of economy, science, and technology on the basis of complete equality and mutual benefit. Foreign economic co-operation is of great political importance, for it helps to strengthen peace and relations of peaceful co-existence between states with different social system. The Soviet Union rejects all forms of discrimination and the use of trade, economic, scientifie and technical contacts as a means of exerting pressure, and will work to ensure the economic security of states.

The CPSU stands for broad mutual exchanges of genuine cultural values between all countries. Such exchanges should serve humanitarian goals, namely, the cultural and intellectual enrichment of the peoples and the consolidation of peace and good-neighbourliness.

The Soviet state will co-operate with other countries in solving the global problems that have become especially acute in the second half of the 20th century and that are of vital significance to the whole of mankind. These include : environmental protection, energy, raw materials, food and demographic problems, peaceful exploration of outer space and the resources of the World Ocean, the overcoming of the economic backwardness of many newly free countries, the eradication of dangerous diseases, and other problems. The solution of these problems calls for joint efforts by all states. It will be much easier to solve these problems if the squandering of efforts and resources on the arms race is stopped.

In the interests of mankind and for the benefit of all nations, the CPSU and the Soviet state stand for an extensive and constructive programme of measures aimed at ending the arms race, achieving disarmament, and ensuring peace and security.

The CPSU, which considers general and complete disarmament under strict and comprehensive international control to be a historic task, is carrying out efforts to achieve it. It shall consistently be working for :

—restriction and narrowing of the sphere of military preparations, especially those involving weapons of mass destruction. First and foremost, outer space should be totally excluded from that sphere so that it will not become a scene of military rivalry and a source of death and destruction. Exploration and development of outer space should be for peaceful purposes only, for the development of science and production, in accordance with the needs of all nations. The USSR stands for collective efforts in the solution of this problem and will actively participate in international co-operation to this end. The Soviet Union will also call for the adoption of measures promoting the non-proliferation of nuclear weapons and the establishment of zones free from these and other weapons of mass destruction ;

– the complete elimination of nuclear armaments to be carried out stage by stage till the end of the 20th century by means of discontinuing the testing and production of all types of these armaments, renouncing the first use of nuclear weapons by all the nuclear powers, and freezing, reducing and destroying all their stockpiles ;

—an end to the production of other types of weapons of mass destruction, including chemical weapons, their elimination and a ban on the development of new types of such weapons ;

– reductions in the armed forces or states, first and foremost those which are permanent members of the UN Security Council and countries that have military agreements with them ; limitations on conventional armaments ; and to the development of new types of these armaments whose yield approximates that of mass destruction weapons, and reductions in military spending ;

—a freeze on, and reductions in, the number of troops and armaments in the most explosive parts of the world, the dismantling of military bases on foreign territory, and measures to build up mutual trust and lessen the risk of armed conflicts, including these that might occur by accident.

The CPSU stands for overcoming the division of the world into military-political groupings. The CPSU is for the simultaneous dissolution of NATO and the Warsaw Treaty Organisation, or, as first step, the disbandment of their military organisations. To lower canfrontation between the military blocs, the Soviet Union advocates the conclusion of a treaty between them on the mutual non-use of force and the maintenance of relations of peace, a treaty which would be open to all other states as well.

The CPSU will make every effort to ensure that questions of arms limitation and averting the threat of war are tackled through honest and strictly observed agreements on the basis of equality and equal security of the sides, in order to preclude any attempt to conduct talks from a "position of strength" and use them to cover up an arms build up.

The Soviet and its allies do not seek military superiority, but at the same time they will not permit an upset in the military-strategic equilibrium that has taken shape in the world arena. Furthermore, they are consistently working to ensure that the level of this equilibrium is steadly lowered, the quantity of armaments on both sides reduced, and the security of all people guaranteed.

The CPSU solemnly declares : there no weapons that the Soviet Union would not be prepared to limit or ban on a raciprocal basis with effective verification.

The Soviet Union does not encroach on the security of any country, West or East. It threatens no one and does not seek confrontation with any state ; it wishes to live in peace with all countries. The Soviet socialist state has been bearing high the banner of peace and friendship among peoples since the Great October Revolution. The CPSU shall remain loyal to this Leninist banner.

The CPSU is a component part of the international communist movement. It regards its efforts to perfect socialist society and advance onward to communism as a major internationalist task, the accomplishment of which serves the interests of the world socialist system, the international working class, and mankind as a whole.

Communists, having always been the most consistent fighters against social and national oppression, are today also in the forefront of the struggle for the preservation of peace on earth and for people's right to life. They know well wherein lie the causes of the threat of war, expose those who are responsible for the aggravation of international tension and the arms race, and strive to develop co-operation with all those capable of making a contribution to the anti-war effort.

The CPSU takes into consideration the fact that Communist and Workers' parties in the non-socialist world are functioning in a complex and controversial situation. The range of the circumstances and forms of thesr struggle is quite broad. However, this expands rather than limits the opportunities available to the movement. The diversity of forms of activity practised by Communists enables them to take better account of specific national conditions and concrete historical circumstances, and of the interests of different social groups and strata of the population.

The CPSU proceeds from the conviction that the Communists in each country analyse and evaluate situations independently, determine their strategic course, policies and means of struggle for the immediate and ultimate goals, for communist ideals. The experience accumulated by the Communist parties is a valuable internationalist asset.

The CPSU thoroughly studies the problems and experience of foreign Communist parties. It regards with understanding their desire to improve their strategy and tactics, to seek broader class alliances on a platform of anti-monopolistic, anti-war activity, and to uphold the economic interests and political rights of working people, proceeding from the conviction that the struggle for democracy is a component part of the struggle for socialism.

The imperialist circles in different countries are closely co-ordinating their efforts aimed against socialism and all the democratic forces and are trying to set Communist parties against one another. In these conditions proletarian internationalism and comradely solidarity among Communist are assuming ever greater importance.

The CPSU believe that disagreement over individual issues should not interfere with international co-operation among Communist parties and their concerned efforts.

In cases when divergences of view on individual problems arise between fraternal parties, the CPSU considers it useful to hold comradely discussions to achieve better understanding of each other's view and reach mutually acceptable appraisals. But when the issue at hand is the revolutionary essence of Marxism-Leninism, the substance and role of real socialism, the CPSU will continue to uphold positions of principle. This also determines the CPSU's attitude to all attempts to destroy the class essence of the Communists' activity and destort the revolutionary nature of the aims and means of struggle for attaining them. Experience has shown that any departure from the fundamental propositions of the teaching of Marx, Engels, and Lentin weakens the potentials of the communist movement.

In its relations with the fraternal parties, the CPSU firmly adhere to the principle of proletarian internationalism, which organically combines revolutionary solidarity with the recognition of the full independence and equality of each party. On the basis of this principle, the CPSU is actively developing its ties with the Communist and Workers' parties, exchanging information, and participating in bilateral and multilateral meetings and regional and broader international conference held as the need arises.

The Soviet people always side with their class comrades in the capitalist world. The CPSU will use its international prestige to defend Communists, who fall victim to the arbitrary rule of reactionaries. It has a high regard for the solidarity of the fraternal parties and for their struggle against anti-Sovietism. The mutual support of the Communist and Workers's parties in the socialist and non-socialist countries is an important factor for social progress.

The CPSU will continue its policy of developing ties with socialist, social-democratic, and labour parties. Co-operation with them can play a significant role, first and foremost, in the effort to prevent nuclear war. However great the divergences between various trends of the working-class movement might be, they present no obstacle to a fruitful systematic exchange of views, parallel or joint actions to remove the threat of war, improve the international situation, eliminate the vestiges of colonialism, and uphold the interests and rights of the working people.

The CPSU attaches great significance to stimulating co-operation among all contingents of the international working-class movement and expanding interaction between the trade unions of diverse trends and youth, women's present and other democratic organisations in various countries.

Being full aware of its historical responsibility to the world's working class and its communist vanguard, the CPSU will continue to work in the following directions :

—to uphold the revolutionary ideals and the fundamentals of Marxism-Leninism in the world communist movement, creatively develop the theory of scientific socialism, consistently flight against dogmatism and revisionism, against all the influences of bourgeois ideology on the working-class movement ;

—to do its utmost to promote cohesion and co-operation among fraternal parties and the international solidarity of Communists and to increase the communist movement's contribution to the cause of preventing world war ;

—to pursue a consistent policy aimed at achieving unity of action in the international working-class movement, among all working people in the struggle for their common interests, for a lasting peace and the security of peoples, for national independence, democracy, and socialism.

CHAPTER EIGHTEEN

PROSPECTS THE GREAT DEBATE

THE Soviet Union appeals to all countries of the Asian-Pacific region-and not only to them-with a call for cooperation for peace and security.

The Asian-Pacific field of the Soviet Union's foreign policy is a component part of the general platform of the CPSU's international activity, which was outlined at the April 1986 plenary meeting and the 27th Party Congress. The course of events in that part of the world is of a national, state interest to the Soviet Union. Yet this is by no means a claim for some privileges, not an effort to ensure benefit to the detriment of others, no attempt to strengthen our security at other people's expense.

The Soviet Union sees its interest in joining efforts, in cooperation with full respect for the right of each people to live as they choose, to resolve their problems independently in conditions of peace.

This view of international and general security has been once again reaffirmed in the statement by the General Secretary of the CPSU Central Committee on Soviet television on August 18, 1986 on the USSR's intention to extend its unilateral moratorium on all nuclear blasts till January 1987.

It takes urgent measures to include the Asian-Pacific region into the process of creating a comprehensive international security system. Speaking in Vladivostok on July 28, 1986, Mikhail Gorbachev proposed for that a comprehensive programme for action in five directions : the first of which are questions of regional settlement. They concern the situation around Afghanistan, Kampuchea, and the tensions on the Korean peninsula.

The second direction of the efforts is aimed at putting up a barrier in the way of a proliferation and build-up of nuclear weapons in Asia and the Pacific, The Soviet Union proposes as the third element of the programme proclaimed in Vladivostok that naval activity in the Pacific, first and foremost, the activity of nuclear-capable ships be reduced. The fourth is a radical out in the armed forces and conventional weapons in Asia. The fifth direction of the efforts for ameliorating the situation in Asia and the Pacific is a practical discussion of confidence-building measures and non-use of force in the region.

Adverse factors influencing developments in Asia from within have often been the source of tension sharpening or even instigating regional conflicts, Nevertheless, developments on the Asian continent, especially after World War II, clearly show that the main cause of numerous and dangerous conflicts in interference from the outside, on the part of imperialism that takes the following courses of action towards the developing countries of Asia :

It seeks to subordinate also this part of the world expressly to its global objectives by deploying (mainly qualitatively) military means, extending bases and building new ones and using military facilities of developing countries. This is being done on the territories of states with pro-imperialist regimes (South Korea, Oman, Pakistan), in neighbouring seas and on their is lands (this is why the United States hinders decolonization of Diego Garcia and Micronesia).

It makes attempts at a counteroffensive against national liberation movements and revolutions (Iran, Afghanistan). In the case of Afghanistan it resorted to an overt export of counter-revolution.

The United States seeks to strengthen its allies in Asia, differentiating its attitude to developing countries : definite priority in granting assistance has been given to regimes ready to get involved in the plans of imperialism, whereas countries which did not show such readiness have become the targets of ideological subversion and economic pressure. War fleets by the Asian coast serve intimidation purposes as well.

It seeks to coordinate its attitudes and activities with China and to support its plans towards developing countries.

It was greatly due to the policy of imperialism, that the post-war developments in Asia were very dramatic, that nowhere else in the developing world were the links between regional and global conflicts so close and aggressive acts of imperialism so extensive and brutal. Out of some 200 military conflicts in the world in 1945-1983 almost half took place in Asia.

The tense situation prevailing in Asia and the adjoining seas and oceans urgently requires the Asian states to conduct a highly responsible policy that is aimed at averting nuclear danger and star-wars, achieving peaceful solutions to all controversial issues, and resolving conflict situations by political means. This is a choice that Asia can and must make.

The United States has long been practising banditry wherever possible. Small wonder that terrorism and US policy have long become synonimous for the peoples of Afghanistan, Kampuchea, Ethiopia, Angola, Nicaragua and a number of other countries, against which the Reagan administration is waging undeclared wars.

While discussing the problem of regional conflicts the USA refrains from condemning the atrocities of apartheid in South Africa and the acts of aggression perpetrated by that country against its neighbours, the wars waged by US stooges in Central America and South-East Asia and Israel's banditry in the Middle East. Moreover, Washington would like to equate the lawful governments of the states following the road of national liberation and social progress, on the one hand, and counter-revolution, on the other.

Even the U.S. media itself has admitted more than once that the regional conflicts, the responsibility for which Reagan and his team summarily impute to Moscow, are actually an offspring of the Washington's policy of "new-globalism". The US administration is carrying out a major programme for the destabilisation of the situation in such countries as Angola, Afghanistan, Kampuchea, Nicaragua and Ethiopia. Washington views as indepcndent and sovereign only those countries whieh unconditionally support the USA. A country voting for peace, disarmament and the removal of the nuclear threat in the United Nations falls out of Washington's favour.

As the Soviet leader Mikhail Gorbachev said in an interview to the Algerian magazine *Revolution Africaine* : "Were it not for American intervention int he internal affairs of other countries, ragional conflicts would subside and could be resolved with far less effort and more justice." This, naturally, would provide opportunities for more effective regional cooperation and for the settlement of difficult economic and social problems facing the 'third world' countries.

The Soviet Union has noted with satisfaction that the need to build good-neighbour relations between the Asian nations on the basis of a broad concept of security is being increasingly appreciated on the continent. Awareness of the necessity to improve the international situation in Asia dominates the attitudes of political circles in these countries toward peace initiatives of the Soviet Union.

Needless to say, it is not the intention of the Soviet Union to impose on other Asian states a recipe or ready-made formula that guarantees all-Asia security. Nothing less than collective efforts are required for working out the basic elements of this concept. The Soviet Union has called on the Asian nations to participate in the joint elaboration of these elements by means of bilateral as well as multilateral contacts. And it is certainly a most urgent matter to first coordinate and then pool efforts in the search for a political settlement of conflict situations in Asia; the idea is to blunt the edge of the military confrontation there, to extinguish the flashpoints of military danger.

Evidently, the elaboration and implementation of the concept of Asian security is a long-term task that cannot be resolved in one stroke. To realize it a stage-by-stage approach must be taken that effects a transition from simple to more complex forms. By this we mean that the Asian states must even now more, step by step, from those bilateral or multilateral accords which are already achievable in this or that part of the continent toward more complex accords, thereby gradually expanding the base for lasting peace and stability on the continent as a whole.

The ultimate result of these joint efforts, their logical conclusion, could be the holding, in the foreseeable future, of an all-Asian debate to consider the entire complex of issues concerning the ensuring of security and equitable cooperation among the Asian nations.

The Soviet concept of Asian security, which, by pooling the efforts of all the states on the continent, provides for a joint search for ways of ensuring peace in Asia and for paying due regard to the experience accumulated by the Asian nations themselves and by states of other continents-constitutes a solid and realistic basis for deepening mutual understanding and cooperation between the Asian states, for establishing lasting peace and reliable security there. This is what the peoples of that great continent are vitally interested in.

The above-mentioned initiatives of Asian countries, which provide for a settlement of the conflicts and differences prevailing on the continent, constitute a good basis for working out an all-Asia security system that would meet the interests of each and every state in the region and help to turn Asia into a continent of lasting peace and mutually beneficial cooperation.

Gorbachev wants that since the world is too small a place to have the effects of nuclear war, it is better to develop comprehensive system of security-call it global, common, universal or a set of regionally determined security arrangements or some kind of international security. Any arrangements has to satisfy two objective conditions (a) US and USSR are the core of the strategic environment; and (b) countries of Asia, Africa, Latin America washed by not only the seas but also by blood want convincing regional stability and strategic and economic security. Will the Soviet Union succeed? WIll the Soviet Union handle Europe, US, developing countries of Africa, Asia and Latin America in a manner that (a) it secures itself, (b) secures its allies and friends, (c) secure the world from nuclear holocaust, (d) save US-Soviet relations from the earthquake that the Reagan Administration wishes to cause so that the next 15 years are spent in repair, even before any one can think of detente-that is if the world can be saved. Who wishes to wear this crown of thorn? India and Soviet Union need to think about Asia-Pacific. Will Gorbachev visit to New Delhi allay 'India's fears' and deepen Indo-Soviet relations in security arena of Asia? America does not want it[1].

What are the possibilities and prospects of solving the problems of Asian security? Compared to Europe, security in Asia is much more connected with the internal situation in the countries of the continent, and their relative stability. The great differences between Asian countries make it difficult to achieve an identity of views on the main directions, forms and sources of threat to security and, vice versa, on how this security could be strengthened. Proclaimed interests of security of one state sometimes pose a threat to another one, to the region concerned or even to Asia as a whole.

Another specificity of Asia is the fact that the economic aspect plays an important role in its security. Progress in satisfying the developing countries' demands, requires also their co-operation.

Concretization of the most important principles of international relations with regard to the situation in that area and their consistent assertion could be the main and realistic content of the

1. Rakesh Gupta, *op. cit.*

present endeavour to solve security problems in Asia. Corresponding to this is the Soviet proposal for Asian collective security emphasizing the following principles: non-use of force or threat of force in international relations, respect for the sovereignty and inviolability of frontiers, non-interference in the internal affairs of otherstates and the development of wide-ranging co-operation in the economic and other spheres on the basis of equality and mutual benefits. These principles are basically identical with many of the principles mapped out by the Movement of Non-Aligned Countries. The problem does not rest in non-existence of principles but rather in their different interpretations and concrete applications. The above mentioned principle of a collective attitude to the Asian security problem does not imply the necessity that all states participate in all steps from the very beginning. The less so does it presuppose an attitude only on an all-continent level. The differences existing within Asia and its regions and the complexity of problems within the continent as well as in its countries' external relations will necessitate a suitable combination of attitudes on both regional and all-continent levels.

Certain experience in strengthening security has already been gained in the different Asian regions. Relatively the greatest progress has been made in efforts to turn the Indian Ocean into a zone of peace. This positive result is undoubtedly also due to the relatively great unity of the states in that region in basic questions, while the advanced capitalist states in particular hold negative stands. So it is evident that the road towards security on the largest continent in the world will be neither easy nor short.

In his timesly and reflective article on the subject of: "why not discuss Asian Security (?)", in *Mainstreams*(August 9, 1986). P.N. Haksar rightly stresses therein that "there exists a real problem of Asian security, which is no less legitimate and valid than the problem of security in Europe." Or for that matter, one may add in this age of the UN Charter when all States are legally treaty-bound to the question of Security, to that of the whole-world.[2]

2. See Iqbal Ithar. Asian Security. *Mainstream* 29 September, 1986.

Then after rightly mentioning successively Holland's vain neocolonialist attempt with Western (British) aid to "regain its lost Empire in Indonesia . . .in 1949", the US interventionist wars, first in Korea and then in Indo-China, after the stunning French defeat at Dien-Bien-Phu, the current US-Pakistan-sponsored military intervention in Afghanistan, China's punishing foray in the late 1970s into Vietnam, and the ASEAN running intervention in Kampuchia, he rightly and relevantly concludes that "the dangers inherent in the situation (obviously such as those of neighbouring Afghanistan and West Asia etc.) impinge upon India's security interests." And argues from that, that he "hopes" that "he has established the validity of the argument that the Asian continent has several reasons to address itself to the problem of security. . . in Asia." Finally concluding wlth the question as to why it should be difficult in Asia to create a forum where countries could exchange views on problems of Asian Security (?) And why a country like India, a leader of the Non-aligned movement whose aim is peace, should shy away from discussing "initially" at any rate, the question of Asian Security? Which seems to imply that some doubts subsist at the official level in India, about the question, despite the formidable list of example past and present. given by Haksar, that have contributed to keep the question of Asian Security alive, not only all the past years since World War II, but which continue—as in Indo-China, in Kampuchia, or in Afghanistan, plus in West Asia, as a result of the Israeli-Palestine conflict, to keep the question of security and insecurity of all, at a boil.

It can thus be claimed that for Asians, the question of their security has never in all these years, or even currently, been a purely academic one, but one of continuing harsh reality. As also one that in the earlier Nehru period, India – as history records—actively and energetically came to grips with, through its nonaligned policies, year in and year out, on the basis of its formal and solemn commitments to the UN Charter. To maintion some of the principal occasions:

(1) When, on October 7, 1949, the UN General Assembly under the impulsion of its Western majority, quite illegally, for

that is not its role under the Charter, adopted a Western-sponsored resolution purporting to sanction a US-led invasion of North Korea, across the 38th parallel, against the opposition of the Socialist States, and with five Asian States (including Nehru's India) abstaining. And which then explained thelr abstention with the argument, that the resolution "would impair faith in the UN (and obviously its security apparatus) if we were to authorise the uniification or Korea by force. . ." That courageous action then representing the first fruits internationally-speaking. of the doctrine of nonalignment, under Indian (that is to say, under Nehru's) influence.

(2) India's bid to bring China out of its international isolation to which the West had consigned it, by reason of its actions during the Korean war, by the Public exchange of visits at Prime Minister-level, and the issue of communiques at both the Peking and Delhi ends, pledging both countries to act by the principles of Peaceful Coexistence finding expression in the UN Charter, in the pursuit of their respective foreign policies, which were thus a considerable steps in the direction of helping to ensure Asian security.

(3) The extensive efforts at the diplomatic level deployed by by nonaligned India in 1954, with Soviet parallel backing, to defuse for a good while, as it happened, what could have blown up there and then into an East-West confrontation in East Asia, on a much vaster scale than the Korean War, when they together succeeded in getting the US to sit down at the same conference table with the three quarantined communist States, China, North Korea, and North Vietnam, at the famous Geneva Conference. A political consummation, which then helped put an end to what might be called the European phase of the conflict in Indo-China.

(4) Following that, in the next year in the same context, interalia, of Asian Security, India then helped convene the important Afro-Asian Conference at Bandung, in 1955, which resulted as we all know, in the formulation of the Ten Principles of State Conduct, which were to constitute not only a sort of Charter both for Afro-Asian security, as also for the nonaligned movement, but

at the same time went towards helping communist China by its presence at the Conference, to enhance the international respectability it had already acquired earlier tentatively, through Indian and Soviet backing, by its presence at the Geneva international conference, a fact that China was to soon forget.

Nor can one ignore the various concrete steps taken by the Soviet Union over the whole period, with the UN, in its annual proposals for graduated of complete disarmament, and/or greater international cooperation, as required by the UN Charter, plus its many contributions to Asian Security far and wide, when it guaranteed China's security to begin with, through a Mutual Security Pact shortly after the foundings of the People's Republic in 1949. And then its use of the Veto in the Security Council on several notable occasions, which prevented the internationalisation of the so-called Kashmir problem, and thus furthered the cause of security in the Indian peninsula; then its mediation at a critical time at the famous Tashkent Peace and Security Conference, in early 1966, between the previously warring States of Pakistan and India, and eventually its mutual security Agreement with India at another critical point in history, one result of which was the emergence of Bangladesh to indepedent statehood.

All the which convincingly shows that the question of Asian Security, raised by Haksar, has never been merely academic one for the majority of the people of Asia, fit only for "seminars and conferences of intellectuals," but a question of everyday continuing reality, specially for the poor who have always to make such extreme sacrifices in the last resort for it, and to which then the Non-aligned States, in particular, must always pay close and constant when formulating their foreign policy concerns and options at any given time.

So far as India is concerned there is much evidence to show that in the Nehru period, with his unmatched ability to get unfailingly to the heart of any political problem or situation as it arose, and when the question of setting up and or implementing the realisation of a "socialist pattern of society," as the Constitution says, was very much to the fore, the related question of security too, w hether world-wide, or regional, was ever in his mind. If therefore it has since become somewhat, if not wholly, academic, as it sometimes seems to be, then that must obviously be due to the errors and failings of its western-educated and often western-prone bureaucracy-cum-politicians, and also the "framework of capitalism" to which everything might well have become a prey.

It is high time the United States and its closes European partners heeded the voice of reason and peace, the proposals coming from Moscow and New Delhi, Mexico and Wellington, the voice of rapidly growing anti-war organisations in the West itself. It is high time they realised that attempts to wear the Soviet Union down economically are doomed to failure. Time urgently demands entirely different solutions, a different approach. Every new nuclenr explosion, every missile produced by the military-industrial complex conveyors increases the responsibility of those who, defying the will of the peoples, are following the line of militarism and are buildtng tension in the world.

The Soviet Union has made a positive contribution in the thought process of evolving some instruments for security of Asia and the Pacific. These proposals can become a starting point for discussions among the leaders and people of this region. It is not necessary to dogmatically stick to the Soviet proposals, these should be examined on merit and an alternative package of proposals too can be evolved. But the crux of the matter is that an open debate on this problem which has a direct bearing on the peace of this region should begin and there is no reason why India should not take a lead in this direction.[3]

---

3. V.D. Chopra. Security of Asia and the Pacific. *Patriot* 18 August 1986; p. 4.

A SELECT BIBLIOGRAPHY

Abrams, Garry. Group (Foundation for the Twenty-First Century) aims to improve U.S. influence in Pacific. *International Herald Tribunel* 13 October 1986; 4.

Adomeit, Hannes. Consensus *v*. conflict: the dimentions of foreign policy. In *Domestic content of Soviet foreign policy* Ed. by Seweryn Bialer. Boulder, Westview Press, 1981.

Alford, Jonathon. *Soviet Union and the Third World*. New York, St. Martin Press, 1981.

Amelko, Admiral N. Mutual confidence and restraint on high seas are indispensable. *Soviet Land* (New Delhi) (19) October 1986; 17.

Anand, Javed. Why star war is unthinkable. *Sunday Observer* (New Delhi) 19 October 1986.

Anderson, Kym. Prospects for trade growth among Pacific basin countries. *Developing Economies* 21(4) December 1983; 376-85.

Armitage, Richard L. Regional security problems of Southeast Asia in the 1980s. In *Economic, Political and security issues in Southeast Asia in 1980s*. Ed. by R.A. Scalapino and Jusuf Wanandi. Berkely, 1982.

Asian security. Tokyo, Research Institute for peace and Security, 1979-1984.

Attar Chand. *Asian collective security: A bibliography of selected readings*. New Delhi, Sterling, 1976; Pp. 64.

Attar Chand. Asian collective security. *Link* 8 February 1976; 31.

Attar Chand. Asian collective security. *National Herald* 18 October 1973; 5.

Attar Chand. Asian security. *Patriot* 27 November 1973; 2.

Attar Chand. China, Japan and Asian collective security, *Women on the March* (New Delhi) May 1974; 18-20.

Attar Chand Collective Asian security. *Shakti* (New Delhi) 27 2 February 1974; 2.

Attar Chand. Collective security. *National Herald* 25 December 1973; 5.

Attar Chand. Collective security in Asia. *National Herald* 30 December 1975; 5.

Attar Chand. Ever deepening friendship and cooperation between India and USSR. *Soviet Review* (New Delhi) 11 July 1974; 46-50.

Attar Chand. Foreign debt crisis and development. *Indian Nation* 19 July 1986; 4.

Attar Chand. Global security: The great debate. *Indian Nation* (Patna) 11 October 1986; 4.

Attar Chand. Harare Summit: Peace and development. *Indian Nation* 29 September 1986; 4.

Attar Chand, India, USSR and collective security in Asia. *Soviet Review* (New Delhi) 2 May 1974; 57-60.

Attar Chand. Indian National Congress and CPSU. *Patriot* 25 February 1976; 2.

Attar Chand. Indian Ocean: Peace and security. *Patriot* 27 September 1986; 4.

Attar Chand. Indo-Soviet amity abiding. *Socialist Congressman* (New Delhi) 7 March 1968; 20-21,

Attar Chand. Indo-Soviet relations: A stabilising factor in Asia. *NIF Weekly* 30 April 1978; 1287-88.

Attar Chand. Indo-Soviet trade ties. *Economic Times* (New Delhi) 24 May 1975; 3.

Attar Chand. Model of Asian collective security: An outline. *Socialist India* (New Delhi) 13 April 1974; 18-19.

Attar Chand. Multinationals and new economic order. *Indian Nation* 3 October 1986; 4.

Attar Chand. New approach towards arms control. *Indian Nation* 20 August 1986; 4.

Attar Chand. Neoglobalism and strategic interest in Asia. *Indian Nation* 31 July 1986; 4.

Attar Chand. Nuclear-free Pacific peace zone. *Patriot* 13 August 1986: 4.

Attar Chand. Peace and progress among nations· Major aspects of Soviet foreign policy. *NIF Weekly* 24 April 1977; 1541-44.

Attar Chand. Peace in Asia. *National Herald* 29 June 1974; 5.

Attar Chand. Peace in Asia. *National Herald* 21 December 1975; 5.

Attar Chand. Peace in Asia. *Link* (New Delhi) 3 February 1974; 2.

Attar Chand. Politics of "Star Wars". *Indian Nation* 23 September 1986; 4.

Attar Chand. Regional economic cooperation and collective security in Asia. NIF Weekly 26 September 1976; 2333-35. *Society and Commerce* (Calcutta) October 1976; 217-18.

Attar Chand. Solidarity makes India, Soviet Union strong nations. *NIF Weekly* 24 February 1980; 389-91.

Attar Chand. *Southeast Asia and the Pacific*. New Delhi, Sterling, 1979. Pp. 378.

Attar Chand. Soviet economic planning and Asian security. *NIF Weekly* 19 June 1977; 1881-82.

Attar Chand. Stability in Southeast Asia. *Economic Times* 19 October 1976; 5.

Attar Chand. Strategic Arms Limitation: Soviet-American peace treaty for entire humanity. *NIF Weekly* 9 September 1979; 2061-62.

Attar Chand. Threat to Asian security. *Indian Nation* 28 June 1986; 4.

Attar Chand. US neoglobalism: An apology for colonization *Clarity* (Bombay) 17 August 1986.

Betts, Richard K. Incentives for nuclear weapons; India, Pakistan, Iran. *Asian Survey* November 1979.

Bhargava, G.S. *South Asian security after Afghanistan*. Aldershot, 1983.

Bhatia, Vinod. *Indian National Congress and Soviet Union.* New Delhi, Panchsheel Publications, 1985.

Bialer, Seweryn. *Domestic context of foreign policy.* Boulder, Westview, 1981.

Borisov, K. Great responsibility. *New Times* (Moscow) (6) 1986; 3-5.

Brunei: Sir Omar is gone. *Asia week* 21 September 1986; 42.

Buszynski, Leszek. On the assessment of foreign policy. In *Soviet foreign policy and Southeast Asia,* London, Croom Helm, 1986; 1-8.

Buszynski, Leszek. Soviet collective security proposal and ASEAN reactions. In *Soviet foreign policy and Southeast Asia.* London, 1986; 40-96.

Buszynski, Leszek. Soviet foreign policy and Southeast Asia. London, Croom Helm, 1986; pp. 303.

Buszynski, Leszek. Soviet Union and the regional balance of power. In *Soviet foreign policy and Southeast Asia.* London, 1986; 247-68.

Buzam, Barry and Gowher, Rizvi. Future of the South Asian Security complex. In *South Asian insecurity and the great powers.* London, Macmillan, 1986; 235-252.

Buzan, Barry. Peace, power and security: contending concepts in the study of international relations. *Journal of Peace Research* 21(2) 1984; 109-25.

Buzan, Barry. *People, states and fear: the national international relations.* Brighton, 1983.

Buzan, Barry and Gowher Rizvi *eds. South Asian insecurity and the Great Powers.* Ed. by Barry Buzan and Gowher Rizvi. London, Macmillan, 1986; Pp. 257.

Chaudhuri, Sailen. *Beijing, Washington, Islamabad entente: Genesis and development.* New Delhi, Sterling, 1982, Pp. 168.

China and the Soviet Union: Down to business. *Asia week* 21 September 1986; 19

Chopra, S.N. Gorbachev will press for Asian security plan. *Sunday Observer* (New Delhi) 28 September 1986.

Chopra, V.D. Soviet perspective; Desire for peace. *World Focus* June 1986; 9-13.

Choudhury, G.W. Pakistan and the Communist world. *Pacific Community* October 1974.

Chubin, S. *Security in the Persian Gulf.* London, IISS, 1981.

Clough, Ralph *N. East Asia and U.S. security.* Washington, 1975. pp. 248.

Cohen, Stephen F. Gorbaehev's detente : Dangerous illusion ? *International Herald Tribune* 3 June 1986; 4.

Colbert, Evelyn. Changing relationship in Southeast Asia, ASEAN, Indonesia and the Great Powers. *Contemprory Southeast Asia* 4(1) June 1981.

Collective security in Asia. *Searchlight* (Patna) 30 November 1973: 4.

Connolly, Violet. Soviet-Japanese cooperation in Siberia. *Pacific Community* October 1970; 55-65.

Cotton. Timothy J. Soviet Union under Gorbachev. *Current History* October 1985.

CPI hails new Soviet proposals for N-ban. *New Age* (New Delhi) 26 January 1986.

CPI hails Soviet N-test moratorium. *New Age* (New Delhi) 24 August 1986.

CPSU and the international communist movement. *Party Life* (New Delhi) April 1986; 18-22.

Dallin, Alexander. *Soviet foreign policy after Stalin.* London, Methuen, 1960.

Darshan Sing. *Soviet foreign policy documents 1985.* New Delhi, Sterling, 1986.

Dash, P. L. After advant of Mikhail Gorbachev : Far-reaching Kremlin changes. *Clarity* 23 March 1986; 7, 12.

Denas, Michael J. Soviet assessment of the correlation of world forces : Implications for American foreign policy. *Orbis* 20 (3) 1976.

Designs on Asia. *Patriot* 4 February 1974; 2.

Dibb, Paul. Soviet Capabilities, interests and strategies in East Asia in the 1980s. *Survival* 24 (4) July-August 1982.

Dorodjatun, Kuntjoro-jakti. Armed conflict in Indonesia : Its history and future. In *Armed communist movements in Southeast Asia*. Ed. by Joo Jock Lim and S. Vani-Gower, 1980.

Duiker, William J. Vietnamese revolutionary doctrine in comparative perspective. In *Vietnamese communism in comparative perspective*. Ed. by William S. Turley. Boulder, Westview, 1980.

Dutt, V. P. *India's foreign policy*. New Delhi, Vikas, 1984.

Dutt, V. P. New Panchsheel for Asia. *States* (New Delhi) 22 December 1973; 13-14.

Dutt, V. P. Soviet collective proposals : Fact and fiction. *National Herald* 20 August 1969; 5.

Feeney, William R. Pacific basing system and US security. In *US foreign policy and Asia-Pacific security* Ed. by W. T. Tow and W. R. Feeney. Boulder, Westview, 1982.

Foot, Rosemary. Sino-Soviet complex and South Asia. In *South Asian insecurity and the great powers*. Ed. by Barry Buzan and Gowher Rizvi. London, 1986; 181-206.

Garver, John. Sino-Vietnamese conflict and the Sino-American rapproachment. *Political Science Quarterly* 96 (3) 1981.

George, Timothy *et.al Security in Southern Asia : India and* the great powers. Aldershot, 1984.

Ghebhardt, Alexander. Soviet System of collective security in Asia. *Asian Survey* 13 (12) December 1973.

Girling J.L.S. Soviet attitudes towards S.E. Asia. *World Today* 29 (7) July 1973.

Global problems of mankind and the state : Social science today. Moscow, USSR Academy of Sciences, 1985. Pp. 210.

Gorbachev, Mikhail *Selected speeches and articles*. Moscow, Progress Publishers, 1986. Pp. 480.

Gorbachev, *Mikhail. Speech at Vladivostok July 28, 1986*. Mosco, 1986. Pp. 40.

Gorbachev announces new moratorium. *New Age* 24 August 1986; 7.

Gorbachev calls for open discussion. *New Age* 10 August 1986; 11.

Gorbachev explains what happend. *New Age* 19 October 1986; 10.

Gorbachev line *Statesman* 6 March 1986; 6.

Gorbachev message to Japanese mayors. *New Age* 23 February 1986; 13.

Gorbachev proposals. *Times of India* 27 January 1986; 8.

Gorbachev seeks peace chance. *China Daily* (Beijing) 4 October 1986; 8.

Gorbachev's call to rid world of N-arms. *Patriot* 30 January 1986; 7.

Gorbachev's Japan visit on the agenda. *Japan Times Weekly* 13 September 1986; 1.

Gorbachev's moves. *Hindustan Times* 7 March 1986; 9.

Gorbachev's peace proposals. *People's Democracy* (New Delhi) 26 January 1986; 1-2.

Gorbachev's proposals intrigue Philippines. *Far Eastern Economic Review* 11 September 1986; 14.

Goroachev's visit to India confirmed. *Statesman* (New Delhi) 15 August 1986; 11.

Gordon, Bernard K. United States and Asia in 1982 : Year of Tenterhooks. *Asian Survey* 23 (1) January 1983.

Goryanov, Mikhail. *Nonalignment and Asian peace and security.* New Delhi, Allied, 1987. Pp. 52.

Greene, Fred. *U.S. policy and the security of Asia.* New York, McGraw Hill, 1968, Pp. 429,

Griffiths, Franklyn. Ideological development and foreign policy. In *Domestic context of Soviet foreign policy.* Ed. by S. Bialer Boulder, Westview, 1981.

Gupta, Bhupesh. Asian collective security need of the hour. *New Age* 21 October 1973; 1, 8-9.

Hayden, W.G. Soviet naval presence in the Indian Ocean : Implications for Australian defence policies. *Australian Outlook* 31 (1) April 1977.

Heinzing, Dieter. Role and interests of the USSR in Indochina. In *Indochina and problems of security and stability in Southeast Asia.* Ed. by Khien Theerawati and M. Brown. Bangkok, 1981.

Hoffman, Eri K. and F.J. Fieron. *Condnct of Soviet foreign policy.* New York, Aldine, 1980.

Horelick, Arnold L. *Soviet Union's Asian security proposals* Santa Monica, Rand Corporation Monograph, 1974. No. P. 5195.

Horn, Robert C, Soviet influence in Southeast Asia : Opportunities and obstacles. *Asian Survey* 15 (8) August 1975.

Horn, Robert C. Soviet-Vietanamese relations and the future of Southeast Asia. *Pacific Affairs* Winter 1978-79.

Horn, Robert C, Soviet Union and Asian security. In *Changing patterns of security and stability in Asia.* Ed. by Chawla Sudershan and D.R. Sardesai. New York, Praeger. 1980,

Hosmer, Stephen T. and Thomas W. Wolfe. *Soviet policy and practice toward third world countries.* Lexington, 1983.

Hough, Jerry F. Gorbachev's strategy, *Foreign Affairs* Fall 1985.

Hsiung, James C. US interests in larger Asia. In *Asian and US foreign policy.* Ed. by J.C. Hsiung and Winberg Chari. New York, Preager, 1981.

In full control (Mikhail Gorbachev). *Free Press Journal 8* March 1986; 4.

Inder Sing, Anita. Superpower global complex and South Asia. In *South Asian insecurity and the great power.* Ed. by Barry Buzan and Gowher Rizvi. London, 1986; 207-34.

India and Gorbachev plan. *Newstime* (Hyderabad) 8 October 1986; 7.

Initiative in S. E. Asia. *Hindustan Times* 22 October 1986; 9.

Isayev, Mikhail. *Peace option for Asia,* Moscow, 1986. Pp. 48.

Jetly, Nancy. India: Domestic dimentions of security. In *South Asian insecurity and the great powers.* Ed. by Barry Buzan and Gowher Rizvi. London, 1986; 37-59.

Jukes Geoffrey. Soviet Union and Southeast Asia. *Australian Outlook* 31 (3) April 1977.

Jukes, Geoffrey. *Soviet Union in Asia.* Melbourne, Angus and Robertson, 1973.

Kanot, Wongtrangon. Revolutionary strategy of the Communist Party of Thailand. In *Armed communist movements in South-east Asia.* Ed. by Lim Joo—Jock and S. Vani. Gower, 1984.

Kaplan, Stephen S. *Diplomacy of power : Soviet armed forces as a political instrument.* Washington Brookings, 1981.

Katz, Mark N. *Third World in Soviet military thought.* London, Croom-Helm, 1984.

Kaufman, Bernd. Prospects for detente in Asia. In *US foreign policy in Asia : An appraisal Ed.* Yung-Hwan Jo. California, 1978.

Kaushik, Devendra. Asian security concepts. *World Focus* June 1986; 3-8.

Khalilzad, Zalmay. *Security in Southern Asia. I—The security of Southwest Asia.* Aldershot, 1981.

Klein, Angela. How far do Gorbachev's proposals go ? *International Viewpoint* 28 October 1984; 3-4.

Koji, I. Y. *et. al.* Trade and industrial adjustment in Pacific Asian countries. *Developing Economics* 21 (4) December 1983; 281-312.

Korany, Bahgat and Ali E. Hillal Dessouki. *Foreign policies of Arab states* London, 1984.

Kroef; Justus M. Vander. National security defence strategy and foreign policy. Perceptions in Indonesia. *Orbis* 20 (2) Summer 1976.

Kroef, Justus M. Vander. Recent trends in Indonesian—Soviet relations. *Pacific Community* 5 (4) 1974.

Kulkarni, Sudheendsa. U.S.S.R. under Gorbachev : Criticism has no ceiling. *Daily* (Bombay) 22 September 1986; 8-9, 13.

Kumar, C. Indian Ocean : The arc of crisis or zone of peace. *International Affairs* (London) Spring 1984; 234-46.

Langer, Paul. Soviet military power in Asia. In *Soviet policy in East Asia.* Ed. by Donald S. Zagoria. Yale University, 1982.

Lebedev, Igor A. Soviet policy considerations regarding the Indian Ocean. *Australian Outlook* 31 (1) April 1977.

Leifer, Michael. *Indonesia's foreign policy*. London, George Allen & Unwin, 1983.

Leifer, Michael. Kampuchea and Laos, critical issues for ASEAN. In *Economic and Political Security issues in Southeast Asia in the 1980s*. Ed. by R.A. Scalapino and J. Wanandi. Berkeley, 1982.

Leifer, Michael. Security of the sea-lanes in Southeast Asia. *Survival* 25 (1) January—February 1983.

Leifer, Michael. Soviet Union in Southeast Asia· In *Soviet Union and the Third World*. Ed. by E.J. Feuchtwanger and Peter Nailor. New York, 1981.

Lenin, V.I. *Imperialism : the highest stage of capitalism*. New York, 1939.

Linder, Staffan Burenstam. *Pacific century*. Stanford University Press, 1986; Pp. 154.

Litwak, R. *et al. India and the great powers*. London, IISS, 1984.

Loescher, G.D. Power politics in Indochina. *Yearbook af World Affairs, 1983*. London, 1983. Vol. 37.

Malhotra, Inder. Political commentary : Soviet Union's "China card". *Times of India* 23 October 1986; 8.

Mclane, Charles B. *Soviet strategies in Southeast Asia*. Princeton, 1966.

Mandel, Ernest. First six months of Gorbachov's reign. *International Viewpoint* 30 September 1985; 3-5.

Mandel, Ernest. Gorbachov's reforms. *International Viewpoint* 14 October 1985; 13-16.

Mediansky, F.A. anc Dianne Court. *Soviet Union in Southeast Asia*. Australian National University. 1984.

Medvedev, Zhores. *Gorbachev*. London, Basil Blackwell, 1986.

Menon, Rajan. India and the Soviet Union. *Asian Survey* July 1978.

Mikhin, *V. Indo—Soviet treaty : Fifteen years*. New Delhi, Sterling, 1986; Pp. 133.

Mishra, Girish. Soviet help to Third World. *Economic Times* 17 March 1986.

Mohan Ram. Come closer, comrade (India and the U.S.S.R.) *Far Eastern Economic Review* (Hong Kong) 30 January 1986; 32.

Morrison, Charles E. and Astri Suhrke. ASEAN in regional defense and development. In *Changing patterns of security and stability in Asia.* Ed. by Sudershan Chawla and S.R. Sar Desai. New York, Praeger, 1980.

Mr. Gorbachev plans. *Telegraph* (Calcutta) 28 February 1986; 6.

Muni, S.D. Subcontinent : Mobilising Asian opinion. *World Focus* June 1986; 20-22.

Nogee, Joseph L. and Kobert H. Donaldson *Soviet foreign policy since world war two.* New York, 1981.

Noorani, A.G. Gorbachov's Asian gambit. *Indian Express* 25 August 1986; 6.

Nuclear-free world. *Pioneer* (Lucknow) 26 January 1986; 6.

Palmer, Norman D. United States and the security of Asia. In *Changing patterns of security and stability in Asia.* Ed. by Sudershan Chawla and D.R. Sar Desai. New York, 1980.

Pauker, Guy J. *Soviet Union and Southeast Asia.* Santa Monica, Rand Corporation Monograph, 1973.

Parker, I. Charles. Third World in Soviet strategy. *Asian Affairs* 7 (6) July—August 1980.

Prasad, K. Pakistan—Iran relations. In *Perspectives on Pakistan's foreign policy.* Ed. by S. Chopra. Amritsar, 1983.

Prime Minister Rajiv Gandhi visits U.S.S.R. New Delhi, Soviet Land Booklets, 1985. Pp. 47.

Rahul Kumar. Indo—Soviet trade ; Need for dynamic approach. *Economic Times* (New Delhi) 13 October 1986; 4.

Rajiv Gandhi visits U.S.S.R. *Indian and Foreign Review* 15 June 1985; 10-12.

Ray, N.K. Moratorium and Pacific security. *Patriot* 23 October 1986; 4.

Relieving mankind of N-Weapons. *New Age* 23 February 1986; 11.

Rizvi, Gowher. Pakistan : The domestic dimensions of security. In *South Asian insecurity and the great powers.* Ed. by Barr Buzan and Gowher Rizvi. London, 1986; 60-92.

Rizvi, Gowher. Rivalry between India and Pakistan. In *South Asian insecurity and the great powers.* Ed. by Barry Buzan and Gowher Rizvi, London, 1986; 93-126.

Rizvi, Gowher, Role of the smaller states in the South Asian complex. In *South Asian insecurity and the great powers.* Ed. by Barry Buzan and Gowher Rizvi. London, 1986: 127-58.

Roberson, B.A. South Asian and the Gulf complex. In *South Asian insecurity and the great powers.* Ed. by Barry Buzan and Gowher Rizvi. London, 1986; 159-80.

Rubinstein, A.Z, *Great game.* New York, 1983.

Scalapino, Robert A., *ed. Asian political institutionalisation.* Berkeley, University of California, 1986; Pp. 313.

Sen Gupta, Bhabani. Indo—Soviet ties on firm footing. *Hindustan Times* 13 October 1986; 1, 16.

Shinohara, Miyohei. Real exchange rates and patterns of industrialization in East and Southeast Asia- *Developing Economies* 21 (4) December 1983; 357-75.

Soviet strategy of peace and social progress. *International Herald Tribune* (7) July 1986; 3-8.

Starr, John Bryan. *Future of US—China relations.* New York, 1981.

Subrahmanyam, K. Pakistan's nuclear capacity and India's response. *Link* 2 December 1984.

Summit of interest (Sino—Soviet relations) *Asiaweek* 21 September 1986; 11-12.

Tai, Zhong. South Asia : Advancing regional co-operation. *Beijing Review* (31) 30 July 1984; 12-13.

Tanaka, Takuo *et. al.* Economic development and the structural change of trade in the Pacific Asia region, *Developing Economies* 21 (4) December; 340-56.

Thomas, Raju, *ed. Great power triangle and Asian security.* Lexington, 1983.

Twenty-seventh Congress of the CPSU. *People's Democracy* 30 1986; 3.

Twenty—Seventh CPSU Congress. *International Herald Tribune* (7) July 1986; 3-114.

Twenty—seventh CPSU Congress : Documents and resolutions. New Delhi, Allied, 1986. Pp. 447.

Towards 21st century. *Economic Times* 17 March 1986.

Vanaik, Achin. CPSU Congress. *Times of India* 13 March 1986; 8.

Vayrynen, Raimo. Regional conflict formations : An intractable problems of international relations. *Journal of Peace Research* 21 (4) 1984; 337-59.

Watanabe, Toshio and H. Kujiwara. Pacific manufactured trade and Japan's options. *Developing countries* 21 (4) December 1983; 313-39.

Zimmerman, W. and R. Axelrod. Lessons of Vietnam and Soviet foreign policy. *World Politics* 34 (1) 1981.

INDEX